COLLECTED T.V. PLAYS
VOLUME ONE

COLLECTED T.V. PLAYS

PLAYS

VOLUME ONE

Where the Difference Begins
A Climate of Fear
The Birth of a Private Man

DAVID MERCER

JOHN CALDER
LONDON

First published as *Collected T.V. Plays Volume One* 1981 by
John Calder (Publishers) Ltd.,
18 Brewer Street,
London W1R 4AS

Originally published as *The Generations: A Trilogy of Plays* by
John Calder (Publishers) Ltd in 1964

BRITISH LIBRARY CATALOGUING IN PUBLICATION DATA

Mercer, David, *b. 1928*
  Collected TV plays.
  Vol. 1
  I. Title
  822'.9'14   PR6063.E7

ISBN 0 7145 3722 5 casebound
ISBN 0 7145 3723 3 paperbound

Printed and bound in Great Britain by
Redwood Burn Limited, Trowbridge & Esher

To my
Mother and Father

CONTENTS

Men may genuinely sympathise with the demand for a radical change. They may be conscious of social evils and sincerely anxious to remove them. They may set up a new department, and appoint new officials, and invent a new name to express their resolution to effect something more drastic than reform, and less disturbing than revolution. But unless they will take the pains, not only to act, but to reflect, they end by effecting nothing.

R.H. TAWNEY

We learn to pity and rebel.

W.H. AUDEN

We are discovering reality anew, and with our conscience, our indignation and our love we are committing ourselves again to that Revolution.

WIKTOR WOROSZYLSKI

WHERE THE DIFFERENCE BEGINS

CAST

WILF CROWTHER, an engine driver	*Leslie Sands*
RICHARD ⎫ his sons	*Barry Foster*
EDGAR ⎭	*Nigel Stock*
GILLIAN	*Olive McFarland*
MARGARET	*Pauline Letts*
AUNTY BEATIE	*Hylda Baker*
UNCLE GEORGE	*Beckett Bould*
AUNTY BESSIE	*Jane Eccles*
JANET	*Ellen McIntosh*
WILF'S WIFE	*Rosemary Matthews*
MAN IN BUFFET	*Frank Seton*

Designed by FREDERICK KNAPMAN
Produced by DON TAYLOR
B.B.C. TELEVISION TRANSMISSION: *15th December, 1961*

Outside the engine sheds in a Yorkshire town. Winter. Late afternoon.

Open on locomotive steam valve and whistle blowing. Wilf is at the cabin window. Coal falling into the tender. The fireman opens the fire door in the cab, lifts fire bars and begins to rake the fire. Wilf leaves the cab, goes down the line and through the shed. He is a big man in his early sixties, with close-cropped grey hair.

CUT TO:
Wilf coming up the street behind a row of terrace houses near the railway. He turns into one of the yards and crosses it to the door.

Scene 1

The Crowthers' Living Room and Kitchen.

> *Wilf enters the kitchen from the back door. He takes off his top coat and hangs it on a hook behind the door. Sits on a stool by the door and begins to unlace his clogs. Richard comes in from the living room. He is a rather bitter man in his early thirties.*

RICHARD: Hello Dad. How are you?
(Wilf stands up and they shake hands)
WILF: I'm all right, lad. How's your mother?
(Wilf pulls off his clogs and puts them under the stool)
RICHARD: I haven't been up yet. Aunt Beatie's with her. She says mother's been sleeping since two. We only got here about an hour ago.
(Richard goes back into the living room followed by his father. Gillian, Richard's girl, is sitting in an

armchair by the fire. She is twenty-three, attractive, gentle, noticeably pregnant. Wilf looks questioningly at her)

RICHARD: Dad, this is Gillian. You did get my letter didn't you?

(Gillian stands up. All three look awkward. Wilf goes to her and they shake hands)

WILF: I did an' all. How d'you do love. *(Looks at her stomach)* When you getting married then?

RICHARD: As soon as the divorce is final. It should be through in about a month.

WILF: It's a reight kettle of fish, and no mistake!

GILLIAN: We're both ... both glad about the baby, Mr. Crowther.

WILF: Why, I should think you are and all love. Tha knows, Margaret—that's his brother's wife— Margaret told me their two were summat as she called a planned family. If them's a planned family, give me a honest to God accident any time on t'year. Sit yourself down love. I'll go and get washed and out on me muck. *(Gillian sits down. Wilf goes up to her)* Don't fret thisen love. Tha's reight welcome here. Tha's welcome.

(He takes a towel which is hanging by the fireplace and goes out into the kitchen, shutting the door)

GILLIAN: I wouldn't have thought he could be as nice as that. *(She puts a hand on her stomach. Richard sits on the arm of her chair)* I thought I'd feel ashamed, but I don't.

RICHARD: Well he liked you.

GILLIAN: In a way, I wish I'd known your wife. How can they avoid making comparisons? And it's a bad start, like this. *(Pause)* Did she get on well with him?

RICHARD: Look Gillian, don't let's start worrying about Janet.

GILLIAN: I wonder what they thought, your marrying a rich and elegant woman like her. That photo of her makes me feel tatty just to look at it.

RICHARD: Does he look the sort of man who'd give a damn whether somebody's rich and elegant? *(Knock on the door)* That'll be Edgar.
(Richard goes to the front door and lets in Edgar and Margaret. Edgar is stocky and irritable-looking, forty-two. Margaret is about the same age—a sharp, complex, edgily tired woman)

EDGAR: Is mother still—

RICHARD: Yes. *(Pause)* She's asleep at the moment. Aunty Beatie's—

EDGAR: I'll sue that bloody garage one of these days. We had a puncture outside Doncaster. When I got the spare out it was as flat as hell, and—
(Margaret pushes past him into the living room. Puts her case down)

MARGARET: And I've had a lecture on the idleness of the modern workman for the last twenty miles. *(To Richard, with a sideglance at Gillian)* How are you darling? Where's father?

RICHARD: He's just getting washed. *(Takes Gillian's hand. She gets up, looking very anxious)* Margaret, Edgar, this is Gillian Moore.

MARGARET: Hello Gillian. *(Shakes hands)* Richard rang me to say he was bringing you with him.

EDGAR: *(Still at the door)* You didn't tell me he'd said that!

MARGARET: I had no intention of listening to you wittering on about it for five hours in the car.

EDGAR: I told you when Janet started the divorce I'd no intention of meeting your new girl friend. *(Gillian sits down. Edgar removes his coat and scarf, speaking angrily)* What you do with your life's your own affair, but—

MARGARET: But what *you* do with his life is *your* affair, isn't it darling?

EDGAR: You keep out of this Margaret---
          (Margaret flops into a chair and lights a cigarette)

GILLIAN: *(Almost crying)* When Richard asked me to come, he told me what you'd say. Now you've said it, I don't mind it as much as I expected. But I think since I am here—

EDGAR: I'm not attacking you personally—

MARGARET: Then who the hell are you attacking?
          (Edgar comes to the fireplace and stands with his back to it)

RICHARD: How like you to start moralising as soon as you get through the door! Do you think I was going to leave Gillian alone eight months pregnant just because you—
          (Wilf enters during Richard's speech. He is bare to the waist and is drying himself)

WILF: What the bladder of lard's going on in here? Are you fratching afore you've gotten into t'house?

MARGARET: Father—*(Goes to Wilf and kisses him)* We were so terribly sorry to hear about mother.

EDGAR: *(Shakes hands with Wilf)* How are you Dad? Just how bad is she?
          (Margaret sits down)

WILF: As bad as she could be, I'm sorry to have to say lad. Doctor came afore I went to work this morning and—

EDGAR: You mean to say you've been to *work?*

WILF: Why, does ta think I get me brass sitting on me backside surry?

EDGAR: With my mother dangerously ill?

WILF: Don't let it turn thy stomach. I haven't been working for mesen. I've been working for t'tax man.

EDGAR: I give up!

WILF: Nay, tha mun never give up lad! You'll have

been introduced to Gillian then? *(Winks at Gillian)* It isn't what you might call planned, but it'll be all reight. *(Turns back to Edgar, who is very angry)* And what's up with thee, like? Has ta lost a shilling and found a tanner? Or what?

(Beatie comes in from the stairs)

BEATIE: Wilf, they'd best come up.

(Wilf takes a clean shirt from the oven door, where it has been put to air)

WILF: You hear what your Aunty Beatie says.

(Edgar, Margaret and Beatie go upstairs. As Richard is leaving the room he looks at Gillian, hesitating)

GILLIAN: I'll stay down here with your dad. *(Richard goes out)* Aunt Beatie said she left you some dinner in the oven. Shall I put it out?

WILF: I don't know as I feel like eating owt love, thank you. It'd nobut stick in me gullet. Is there any tea in t'pot?

GILLIAN: *(Getting up)* I don't think it'll be hot. I'll make some more anyway, shall I? *(Goes to kitchen)*

WILF: This'll do me. Don't trouble thisen lass. I'll sup it, as long as it's not stewed.

GILLIAN: *(Calling from kitchen)* You don't mind my coming up with Richard, do you Mr. Crowther?

(She comes back with cup and saucer, puts them on the table and pours the tea)

WILF: Mind? Why should I mind? Tha's one on t'family now, int ta?

GILLIAN: Not as far as Edgar is concerned.

WILF: Nay, take no notice on Edgar, Gillian. This is *my* house, tha sees. Not his. If you and Richard's happy, that's all I care about.

GILLIAN: You know, Richard thinks he's been a disappointment to you.

WILF: Gillian, I'll tell you straight love. When him
           and Janet got married we wondered if they'd
           make a go on it. They spent their time gadd-
           ing round t'world on her money. He should
           have kept his independence from the start.
           *(Wilf pauses. He looks at the picture over the
           mantelpiece—a pseudo Van Gogh)*
           Then all that painting and writing and nowt
           come on it.
           (He points at the picture)
           He painted yon picture over t'mantelpiece.
           One on his first.

GILLIAN: Do you like it?
           (Gillian looks up at the picture doubtfully)

WILF: His mother does. I've never seen flowers like
           them in nature, mesen. Yon looks like summat
           t'cat's thrown up.
           (Wilf sits down at the table and rolls a cigarette)

GILLIAN: That's what Richard thinks now.

WILF: Oh aye, *now!* But he thought it were a master-
           piece *then.* Don't ask me though. It's his
           mother has an eye for colour, you know.

GILLIAN: I wish I'd been able to know Mrs. Crowther.

WILF: I wish you had an' all love. But tha's come too
           late.

GILLIAN: Have you thought about what you'll . . . what
           you'll do?

WILF: What I shall do?

GILLIAN: I mean, will you stay on here?

WILF: Canst think on any good reason why I
           shouldn't, love?

GILLIAN: It's just, Richard says you're due to retire in
           six months.

WILF: Aye, I've been thinking about it. *(Pause)*
           Here, would you like to see what British Rail-
           ways has given me for forty years hard labour?
           (Wilf crosses to the sideboard and opens a drawer.

	He comes to Gillian with a small white cardboard box)

GILLIAN: *Forty* years?

WILF: Aye, I went on t'London Midland and Scottish in nineteen twenty.

(Wilf takes a gold watch from the box and gives it to Gillian. She examines it closely)

What's ta think on that, then? It's what they give thee instead on a pension, tha sees.

GILLIAN: It's lovely.

WILF: Solid gold silver plated tin. *(He smiles at Gillian)* Has ta seen t' inscription? To Wilf, from Brian.

(Wilf turns the watch over in her hand. There is an inscription on the back)

GILLIAN: Brian?

WILF: *Sir* Brian! He's gone way of all flesh now.

(They both laugh and Gillian hands him the watch back. He stands by her, looking at it)

There, that copt thee didn't it?

GILLIAN: Do you like being an engine driver?

WILF: Oh aye, being a driver's all reight. It's British Railways as gets up my back.

GILLIAN: But I'd have thought you'd be all *for* nationalisation.

WILF: I am an' all love. It's British Railways sort of nationalisation I'm talking about.

(Wilf puts the watch in its box and goes to put it away)

Dost know, we getting to have as many bosses as t'parson preached about. And they know as much about the inside of an engine as I know about the inside on Buckingham Palace. Still, t'trouble's on both sides. We don't get sort of young lads firing that we used to. Good ones won't come on t'railway.

GILLIAN: I've always wanted to go on an engine.

(Wilf looks at her, disbelieving but amused)

WILF: What, on t'footplate? Tha'd change thy mind
               if tha travelled a few mile tender first. Specially
               on some of t'old rattlers we have nowadays.
               (He sits down at the table) Tha knows, they call
               me t'poet driver down at sheds.

GILLIAN: Why do they call you that?

WILF: Well, when you take an engine back you have
               to fill a report card in, if there's owt wrong
               with it, for t'fitters. I always put summat
               down as'll give them food for thought,
               like. Take this one last week. Reight shook us
               insides up it did. So I put on t'card: this
               engine has square wheels and oval axle boxes.
               You should've seen t'foreman's face.
               *(They both laugh. Beatie comes in from the stairs
               door. She is crying)*

BEATIE: You'd best go up now Wilf lad.
               *(Wilf gets up. He is suddenly very old and tired. He
               stops to look at the two women by the fire as he goes
               out)*
               Aren't you going as well, love?
               *(She sits down by the fire and cries softly, holding her
               apron to her face)*

GILLIAN: I think I'd better not.

BEATIE: Perhaps it's best. It's no fit thing for a lass in
               your condition.

GILLIAN: It's not that. But, things being what they
               are—

BEATIE: Eh love, there's plenty in our family been glad
               to get to church in time, I can tell you.
               *(Beatie dries her eyes and gets up. She collects the cups
               and saucers on the table)*
               I think she's going to go peaceful though, and
               that's a mercy. What'll become of our Wilf I
               don't know. He's that stubborn.
               *(She carries the crockery into the kitchen, Gillian
               opening the door for her)*

GILLIAN: Do you think he'd come to us?
               (Beatie talks as she fills the kettle and puts it on the fire in the living room)

BEATIE: He'll go to nobody, Gillian. He's right proud is their father, when it comes to t'bottom on him. That's one on t'things our Edgar and Richard don't understand.

GILLIAN: I think Richard understands.

BEATIE: Maybe he does and maybe he doesn't. It's my honest opinion them lads has gotten above theirsens. An' that's what comes on sending them to t'grammar school.

GILLIAN: But, don't you think Mr. and Mrs. Crowther were doing something worthwhile? Trying to give their children something better than they'd had?

BEATIE: Happen they were. But what I remember is t'way they pinched and scraped to do it. An where's it got them? There isn't one on my three lads making less than fifteen pound a week, without all that education, neither. They look after me, they do, and not one on them lives more than ten minutes walk away. There, they're coming down—

Scene 2

Wilf's Bedroom.

Richard, Margaret and Edgar leave the bedroom and go downstairs. Wilf is in the bedroom looking at his wife's face. Sound of shunted trucks clanking to a standstill. Close up Mrs. Crowther's face—she is dying.

Scene 3

Living room, a few minutes later.

EDGAR: What gets me is that you should bring Gillian
               with you. We could have done without that.

RICHARD: Edgar, lay off will you? Save it.

EDGAR: Save it for when? I've no intention of seeing
               either of you for a bloody long time, I'll tell you.

RICHARD: Suits me.

BEATIE: Eh, will you both not stop it? With your mother
               dying upstairs like she is. Y'ought to be
               ashamed on yersens.

RICHARD: Aunt Beatie, he's my brother. I can't just shut
               my ears and pretend he's a gibbering puppet,
               even if he acts like one. He's got to be
               answered.

MARGARET: Richard, for God's sake—

RICHARD: Do you think I don't care what's going on
               upstairs? Do you think I don't want to shut my
               mouth and let her die in a peaceful house?

MARGARET: Well then?

               (Richard subsides a little, continuing more quietly)

RICHARD: You know, she's actually proud of us! That's
               what cuts me. *(Wearily)* Proud of all the wrong
               things, like Edgar making as much in a week
               as my dad makes in a month.

BEATIE: Now Richard. You've both gotten on, and
               that's what she wanted.

RICHARD: Haven't we! But what about what we are,
               apart from what we've got? *(To Edgar)* The
               worst is, Edgar, you don't even care *why* Janet
               and me had to pack it in. That's a mere detail.
               Only you know, you do live in a world where
               people marry the wrong people, and sleep
               together when they're not married, and all the
               rest of it.

EDGAR: I do know it's wrong to marry a woman who loves and trusts you, then drink yourself silly and get off with other women, till she can't stand you any more!

BEATIE: Our Edgar!

EDGAR: Ask him. Ask Gillian. I expect she knows as well as I do.

RICHARD: The thing is you see Aunt Beatie, Edgar married a woman who loves and trusts him, and he wouldn't have a divorce even if they were tearing each other's hearts out!

MARGARET: Now just a minute Richard—

RICHARD: I don't suppose you are! I hope you never do either. If you ever had to point out to Edgar that he was driving you round the bend he'd tell you to start learning a foreign language.

MARGARET: I think we've had enough of this—

RICHARD: He's dreaming the great middle class dream, is Edgar—

MARGARET: Stop it!

RICHARD: Well, that's the irony of it. If only my mother and father could have seen it. To educate us, you see, so we'd be richer than them . . . in every sense. And I'm wondering if we haven't become the image of everything they lacked the insight to despise!

(Richard turns away. Edgar has half taken the point. Speaks awkwardly.)

EDGAR: I thought we'd get round to class talk before he'd finished.

RICHARD: *(Turning)* It's more than that.

EDGAR: Is it? What about the great working class dream? What about all that fame is the spur stuff? That table! I've spent some hours of agony there, I can tell you. And if you let up for a minute, it was: Get on wi' thy work, if tha wants to make owt on thisen! You don't

think my father thought he was bringing up
two future intellectuals for the Labour Party,
do you? It was *brass!* Anyway, the kind of
socialism he went in for, it's as dead as the
dodo.

Scene 4

*Wilf closes his wife's eyes. He crosses her hands on
her breast. He stands up, looks down at her. He
looks at the framed photograph on the chest of
drawers—of two men at an open-air bookstall with
posters—"Join The Left Book Club". Again he
looks at his wife's face—and then back to the
photograph.*

Scene 5

Living Room a few minutes later.

EDGAR: You're about twenty-five years out of date
Richard. Your so-called working classes want
things. Just like everybody else. And in those
days socialism—you know what it really boiled
down to with people like my father? It meant
pushing little sods like you and me on to
university so's we'd be able to push our noses
further down into the feed-bag. So as we'd get
to be bosses. You don't think they educated us
to be *socialists?* Not on your life! It was to get
us out of *this.*
(*He waves his arm at the room. Wilf appears at the
door and comes slowly into the room*).

WILF: Well, tha has gotten out on it, hasn't ta? And
so has thy mother.

BEATIE: *(Crying)* Eh, Wilf, Wilf.
WILF: And I've nobut one question to put to thee,
            Edgar.
EDGAR: What's that?
WILF: What's ta going to do with thy two lads?

Scene 6

*Gillian and Margaret's bedroom, later the same
evening. Gillian and Margaret are in their bedroom. Gillian is unpacking, Margaret is sitting at
the dressing table, putting pins in her hair.*

MARGARET: I hope you don't mind sharing a bed with me.
            I snore.
GILLIAN: It's Edgar who's going to mind, isn't it?
MARGARET: Oh, he's long past caring.
GILLIAN: But I meant—
MARGARET: Oh don't mind me darling. It's nice to have a
            bitch, now and then. Anyway, you'll soon find
            out about Edgar. When a situation makes him
            angry, it's usually because it's one he knows he
            has to accept.
GILLIAN: Have he and Richard always quarrelled like
            that? Or is it only because of me?
MARGARET: As far as I can make out, they've quarrelled
            ever since they could spit. But for the last ten
            years it's mostly been about politics. Mutual
            insults are all they've got left to show they're
            still fond of one another.
GILLIAN: Well, if they're both sleeping downstairs
            to-night, I hope they don't get on to either me
            or politics.
MARGARET: Believe it or not, Edgar was practically a com-
            munist when I first met him. We were both
            in our first year at college. Still, that was
            nineteen thirty-eight. In those days, if you

weren't on the left it meant you were probably
psychotic, or something. He's changed quite a
bit, has your future brother-in-law. *(Pause)*
How old are you Gillian?

GILLIAN: Twenty three. I'm afraid I'm not very up in
politics, myself.

MARGARET: But you're on Richard's side, aren't you?

GILLIAN: Yes. I am.

MARGARET: I never thought I'd marry so young as I did.
I wanted a first in history, and a career. *(Pause)*
Well, I got the first. Then I married Edgar. I
was full of ideas about, you know, an intellectual sort of life. Books and plays and music . . .
all that. Then there was the war, and the
children. I often wonder if it could all have
been so important to me, if I could let it go so
easily. I make resolutions, you know. I go to
the library and get a stack of books out. Never
touch them from one day to the next. God,
I must be boring your head off!

GILLIAN: Did you come from a—from a working class
family?

MARGARET: No. My father was a bank manager. True
blue.

GILLIAN: What I don't understand is why Edgar should
have changed so *much*. I mean, from the way
he talks now—

MARGARET: I understand it, believe me. Wanting a
different kind of world requires too much
mental effort. You end up with a mortgage,
and a seed catalogue, and a suspicion that
maybe murderers *ought* to be hanged. We did.

GILLIAN: People like Mr. Crowther don't change.

MARGARET: That's only because they've never had the
chance. They stay simple, and—ignorant of
how much everything else has changed.

GILLIAN: So you agree with Edgar, really.

MARGARET: I don't know who the hell I agree with! I'm past it darling.
(She rubs cream on her face)
You must admit, father *is* just a wee bit how green was my valley, isn't he?
(Wipes her fingers on Kleenex. Goes to fireplace and throws Kleenex in. Adjusts a pin in her hair)
I wonder why I've put these in to-night.

GILLIAN: Don't you usually?

MARGARET: Only when I want to scare Edgar away.
(Going back to dressing table)

GILLIAN: I thought you said he didn't—

MARGARET: Very rarely, he does. But I'm damned if I'll have it at his convenience. And if you don't see the point of that, it's because you're so wholesome. Never mind, we're *both* as safe as houses tonight.
(Glances at window)
Why did they have to go round telling the relations straight away? It's raining like hell too. I can't understand why anybody wants to live in Yorkshire at *all*. *(Rounds on Gillian)* Doesn't anything ever make you feel vicious? It's always men who get what they want and not what they deserve. With women it's the other way round. *(Controls herself)* I'm sorry, Gillian. Proper hag, aren't I?
(Sound of door downstairs)

Scene 7

The Living Room

Wilf and Richard come in. Pulling off their rain-coats. Wilf sits down and takes his boots off

WILF: I'm barn to take these boots off and just have

five minutes. *(He sits)*

When your Aunty Mary gets talking she's like a gramophone with t'needle stuck.

(Gillian comes in)

GILLIAN: I thought I heard the front door. Would you like something to eat?

WILF: Dost know, I think I *could* eat summat. Me stomach thinks me throat's cut. There's some cold ham in t'pantry, let's have a sandwich love.

GILLIAN: *(Going out to the kitchen)*

Margaret's gone to bed.

WILF: Hasn't our Edgar come in yet?

(Gillian calls "No" from kitchen)

She seems a reight grand lass, Richard.

(Bends to light a spill at the fire. Straightens up facing the Van Gogh)

Nowt seems to have gone reight for thee up till now, lad. One road or another.

RICHARD: Sometime, I'd like to tell you how it went wrong between me and Janet.

WILF: Nay, I'm not asking for explanations. Nobut, it looked as if tha were never going to settle down.

RICHARD: I never wanted to. Still, I'm getting used to the idea, now.

WILF: An' what's become on thy painting and writing?

RICHARD: I've pretty well given it up. I never seem to be able to finish anything.

WILF: It takes time, lad. Like owt that's worth doing.

RICHARD: It isn't that dad. I've no talent. *(Points at the painting)* You know, it's time we took that bloody thing down. *(Sits down at the table)*.

WILF: Your mother loved that picture.

RICHARD: It ought to come down.

WILF: Not afore your mother's buried.

RICHARD: Did I tell you I've given up supply teaching? I've taken a permanent job in a comprehensive.

WILF: So tha's finally made thy mind up to it.

RICHARD: It's a way of earning a living.

WILF: Is *that* all tha can see in it!

RICHARD: Well I wouldn't exactly say I'd got a vocation.

WILF: Tha's over thirty, lad. If tha'd gotten down to it when tha left college, instead on living on Janet's money, tha'd happen be in a better position today. *(Sits down at the table opposite Richard)*

RICHARD: Well, I've got down to it now.

WILF: I cannot understand why our Edgar's gone one road, and tha's gone another. I can't weigh it up.

RICHARD: I envy Edgar, in a way.

WILF: Tha envies him? What for?

RICHARD: He's a good scientist. He's doing something he wants to do, and he's good at it.

WILF: And is there nowt tha wants to do?

RICHARD: No. Nothing.

WILF: Dost mean to say, if tha can't be some sort on an artist, tha's not playing, like?

RICHARD: Could be.

WILF: Nay, tha wants to pull thy socks up!

RICHARD: You know dad, Edgar and I have opposite views on just about everything. Only his fit the world as he sees it and mine fit the world as I'd like to see it. That's a big difference. I'm tired. I'm so tired that being an adequate husband and father is about as much as I can reasonably expect of myself now. *(Pause)* And that, coming from somebody who's never gone hungry, never been worked to exhaustion, never struggled or *had* to—that's the end. I'm ashamed to say it to you dad. *(Rises)*

WILF: Nay, I know there's more than one kind of struggle, lad, if I know nowt else. *(Pause)* Everything looked a damn sight different when I were your age. Dost know, when we first came here tha could be out in t'fields in five minutes. On a Sunday night we used to put Edgar in t'push chair and thee in thy pram and walk two or three mile along the canal. It wasn't built up then. You could fair smell t'countryside t'other side on t'pit. If tha goes up there now, tha'll see we've almost joined on to Leeds! It's all gone, all that nature. *(Pause)* T'sort of life we had, and all, tha doesn't see that no more neither. Many a time ten and fifteen in here on a Sunday for their teas. We used to get on singing hymns when it were all cleared away, like. Mind, there were nowt solemn about it. We all enjoyed us sens. T'same folk we never see them from one month to t'next, nowadays. Their sons and daughters comes up in their cars to take them for a drive on a Sunday afternoon. But it's not t'same. *(Broods)* Now, we've gotten t'telly, tha knows. Nay, when I were thy age I had thee lads, and thy mother, and I thought t'time'd come when we should have a different road of going on in this country. *(Pause)* By, tha talks about socialism! I were as red as John Penny's eye after a night on t'beer. Socialism had some guts in it in them days. But if it's altered, so has t'working classes. And there's an end on it, for most on them.

RICHARD: It shouldn't be an end of it.

WILF: Eh, what dost expect, if t'sons can nobut turn round and say they tired? Tha grieves me, talking like that. What's up with thee?

RICHARD: You know what your sons are, right enough!

One solid conservative and one shagged-out political idealist.

WILF: Tha says tha's gotten different views from Edgar. *Stand* on them then! Dost want it chucked at thee on a plate?

RICHARD: I'm only trying to say—

WILF: That tha's in a reight pickle!

RICHARD: It's a question of where to begin again, dad.

WILF: Tha mun find thy road, same as we had to, Richard. Nobut, tha's an educated man. Tha mun do better than we *could* have done, with all t'will in the world. And happen being educated, tha'll not let them pull t'wool over thy eyes.

(He bends down to pick his boots up. Gillian comes in with a tray)

GILLIAN: There. It's all ready. Will you have it by the fire?

WILF: Eh love, my appetite's gone again. I'll get mesen off to bed, if you don't mind.

GILLIAN: Are you sure?

(Quite suddenly Wilf is almost in tears)

WILF: Ah mun go up, lass.

(He looks from one to the other as if appealing to them. Gillian goes to kiss him)

GILLIAN: Goodnight, father.

(He puts his arms round her, still holding his boots)

WILF: Tha's a good lass. Good night, both on you. You'll bank t'fire up, won't you? Keep yoursens warm.

(Wilf goes out. He walks upstairs slowly, carrying his boots)

GILLIAN: You haven't been . . . upsetting him, Richard?

RICHARD: I don't know. I suppose I have. I didn't mean to. We weren't arguing, or anything. I was trying to tell him how I feel about . . . well, you know.

GILLIAN: And what about how he feels?

RICHARD: Yes, I know.

GILLIAN: He's so vulnerable, all of a sudden.

RICHARD: I know.

GILLIAN: He's really expected, hoped for quite a lot from you and Edgar. Hasn't he?

RICHARD: Yes. He has.

GILLIAN: Did you know?

RICHARD: I haven't really talked to him for years, till to-night. *(Pause)* Hadn't you better be going up to bed yourself?

GILLIAN: I suppose so. The baby's like a lead weight to-night. *(Pause)* Richard, the room where your dad's sleeping—

RICHARD: What about it?

GILLIAN: Was it yours?

RICHARD: Mine and Edgar's. Why?

GILLIAN: I had to go in for some sheets. I found this. *(Lifts up a cushion from the sofa and brings out a worn and shapeless knitted monkey)* You told me about him, remember?

RICHARD: *(Takes the monkey)* In that chest of drawers? *(She nods)* I thought he'd been cremated years ago!

GILLIAN: So I brought him down to keep you company. Make up for me! *(They both laugh. Richard sets the monkey on top of the clock on the mantelpiece)* Well—

RICHARD: Stay in bed in the morning—there's no need to get up early. Beatie's staying next door, so she'll be in about half past eight. *(Gillian goes to him. They stand with their arms round each other)*

GILLIAN: I shall miss you. It's the first time we've slept apart.

RICHARD: And I shall miss you.

GILLIAN: The blankets and things are in the hall. *(Kisses him)* Good night.

RICHARD: Goodnight love.

GILLIAN: Luv.

(They kiss again. She leaves. Richard pours a cup of tea and takes a sandwich. Sits by the fire. Edgar comes in rubbing his hands, and goes to stand in front of fire)

EDGAR: Everybody in bed?

RICHARD: Yes.

EDGAR: How did my Aunty Mary take it?

RICHARD: Tearfully. Slightly predatory as well. Tea?

EDGAR: Yes please. Why predatory?

RICHARD: *(Pouring tea)* That ring my grandmother gave my mother. Aunty Mary's been after it for years. Have a sandwich.

EDGAR: *(Takes a sandwich, bites into it)* You don't spare anybody, do you?

RICHARD: How did yours go? Uncle George is a bit senile, isn't he?

EDGAR: Hadn't a clue who I was talking about. Still, the poor old sod's nearly seventy-three.
            (For a few seconds they chew, eyeing each other)

RICHARD: Well?

EDGAR: Well?

RICHARD: Made any nice bombs lately?

EDGAR: I must say, you've managed to turn my mother's death into a memorable occasion.

RICHARD: Which otherwise it wouldn't have been, would it?

EDGAR: Now look here, Richard—

RICHARD: All right, all right. Forget it. Let's have a truce, shall we? An armed truce.

EDGAR: I'm perfectly willing to set aside—

RICHARD: No, don't set anything aside Edgar. Just shut up and help me make the beds.
            (Richard goes into the hall. Comes back with a pile

of blankets, sheets and pillowcases) Which will you have, a sofa or two chairs?

EDGAR: Which do you prefer?

(Richard throws blankets on chair and sofa and gets out his cigarettes)

RICHARD: Let's have a cigarette and work out the protocol. *(Lights one)*

EDGAR: You can sleep where the hell you like.

RICHARD: Now, now!

(Takes out a coin and spins it)

Call—

EDGAR: Heads.

RICHARD: Heads it is, brother. Which'll you have? The Dorchester or the Ritz?

EDGAR: I'll have the sofa.

RICHARD: All right then. Let's get on with it.

(They begin to make up a bed on the sofa)

RICHARD: *(Throwing blanket)* Come on.

EDGAR: All right, all right.

RICHARD: Come on, nurse Crowther . . .

(Richard pulls the blanket and Edgar grabs at it. Tug of war. Richard begins to laugh and Edgar too begins to enjoy it)

Scene 8

Wilf's Bedroom.

Wilf is at the door of the bedroom where his wife is lying. He is wearing rough, striped pyjamas. He goes up to the bed foot and stands looking down. Hesitantly he touches her feet where they make a pyramid under the sheet. Moves to the bedside, rubbing his hand across his face.

WILF: An' I mun go on? *(Pause)* Without thee? *(Pause)* Did they please you, our lads? *(Pause)*

What does it all come to? *(He moves closer to her face)*

I wished I were dead myself, tonight. *(Pause)* I've never wished that afore in my life. *(Pause)* Never. *(Long pause)* Where are you? *(Pause)* They frighten me. *(Pause)* When they get on at one another, they make me shiver. I'd sooner it had been me to go. *(Pause)* It's worse to lose their mother.

(Rain drumming heavily against the windows. He rises. Looks to window, goes to the door. Stands looking at the bed).

Ah mun learn to bide it. *(Pause)* We all mun.

Scene 9

The Living Room.

Richard and Edgar are in pyjamas. Richard is arranging a pillow on the armchair. Edgar gargling in the kitchen. Edgar comes in from the kitchen and goes to poke the fire. Richard gets into the armchair and pulls the blankets over him.

RICHARD: Hey, you in the choir!
(He sings, imitating boy soprano)
Oh, for the wings, for the wings, of a dove . . . far away, far away would I . . . that time Billy Munt was pumping the organ and he stopped just when you were on top C. You burst into tears and the organ sounded like a dinosaur breaking wind.
(Edgar lies down on the sofa)
Bill was killed in Cyprus.

EDGAR: Well, if we'd taken a strong line in Cyprus from the start—

RICHARD: Oh, come off it. He'd just finished at Leeds

Art school when he was called up. Because he was an *artist,* see, they set him on painting signs in Greek for the troops to display. Disperse or we fire. Billy was with the Cypriots from the start so he painted the letters as small as he could—

EDGAR: So?

RICHARD: So when they went to break up a demonstration one morning, they couldn't read Billy's writing, it was too small. There was some shooting, and he got killed. The brutal comedies of war, don't y'know.

EDGAR: I thought we were supposed to have a truce?

RICHARD: Don't mind me. I'm passionate. I get carried away. *(Pause)* Well, I suppose it's all old hat, now.

             (Edgar catches sight of the knitted monkey)

EDGAR: What the hell's that?

RICHARD: What?

EDGAR: On the clock.

RICHARD: You ought to know.

EDGAR: What do you mean, *I* ought to know?

RICHARD: It's a monkey.

             (He goes to the mantelpiece and takes the monkey off the clock. Goes back to the armchair)

EDGAR: Never seen it before in my life.

RICHARD: As a matter of fact, you had one of the few real relationships that you ever had in your life, with this monkey. *(Pause)* It was my monkey.

EDGAR: *(Mimicking)* It was my monkey!

RICHARD: To be exact, it's a knitted monkey. Stuffed with kapok. You used to amuse yourself by tying knots in its tail, didn't he? *(To the monkey)* Yes he did. The sadist was well to the fore in your character even in those days.

EDGAR: It stank.

RICHARD: Stank? Every knot in that monkey's tail was a

EDGAR: knot in my tail, chum *(Holds it up, looking at it)* It stank because you were an incorrigible bed wetter.

RICHARD: Yes and why? Because I had to share a bed with a torturer. You'd have made a granite statue wet its bed.

(Edgar bursts out laughing. Richard throws a pillow at him. Edgar throws it back. A pillow fight develops, which ends up with them laughing and wrestling on the floor. Margaret appears in the hall doorway in her nightdress)

MARGARET: Edgar! Richard!

(The two men stare at her, embarrassed)

What the hell do you think you're doing? You were making too much noise to hear it, but your father's crying like a child in his sleep!

(Edgar slowly sits up. Richard and Edgar look at one another helplessly)

Scene 10

The Living Room. The following morning.
Edgar is reading 'The Times' alone at the break-fast table. Margaret comes in wearing a dressing gown, she looks haggard.

EDGAR: You'll have to make some fresh tea. *(He speaks without looking up from the paper)*

MARGARET: *(Weighing the pot)* It's half full.

EDGAR: It's cold.

(Margaret goes to the kitchen. Empties tealeaves in sink. Fills and turns on electric kettle)

MARGARET: Where is everybody?

EDGAR: Richard and Gillian shopping. Aunt Beatie next door. My father's gone to arrange about the funeral.

(He turns to the crossword and takes a pen from his

pocket. Margaret comes in and wanders over to the window)

MARGARET: Still raining.

EDGAR: I know.

MARGARET: There's a dead bird in the gutter. Oh Edgar, it's *flat*. Flattened out.

EDGAR: Run over.

MARGARET: And a lot you care!
(Edgar puts down his paper in exasperation)

EDGAR: I am not the Lord God Almighty! I do not have the welfare of every little sparrow at heart! What are you going to do, report me to the police?

MARGARET: Oh, go back to your crossword! *(Edgar carries on reading)* A room with a view. One goods-yard, a row of tarted up slums and about half a million chimneys. And Aunt Beatie says she wouldn't live anywhere else!

EDGAR: I don't suppose it's the view she's fond of.

MARGARET: *(Imitating Beatie)* Ah've had a 'undred and fowerteen bairns an' there int one on 'em makin' less ner—

EDGAR: *(Looking up irritated)* She showed a damn sight more guts raising her family than you'll ever do with yours.

MARGARET: Now don't start prickling with local pride. If you see Aunt Beatie as a sort of provincial corn goddess that's okay by me but don't expect me to keep a straight face.

EDGAR: *(Going back to his crossword)* I don't even know what a corn goddess is.

MARGARET: No, you wouldn't know, would you? *(She sits down at the table)* I seemed to spend the whole night having nightmares. And Gillian slept like a baby.

EDGAR: Should have taken one of your pills.

MARGARET: Do you know Edgar, I believe if I woke up one

	morning and told you I was dying, you'd say I should have taken one of my pills!
EDGAR:	There's two things wrong with you Margaret. Anaemia and constipation. Both are amenable to treatment—pills.
MARGARET:	I'd better not start telling you what's wrong with you.
	(The kettle whistles and she goes out into kitchen)
	D'you know what Gillian told me last night?
EDGAR:	What?
MARGARET:	She said before she got big, they did it nearly every night.
EDGAR:	Wait till they've been together as long as we have.
MARGARET:	*(In the kitchen doorway)*
	I ought to write one of those articles. *(She comes to the table, carrying the teapot)* I gave myself to a nuclear physicist by Margaret Crowther. Intimate details of what it means to be married to the men who risk the perils of radiation to make *your* bombs.
EDGAR:	*(Filling in a clue in the crossword)* Overdoses of radiation cause sterility, not impotence.
MARGARET:	My God, what's *in* the paper this morning?
	(Puts on an announcer's voice)
	Strontium ninety, up two points. Fission products, a steady fall.
EDGAR:	Very funny!
MARGARET:	*(Pouring tea)* Gillian's scared stiff she'll have a baby with two heads. I told her what you said about fall-out hazards being exaggerated. It's odd isn't it, the way some people go on worrying when they've been told everything's perfectly all right. Well, she said Richard said—
EDGAR:	Richard is a vacillating idealist. He couldn't tell a neutron from a nappy. It's people like

Richard who get mixed up in these marches without knowing a damn thing about radiation except what they read in the weekly papers.

MARGARET: I think Gillian's absolutely all right for Richard. You know, when I met you I thought it was terribly romantic your being a scientist. All those test tubes.

EDGAR: I haven't touched a test tube for years.

MARGARET: Richard's a sort of everything manqué, isn't he?

EDGAR: *(He gets up, puts his pen away and goes to sit on sofa)* I gather you want to talk about Richard and Gillian this morning.

MARGARET: I just want to talk. Sooner or later you'll have to realise that there's no point in treating Gillian like a tart. Has it occurred to you that they show every sign of being happy together?

EDGAR: And has it occurred to you that so did Richard and Janet? He can't spend his life getting married and divorced and marrying his mistresses, can he? And don't tell me it's anything to do with being an *artist*. I don't think the work of art exists that was worth ruining anybody's life for.

MARGARET: I wonder how Richard sees us—

EDGAR: I don't give a damn.

MARGARET: *(Fiercely)* Then you ought to! *(More quietly, to herself)* Sometimes I feel as if I don't exist.

EDGAR: All I can say is, there's a lot of evidence to the contrary!

MARGARET: *(Ignoring him)* Something about Richard and Gillian together. They aren't all the things we *are*.

EDGAR: Such as?

MARGARET: Trivial. Stunted. Absurd, really. We're absurd. *(Pause)* Even you must have your dim

	suspicions. Over forty, married, two children, three thousand a year. What about *you?*
EDGAR:	For heaven's sake what about me?
MARGARET:	Oh, it's both of us! I know. I'm wondering if I could have been different. *(Pause)* What do we care about? What passionately concerns us? You sneer at Richard and the people that go on the bomb marches, but you're a *smaller* man for not even entertaining the idea. Hardly matters if Richard's right or wrong. He and Gillian are a *different kind* from us. I want to know how it is. And why it is. Can't you see what I'm trying to say?
EDGAR:	Oh yes! I can! *(Mocking her)* You and I are trivial, stunted and absurd. You know it and I don't, and in some peculiar way this makes you one up. Richard and Gillian are neither trivial, stunted nor absurd, and this makes *them* one up. Frankly I haven't a clue what it all means. It must be the change of life! *(Margaret's face has slowly contorted as she listened. She bangs her fists on the table suddenly, and upsets the cup of tea. She is crying)*
MARGARET:	*(Crying)* Damn you Edgar! Damn you. Edgar, I'm nearly middle aged. My sons are growing up and I'm empty. I used to be clever . . . interested, when I was young. I was happy then just to lie down in bed beside you. Do you never think about the future at all? Maybe another twenty years, and how am I supposed to spend it? Grovelling in a rock garden and cutting sandwiches?
EDGAR:	*(Goes to her genuinely concerned and upset by her reaction)* Margaret, I honestly didn't know you were so unhappy.
MARGARET:	It's something I've never . . . let into my mind, until now.

EDGAR:	I wouldn't have said we had so little.
MARGARET:	Then why do I *feel* we've got so little?
EDGAR:	I expect you'd like the best of both worlds.
MARGARET:	What worlds?
EDGAR:	Mine . . . and Richard's. I imagine that intelligent women always do.
MARGARET:	*(Harshly)* Don't you *dare* patronise me!
EDGAR:	*(Half smiling)* Oh, Margaret!
MARGARET:	Leave me alone—for a bit. Please.
EDGAR:	*(Showing furtive relief)* Well, I did say I'd pick my father up at the undertaker's.
MARGARET:	Yes, all right.
EDGAR:	We'll talk about all this again. When we get home, Margaret.
MARGARET:	If you want to.
EDGAR:	I'm . . . sorry, Margaret.
	(He goes out of the front door. Margaret is left alone at the table. Her face is tense. She is gripping the teacup with both hands)

Scene 11

Old Folk's Club. The same morning.

The 'Old Folk's Shelter' is a small brick building on a vacant lot in the main street. In its one room are a few shabby armchairs, a table and a coal stove. Uncle George is a frail old man in his early seventies. He sits at the table playing with dominoes. Auntie Bessie sits near him, knitting. Wilf passes the window and comes in. He takes out a packet of cigarettes and puts them in front of George.

WILF:	Now then! I've brought your cigs mesen this week.
BESSIE:	Eh, our poor Alice.
GEORGE:	You what?
BESSIE:	*(Shouting)* I say, our Alice'll not be bringing

your cigs no more. *(To Wilf)* He understands nowt you say. It were good on your Edgar to come and tell us last night. I am sorry, Wilf. Eh, she used to bring him his cigs every Saturday, come sunshine or snow.

WILF: Will you come to t'funeral then?

BESSIE: Nay, he's not fit to take nowhere.

GEORGE: Where's our Alice?

BESSIE: *(Shaking her head at Wilf)* She's passed away, George. Last night. Don't you remember, our Edgar came to tell us?

GEORGE: Aye, they don't care about you when you begin to lose track on yersen. *(He becomes crazily malicious)* Is it Wilf? Wait till you qualifies for t'old folks club lad. Soon be thy turn. We come here to die, tha knows. Aye, I've seen three on them die in front of yon very fire!

WILF: *(To Bessie)* Not much on a place, is it?

BESSIE: It's not so bad when there's a few on them here. You get a bit of company, you know. He still plays his dominoes.

GEORGE: *(Fumbling at the cigarettes)* We had your Edgar round last night.

WILF: I know, George, I know.

GEORGE: Like a dog with two tails, yon one.

WILF: Now what d'you mean by that?

GEORGE: Wants some stick, yon one.

BESSIE: He doesn't know half on what he's saying, Wilf. Take no notice lad.

WILF: What's up with our Edgar, then?

GEORGE: Tha wants to take him away from yon school and put him down t'pit! T'other one an' all. Tha's wasting thy time, lad.

WILF: You're thirty year behind t'times George. Our Edgar's a grown up man. So is Richard.

BESSIE: Two lovely lads they are, an' all.

GEORGE: Just thee wait. Tha'll see when tha's sitting
             here day after day watching folk through yon
             pane of glass. It won't be long.

BESSIE: I sometimes think it'd be a blessing if he were
             taken. What if I go afore him? He can't dress
             his sen. He can't feed his sen. If he has a cig
             you've got to watch him or he's on fire.

WILF: I never thought George'd go like that. He
             were a fine strong feller.

BESSIE: Edgar said Alice went peaceful.

WILF: Aye, she went peaceful. *(Pause)* I've always
             hesitated to ask you Bessie, but are you all
             reight for money? Can you manage?

BESSIE: Eh Wilf, lad, we live on us pension and I've
             enough put by to bury us you know. Our
             Keith sends t'rent, when he bethinks his sen.
             He's a manager now. He has sixty fellers
             working under him.

WILF: They're all getting on, aren't they?
             *(George is getting a cigarette into his mouth, with
             great difficulty. Wilf lights it for him)*
             What we trying to tell you George, our Alice
             has passed on.

GEORGE: Aye, yon lot from Parliment wants to come
             up here and tell some on t'old folk they well
             off, like. They do.
             (Pause. His mind clears a little)
             Three quarters on them that's had families
             round here, they've watched their bairns
             grow up into reight Tories.

BESSIE: It's funny, isn't it. For all his mind wanders
             he can turn owt into politics! *(Pause)* There's
             not so many like him and you left, Wilf.

WILF: Happen it's just as well.

BESSIE: He lived and breathed Keir Hardie when he
             were a young feller. You're going to be lonely
             Wilf. Why don't you join t'Darby and Joan

	Club when you retire?
WILF:	I prefer fishing.
BESSIE:	I suppose you could go to one on t'lads.
WILF:	I want to be dependent on nobody. *(Looks round)* I couldn't bide this place, Bessie.
BESSIE:	Well, it's always warm. And you hear all t'gossip.
GEORGE:	Don't thee listen to her. We come here to die. Then tha sees, t'muck'll cover us, and it's all ower! I won't say I wouldn't sooner have died in t'pit, but tha's got to die somewhere.
BESSIE:	We don't spend all our time here you know, Wilf. We can get into t'pictures for ninepence. Nobut he goes to sleep and many a time I can't wake him. I make t'best on it an watch t'picture round again.
WILF:	Does he still take his gill?
BESSIE:	Does he! He drinks more free beer than he pays for, down at Fox. But I will say, he's worked hard all his life, he's entitled to his glass of beer.
GEORGE:	Young feller come to t'door afore t'last election, he says: I hope we can count on your support, Mr. Ackroyd. He were nobut a little un. A good breath'd have fair blown him ower Ilkley Moor. I says, sitha young feller, tha wants to make thisen scarce, afore I lose my temper. Tha wants to get thisen off to Spain, I says. Fight for them that's making a world fit for t'workers to live in. But ay'm canvassing for the conservative party, he says. Well dost know, I picks up on yon shovel and I has him out on that door like a shot out on a gun! *(Wheezes into laughter)*
BESSIE:	He gets it all mixed up, you know.
WILF:	He's not t'only one! *(Pause)* It grieves me to

see him like this, Bessie.

BESSIE: He were as right as rain till he stopped work. An' mind you don't let it take you like that! You'd think there'd be summat else in a man's life besides his work. Folks nowadays, they know how to enjoy theirsens a bit better. *(Pause)* Well, you've got your bairns, Wilf.

WILF: Nay, when they're grown up there isn't much left on what they were when they were little lads. Nobut I look at them sometimes and it's a reight effort to think on I'm their father. When I hear them talking I sometimes feels as if I were born with my head full of slack coal!

BESSIE: Well you can't expect t'world to stand still, can you?

GEORGE: Alice, did you say? Did you say Alice has passed away?

BESSIE: Yes, owd lad. She has.

GEORGE: Who's going to bring me my cigs then?

BESSIE: Wilf's just given you your cigs! *(To Wilf)* He isn't callous, Wilf. It's—

WILF: Nay, I know. I'll be getting on.

BESSIE: I think we shall sit on here for a bit. Then we'll go and get our dinners. You'll come and see us, won't you Wilf. You an' George were very close, at one time.

WILF: Your fire wants making up.
(He takes a skep of coal and shakes some into the stove).
They ought to give you some better coal.
(Stands looking round the room)
Tha's better off in your own home, than here, Bessie.

BESSIE: Nay, I like to get out and see what folks is doing. What else is there? *(Pause)* T'days is long, when you get old, Wilf. You'll see. Eh, you sometimes wonder what it's all been for, don't you?

GEORGE: I can remember t'first day our Alice went into service, dost know. Setting off with her little tin trunk. She were hardly big enough to see over t'table top.

BESSIE: He can remember t'early days all right. But he couldn't remember summat that happened yesterday!

GEORGE: Thirteen year old, she was. Two year afore t'Kaiser war. *(Pause)* It hasn't been nowt but bloody wars, when you come to look at it. Has it? Still, with a bit of luck we shall be under t'sod afore t'next one. Capitalists has got to go on making wars, tha knows. That's Marx, that is. Karl Marx said that.

BESSIE: I cannot make him understand it isn't like he thinks no more. Our house is a palace compared with what it used to be. We just managed to get it done out afore he give up work.

WILF: I'd best be off.

BESSIE: An' you'll come and see us, Wilf? Our Alice always came round on a Saturday.
(Wilf hesitates by the door, looking from one to the other)

WILF: I'll come an' see you. I'll come round to your house.

BESSIE: Nay, you'll nearly always find us here lad, with t'other old uns.

WILF: Aye. Well I'll be seeing you then. *(He goes)*

GEORGE: Aye. Tha'll see us if I last.

Scene 12

The Kitchen. Later the same morning.
Margaret is now dressed. She is waiting for the
kettle to boil, and stands reading a brass plaque
on the wall, a poem—'Mother'. The kettle boils
and she makes another pot of tea. Wilf comes in the
front door, takes off his coat and comes through to
the kitchen.

MARGARET: Edgar's gone down to the undertakers in the car, to meet you!

WILF: Has he? I thought he wasn't coming so I walked back. I stopped at t'owd folks shelter to give Uncle George his weekly packet of cigs.

MARGARET: Uncle George? Is he still—

WILF: Aye. He's past it. To look at him now, you wouldn't think he were a reight grand speaker. He knew t'history on t'trade union movement backwards. I'll always remember him t'way he used to be. Eh, one Saturday afternoon it's years back now, I heard him heckling somebody speaking for t'Catholic Truth Society, in t'market place. This priest like, he stood it as long as he could, then he turns to George and says: *(Imitates posh voice)* My dear man, if God did not create the world, perhaps you'd be good enough to tell me what you are standing on at this moment! And George, quick as a flash, dost know what George said?

MARGARET: What?

WILF: Quick as a flash George says:—an electro-magnetic flux!
(They laugh)
But he were a reight un! He were a reader, you know. Lenin, Trotsky—he had a go at the lot.

(Pause) He worked till he were seventy, an, all. Now he has to be looked after like a baby. *(Pause)* If that's growing old—

MARGARET: I'm sure you won't go like that! *(Pouring his tea into a cup)*

WILF: I'd sooner be put to sleep like a bloody dog. Tha's a right good lass nobut can I have my mug?

MARGARET: *(Gets mug from shelf)* I always forget don't I?

WILF: I've never asked you how t'bairns are, Margaret.

MARGARET: Oh, they're fine. Edgar's talking of sending them to boarding school.

WILF: Nay!

MARGARET: Don't tell him I told you. He's rather touchy about it.

WILF: It's same as t'bloke said—

MARGARET: What?

WILF: Wonderful, wonderful, what'll happen next!

MARGARET: Now don't you start taking the micky out of Edgar! *(Pause)* I don't know whether I want them to go or not.

WILF: I can see by t'time t'Crowthers gets to t'third generation, we'll have a life peerage in t'family or summat!

MARGARET: Well you started it!

WILF: I'm wondering what I have started!

MARGARET: *(Hesitating)* Gillian's nice, isn't she?

WILF: I've right taken to her. Where are they, any road?

MARGARET: Shopping, for Aunt Beatie. I never got on with Janet.

WILF: I can't say as I took much notice, love. There wasn't a time when she came here without bringing a few fish hooks, or a trout fly or summat. Mind there's nowt to beat t'flies you make yoursen.

MARGARET: I wonder what it's like to be really rich. *(Going to sink)*

WILF: Same as being poor, nobut tha's gotten a lot of money!

MARGARET: *(Slightly resentful)* Whenever I try to talk to you, you always make fun of me.

WILF: What's on thy mind, Margaret?

MARGARET: I can hardly stand this trouble between Edgar and Richard.
(They come into the living room and Margaret stands in front of the fire)

WILF: Dost think I can?

MARGARET: At one time you'd have thought Richard and Janet were the ideal couple.

WILF: There isn't any such thing, a man and woman makes theirsens out on some idea on t'future. And a man's got to be strong. He's got to give a woman strength, for all t'strength she's gotten's for her bairns. An t'world that he wants—she wants it, for if she doesn't she can mean nowt to him.

MARGARET: *(Fiercely)* No! It isn't that. It can't be just that.

WILF: Now what's gotten into thee?

MARGARET: *Nothing's* got into me!
(Wilf looks at her. He takes his tobacco tin and matches from the mantelpiece and rolls a cigarette)

WILF: Dost know, when Richard came home from college he asked if I could get him set on down at sheds? I'd have looked all reight, wouldn't I? Next thing we heard he were a clown in a circus, then he were a navvy, then we got a telegram saying: Married yesterday, leaving for Berlin to morrow. Our Edgar doesn't know the half of it. His mother and me kept that side on it dark, tha sees.
(Richard and Gillian come in, Richard carrying a loaded shopping basket which he puts on the table.

They take off their coats)

There you are then. Have you seen anybody you liked better than yoursens?

RICHARD: I don't reckon much to your new town centre.

WILF: Nay, Gillian, sit thee down love. Take t'weight off your feet.

(Gillian sits down)

Tha munt let nobody hear thee running down t'new centre. They reight proud on it lad!

GILLIAN: It's awful!

WILF: Would tha prefer t'oed slums then, Richard?

RICHARD: I don't like brand new slums!

WILF: Tha sees, t'feller that built them understands Yorkshire folk. He knows they go round with their eyes on t'pavement looking for tanners.

(Beatie comes in and goes to the shopping basket. Begins to unpack it).

BEATIE: Did you get bread, Gillian love?

GILLIAN: It's on the kitchen table.

(Beatie takes the basket into the kitchen)

BEATIE: That's been a reight grand help to me. Mrs. Craven is in a state over Alice. She says they moved in same week as you Wilf and it's just thirty years next week. It's a long time to be neighbours, and never a wrong word neither. *(Feels in her apron pocket and goes back into the living room)* Eh Richard lad I'm forgetting, I copt telegram lad on his way t'front door. There's one for you love. I hope it's nowt. *(Hands telegram to Richard)* And Wilf, you've not drawn them curtains in t'little bedroom.

(Richard reads the telegram. Stands looking stunned)

GILLIAN: Richard! What's the matter?

(She goes to Richard reads telegram aloud over his shoulder)

Arriving two p.m. this afternoon—Janet.

BEATIE: Eh, no!

MARGARET: But how did she—

          (Edgar comes in quietly from the kitchen)

RICHARD: Who told Janet then? Who the hell *told* her?

EDGAR: I did. I asked her to come.

          (Gillian bursts into tears, puts her hands to her face. After a moment she rushes out, upstairs. Richard follows her. To Margaret)

          Well don't look so bloody outraged! *(Pulls his coat off, throws it on a chair)* You knew Richard was bringing Gillian, but you didn't tell me, did you? Oh no! Why do I have to be kept in ignorance of what's going on in my own family? *(Pause)* Let me tell you, marrying Janet was the only thing Richard ever did that brought my mother any happiness—

MARGARET: Why are *you* kept in ignorance? Because your insight into human nature is so profound you think making the best of a bad job is the anglo-saxon contribution to civilization!

EDGAR: Margaret, if either you or Richard had told me, do you think I'd have sent for Janet? As a matter of fact I wired her this morning not to come. Not much hope of being in time I knew, but—

MARGARET: Sometimes you make me *sick!* What were you thinking about? A tender reconciliation under Gillian's *nose?*

WILF: Edgar, I don't rightly know what tha's been up to, an' I'm sure tha nobut had best on intentions. But I'm not stopping in this house to watch you at one another's throats. I'm not! One road and another I don't know where to turn between you. An' if you don't care as it's your mother lying dead up in yon middle bedroom, I care as it's *my wife*. She's dead, and nowt'll bring her back, and I've been trying to weigh you all up for t'last twenty-four hours, but I've had enough. You've given me summat to think about between you—

(Richard comes in as his father stops speaking)

MARGARET: How is she?

RICHARD: *(To Beatie)* Will you go up, Aunt Beatie? She's not so good.

BEATIE: You want to make your minds up to stop it. Stop it. All of you. You'll send your father out of his mind.

(Beatie goes upstairs. Richard sits wearily in the armchair)

RICHARD: I'm sorry about it all, Dad.

WILF: I'm off out, I'm barn to your Uncle Jack's and by God you'd better sort yersens out, for I'll have no more!

(Goes to hall, puts on cap and reappears in the doorway)

When t'undertaker comes your Auntie Beatie'll show him up.

And if Janet turns up, I've no doubt she'll soon see why I'm not at home to see her. I'm leaving you all to it. *(He touches his throat)* I'm up to here with it.

(He goes out. Margaret goes to hall door)

MARGARET: He's not the only one either.

(She goes upstairs. Pause)

EDGAR: I wonder what it is about you that inspires Margaret's loyalty! *(He sits on sofa)*

RICHARD: Maybe she's taken a look at you and come out of the anaesthetic.

EDGAR: And just what do you mean by that?

RICHARD: *(Both angry and tired)* Oh, Edgar! You still haven't really caught on, have you? You're still wondering what all the fuss is about. It's family life chum. *(Puts on an affected voice)*

It's all so *real. (Pause)* You know they're wasting their time when they make documentaries about East End teds and show them to the jaded middle classes. They ought to film us and inflict it on the teds. *(Richard sits at the table)*

EDGAR: *(Speaking slowly)* I knew you were living with Gillian, but I didn't know she was pregnant. *(Pause)* Whether you despise me for this or not, it's the sort of thing that *does* make a difference for me. *(Pause)* I wanted it to make a difference yesterday. And I couldn't. *(Pause)* Do you know, I just couldn't.

(He goes to Richard and leans on table. He speaks with great difficulty)

What is it about me you hate so much? *(Pause)* I'm ... you know, I'm comfortably off now but—for years I've been too busy struggling to get where I am to allow the luxury of stopping to ask whether it's *right. (Pause)* I'm a fairly good sientist.

(He sits down leaning towards Richard)

I don't understand you. Nothing about you. *(Pause)* The years between you and me ... they're more like a generation. Men like me ... came home in nineteen forty-five, and all we saw was this country had to be picked up. Like what I suppose you'd call the bowler-hatted brigade. Only then it was a question of technology ... research. *(Pause)* I'm not a very articulate man, Richard.

(He takes out a pipe and begins to scrape out the bowl)

I prefer the motoring monthly to the stuff you go in for. *(Rises to mantelpiece. Pause)* The reason I'm so concerned about Janet is despite the fact we're brothers, I respect what she's a product of, more than I respect what you stand for. She's decent and she's gentle and she never hurt anybody. Qualities you seem to demand, but you never give. *(Sits)* If I tell you I desperately wanted you and her to make it up—I hope you'll believe me. Now it's my father we've got to think about. *(Richard has been listening neutrally. Now he faces Edgar angrily)*

RICHARD: And we tell Janet we're awfully sorry but there appears to have been a mistake somewhere.

EDGAR: That's a cruel and ugly way of twisting what I tried to tell you!

RICHARD: It's the cruel and ugly truth! *(Pause)* I'll go and meet her at the station.

EDGAR: When Margaret came in last night I was ashamed—but, I hardly know how to say this. For half an hour I felt we were brothers. Do we have to behave like kids, to be brothers?

RICHARD: To be absolutely honest, I have no pleasant feelings about you whatsoever. Not a . . . single . . . spark. You're . . . much more dead for me, than my mother is.
(Edgar sits for a second. Rises and gets coat from sofa)

EDGAR: And do you really mean to tell me that . . . that right at the heart of this, for both of us, it's a political difference? Simply putting the cross in a different place on a voting slip? Do you?

RICHARD: No, I don't.

EDGAR: *(Putting on his coat)* Then what?

RICHARD: Anway, it's very much more than a political difference. It's a difference of choice.
(Edgar is baffled, miserable, still with a trace of habitual bullying contempt)

EDGAR: I honestly don't know what you mean.

RICHARD: Then we're exactly where we started, aren't
              we?

EDGAR: I'm going out for a bit. I love my dad. As
              much as you do. But he was wrong.
              *(Edgar goes out. Richard follows and shouts after
              him from the door)*

RICHARD: That's where the difference begins.

Scene 13

TELECINE: *Station, afternoon of the same day.*
              *(Richard runs up the slope into the forecourt of the
              station, looking at his watch. He gets a platform
              ticket from the machine. The train arrives and as
              he runs up the steps of the footbridge, people from
              the train come across the bridge towards him. He
              pushes through them and sees Janet. She is con-
              ventionally well-dressed—a smart, good-looking
              woman.*

JANET: I'm glad you came to meet me.
RICHARD: *(Taking her suitcase)* You shouldn't be here.
JANET: How is your mother?
RICHARD: She died last night.
JANET: Oh—
RICHARD: Look, Janet. You can't come to the house.
JANET: Why not?
RICHARD: Let's go to the buffet. We've got to talk.

Scene 14

Railway Station Buffet.

*Janet sits at a table in the buffet. Richard is at
the counter.*

MAN: Egg and chips please, miss.

(Richard brings two cups and puts them down on the table)

RICHARD: I don't think there's . . . I'll get some sugar.

JANET: For God's sake, Richard. I'm not going to drink it. I don't want it.

RICHARD: *(Sits down)* I'm surprised you came. For all you were fond of my mother.

JANET: Hadn't you better explain first why we're here and not on the way home?

RICHARD: You were fond of her.

JANET: Yes. I was.

RICHARD: It was cancer.

JANET: I know. She wrote and told me.

RICHARD: Edgar shouldn't have asked you to come.

JANET: I thought it . . . considerate of him.

RICHARD: Despite the circumstances?

JANET: Despite?

RICHARD: Edgar's quite capable of hoping for an eleventh hour reconciliation!

JANET: You can hardly blame your own brother for not wanting to see your marriage break up!

RICHARD: And you?

JANET: I came . . . to be with your mother.

RICHARD: After a day's delay.

JANET: It was impossible to come yesterday.

RICHARD: I wonder what could make it impossible, when she was dying?

JANET: You've still got that habit of interrogating people rather than asking.

RICHARD: Well then, why didn't you come yesterday?

JANET: Edgar's exact words in the telegram were: cannot live more than a few days.

RICHARD: I see. A calculated risk!

JANET: Are you reproaching me for coming, or for not coming? *(Pause)* What do you want me to do, Richard? Take the next train back to London—or what?

RICHARD   And you got the telegram at your flat?

JANET: I was spending a week with John Miller and
           his parents. My mother phoned me. She's
           living with me now.

RICHARD: I heard you'd 'been seen' as they call it, with
           Miller.

JANET: I don't think it concerns you.

RICHARD: Judging from his maiden speech in Parlia-
           ment, Miller ought to be the concern of every
           right-minded citizen. There ought to be a
           lynch Miller campaign.

JANET: What's all this to do with—

RICHARD: He's a vain and stupid man and he's—
           *(Richard pauses. Janet's assurance is wearing thin,
           she becomes nervous)*

JANET: He's what?

RICHARD: He's wrong for you.
           *(Janet seems to be trying to make a decision. In
           deciding, she becomes both defiant and vulnerable)*

JANET: I know. *(Pause)* I see too many people the way
           you would see them, Richard. *(Pause)* I was
           having a violent row with John when my
           mother telephoned, and—we'd been rowing
           all week.

RICHARD: I'm very pleased to hear it!

JANET: Don't make fun of me, Richard.

RICHARD: I'm not making fun of you. Any bastard with
           his ideas should be—

JANET: I don't want him, Richard. I don't want any-
           body, unless I . . . still . . . want . . . you.
           *(The man at their table looks up briefly from his
           egg and chips)*

RICHARD: *What?*

JANET: Do I have to say it again? It's humiliating
           enough once!

RICHARD: No. Once is enough for me. You don't really
           mean to say, at this stage?

JANET: Why not?

RICHARD: Oh, if we ignore everything that's been said
            and done . . . the mutual thumbscrewing, why
            not?

JANET: I don't want to ignore anything.

RICHARD: So the marriage is supposed to rise like a
            phœnix out of its own ruins!

JANET: I don't know what it's supposed to do.

RICHARD: Janet, it was *your* divorce. Your lawyers. Your
            money. Your revenge. I'm the guilty party,
            remember? I'm faithless, unreliable, treach-
            erous—and what was it your barrister bloke
            called me? A morally unscrupulous person. I
            would have thought that makes me pretty
            indigestible!

JANET: It does.

RICHARD: Then for heaven's sake!

            *(They look away from each other. Richard fiddles
            with his cup. We hear the clatter and noise of the
            cafeteria)*

            It's over a year since the final row Janet. I
            remember very clearly what you said. You
            said: I simply don't love you any more. I
            can't love you any more, because I can't love
            somebody I don't trust. And apart from in
            court, I haven't seen you since. It's a bit late
            to come up with this!

            (Pause)

JANET: It seems to me now that . . . if I hadn't been
            so obsessed with whether I could trust you, I
            wouldn't have lost you.

RICHARD: Well, it's finished. You wanted to finish it,
            and you did.

JANET: Can't we go home? I'd like to see your father.

RICHARD: I brought Gillian Moore home with me. She's
            going to have a baby. We're getting married.
            (Pause)

JANET: I see. And does she know . . . all about you
                and me? About what happened?

RICHARD: She knows the facts and my interpretation of
                them. I tried to tell her your side of it as well.

JANET: Did you tell her what happened in Majorca?

RICHARD: Yes . . . I told her, one day I simply decided to
                stop writing. I said I told you, and started to
                get drunk and you walked out. I told her you
                came back that night and found me in bed with
                the Spanish maid. Said you cleared out there
                and then. *(Pause)* I must say, it sounded a bit
                farcical in the retelling. That's the trouble with
                facts.

JANET: And did you tell her the rest? That you
                couldn't stand my money, or my friends, or
                my family? Did you tell her what a phoney
                puritan you are? *(She becomes hysterical)* Did
                you tell her you thrived on my *shame*, for every-
                thing I'd had and you hadn't? For all the
                phoney values I'd swallowed and you'd seen
                through? Like hell you did! You probably con-
                fined yourself to telling her that I couldn't
                forgive you for not being a success!

RICHARD: Well, that's true, isn't it?

JANET: I just hope you don't wear *her* out expecting
                her to think that coming from a working class
                background is some kind of virtue in itself!
                *(Janet begins to cry. She cries helplessly, as if she
                desperately wants not to and is shamed by not being
                able to control it)*
                I'm saying everything I intended not to say!
                (Pause) How dreadful it all must be for your
                father—

RICHARD: He probably wishes we were all back where
                we came from. I don't blame him if he does,
                either.
                (Pause) You know how I always felt when you

and I went home—
(Janet stops crying. Dries her eyes)

JANET: You made a damn sight more fuss about the gulf between you and your parents than I ever did. And that's funny! I was supposed to be the bourgeoise!

RICHARD: Janet—all your life you've been able to share things with your parents. In families like ours the children are alien. They're split right down the middle.

JANET: Anybody'd think you'd have been happier if they'd sent you out to work when you were fourteen!

(Pause. Richard pushes away his cup. Leans on the table. Speaks abstractedly)

RICHARD: One half of me loves my mother as somebody about three feet taller than myself, with big red arms and an apron that smells of new bread . . . hanging the washing out in the yard. And my dad—a giant in overalls that smell of engines and dark shag. And behind *them* . . . the chimneys and soot and mills and the goodsyard. Soapy water running in the gutters and the tealeaves drying on a square yard of soil round a dead rose tree.

(He sits back, staring vacantly past Janet)

The other half of me sees them with a sort of aching detachment. My mother worried about her home-made clothes on Edgar's convocation day . . . and saying "Now Wilf!" when my father talked too much after a couple of cocktails at one of Margaret's parties. *(Looks Janet in the eyes)* To watch you being 'nice' to them was like watching a bloody duchess on a district visit!

(Gillian comes into the buffet. Dragging a suitcase with difficulty. She looks utterly defeated. She does

	not see Richard and Janet, but goes to counter)
GILLIAN:	Cup of tea, please.
JANET:	Let's stop it, Richard. Let me just go back to London and forget I ever came. I know it's my own fault for coming, but anyway I can't stand any more. Just go, Richard.

(They look at each other for a moment, then Richard gets up and walks away. As he goes he sees Gillian turning from the counter holding a cup of tea. She reaches down for her case and upsets the cup. Richard goes to her, picks up the cup and puts it and the saucer on the counter. He takes Gillian's arm—she is trembling, looking over his shoulder towards Janet)

RICHARD:	Gillian, what are you doing? What do you think you're doing?

(Janet picks up her bag and case. Glances at Richard and Gillian, walks out quickly)

GILLIAN:	Janet?
RICHARD:	Yes but—why are you . . . What made you leave the house? And your case?

(He leads her to a table)

GILLIAN:	I was going home.
RICHARD:	Home?
GILLIAN:	Back to London. Back to your flat, I suppose.

(They sit, holding each other's hands across the table)

It all suddenly seems so utterly hopeless.

RICHARD:	I *told* you I wouldn't have Janet come to the house—
GILLIAN:	I know. When you'd gone, that was what struck me as being so, so *bad!*
RICHARD:	I don't know why the hell Beatie didn't stop you—
GILLIAN:	She didn't see me. She was getting bathed. And Edgar and Margaret had gone out. Everything Edgar's said, it looked exactly like

	that to *me*. I felt as if I'd no place there. No right there.
RICHARD:	And you imagine you could just walk out? Just get a train and go back? Like that?
GILLIAN:	Whatever's happened, Janet has a right to be there—if she wants. *(Pause)* I suppose she's gone?
RICHARD:	You don't really think she would have stayed, do you?
GILLIAN:	I was . . . in a panic Richard. *(Pause)* Don't let's stay here—
RICHARD:	I wish you . . . hadn't to face all this, Gillian—
GILLIAN:	She's very attractive. Like in that photo. Sort of well-bred, or whatever it is.
RICHARD:	Janet always was bred—
	(They manage to half smile at each other)
GILLIAN:	I feel better now. I thought I was going to sick the baby up when I read that telegram. Don't let's stay here.
RICHARD:	Come on then—
	(They get up, and Richard takes her case in one hand, Gillian's arm in the other. They slowly walk out of the buffet)

Scene 15

Living Room – Later in the afternoon

Gillian is lying on the sofa in her dressing gown, with a travelling rug over her legs. Beatie is tucking the rug in, Richard is watching.

BEATIE:	Now shall I send for t'doctor?
GILLIAN:	I'm all right, honestly.
BEATIE:	You want some stick, going out like that. If you lose your baby you *will* have summat to get worked up about.

GILLIAN: But I—

BEATIE: Now that's quite enough for one afternoon. You rest yoursen for a bit, and thank your lucky stars it's no worse.

RICHARD: Can I do anything?

BEATIE: *(Straightening up)* You and our Edgar between you, you've done enough I should think! I hope never to see t'like again! Your dad mortally offended, this poor lass next door to a miscarriage, you and Edgar at daggers drawn . . . I wonder what I've come into, I do an' all.

RICHARD: There's no question of a miscarriage—

BEATIE: Oh, and since when have you been an expert, like? Have you had any bairns?

RICHARD: What d'you think I am, a hermaphrodite?

BEATIE: *(To Gillian, who is giggling)* What's he say? Summat blue, I've no doubt. *(To Richard)* Now you stop with her, I've got some baking to do.

            (Beatie goes into the kitchen, closing the door behind her)

GILLIAN: I feel sleepy now.

RICHARD: Try to sleep then.

            (He sits on the arm of the sofa and she rests her head on his lap)

GILLIAN: When you love somebody, you can love everybody else a bit more, can't you?

RICHARD: What's that supposed to connect with?

GILLIAN: I was just thinking. I was frightened of Janet. *(Pause)* I know it isn't going to be easy for us, Richard. *(Taking his hand and putting it to her face)*

RICHARD: Don't be daft.

GILLIAN: But I know it isn't. I want to face it.

RICHARD: Well not now. Try to sleep.

            (He gets up and goes to the armchair near her)

GILLIAN: Tell me a story.

RICHARD: Why tell you a story?

GILLIAN: *(Feels the baby)* Tell *it* a story then. You'll have to get into the habit some time.

RICHARD: That's a boorjuice habit.

GILLIAN: I don't care.

(Richard makes a performance of settling down in his chair)

RICHARD: Well then. Let's see, a story. Well it was like this, see. Once upon a time there was a little house—

GILLIAN: By a silver river with frogs sitting on lilly-pads—

RICHARD: No, as a matter of fact it was by a mucky canal full of dead dogs and illegal sewage.

GILLIAN: Social realism for little tots!

RICHARD: That's it. Well this house by the canal was just at the end of the snicket from the gas works to the slaughterhouse. And in it there lived a little person. A social realist. He was three feet high and he could use a knife and fork, and when the story begins he'd just heard how the world was created . . . from the big people. They told him: in the beginning was Keir Hardie and Keir Hardie was with God and Keir Hardie practically *was* God. Course he didn't create the world. A devil created the world. A capitalist devil who said: let there be factories and there were factories. Let there be muck and there was muck. Let there be brass and there was brass . . . for some folk. *(He gets up, walks to the fire, stares into it. Looks at the Van Gogh)* All the big people had been working for the devil for as long as they could remember. *(He kneels down in front of the fire)* Mostly for brass, but partly because he was a gentleman and

he knew how to run the country. Like all the best devils he had a lot of faces as well. He was on the council, he had a posh office at the pit, he owned the railways, he was on the school board of governors . . . he was a magistrate. And he even went to church and took the collection for the other god, the one in the sky. Both Mam and Grandma had a foot in both camps. They were sort of heretics. They knew the world ought to be like Keir Hardie and Dad wanted it, only when they talked about when they'd been in *service* . . . they made it sound all right. *(Pause)* All that lovely table linen and silver and everybody knowing his place, even the master. And then when they said that Dad gritted his teeth and told them to wait till t'working classes takes over. We s'll wipe us noses on t'table linen. Dad thrilled and terrified at the same time—Mam and Grandma were just womenfolk. Dad wanted the people to own everything and everybody to have an inside lav. He said that was socialism, in case they didn't know it.
(Pokes the fire. Stays silent)

GILLIAN: What happened then?
              (He stands up with his back to the fire)

RICHARD: The little person gradually worked out Dad's ideas for himself. They had to get the devil out and put Labour in . . . get rid of the old factories and t'muck and share out t'brass. This involved going to college so you could meet the devil on his own terms and so you wouldn't have the sort of life the big people had.
              (He goes to sit at the table)
              Eventually the little person grew up and went away. *(Pause. Richard's face is sad and strained)*

And got educated and a lot of other things. What's the use of telling stories to a foetus?

GILLIAN: What's the matter Richard?

(Pause)

RICHARD: Nothing. Nowt. It makes a good fairy story. That was part one. Part one's the best because it's the ideological part. In part two the devil changes his spots and everybody gets in a proper muddle. Dad's getting on in years and doesn't quite get the hang of the changes. He sees the slums come down and the rocket sites go up. He gets subsidised teeth, free glasses for reading, and a gold watch for devoted service. The day comes when Mam says well there's no getting away from it we're better off now than we've been for many a long year.

(Pause)

And practically all there is left to do is shout where do we go from here? Shout: where do we go when the cities aren't fit to live in, when we all have everything to live with and nothing to live *for?* Where do we go, when all the black men have got their independence, when all the coolies are riding round in mini-cars?

(There is a knock at the back door)

When we're all fed and inoculated, where do we go? When the life expectancy's raised to 150, where do we go?

(Repeated knocking. Beatie opens the living room door)

When we—

BEATIE: It's the undertaker Richard.

RICHARD: The undertaker *(Begins to laugh)* That's it—that's where we go!

Scene *16*

Living Room. late the same evening.

*Beatie is at the table with her workbasket, darning
socks. Margaret is flicking through a magazine.*

BEATIE: Their Uncle Fred and Auntie Mary'll be
              coming, that makes five. Then there's Eunice,
              Jack and his wife, and Auntie Cora from
              Barnsley. Eh, she's a brave un, is Cora.

MARGARET: What's the matter with Auntie Cora?

BEATIE: She's had everything taken away, you know.

MARGARET: She's what?

BEATIE: Eh, it's wonderful what they can do nowadays,
              isn't it? She were in Leeds Infirmary ten weeks
              and if she hadn't gone when she did, she
              wouldn't have lived. Mind, some of them
              young doctors nowadays they treat you like
              muck, don't they. I were saying to—

MARGARET: Just how many *are* coming to tea after the
              funeral?

BEATIE: Well I make it fourteen love, including
              t'missis next door.

MARGARET: In here?

BEATIE: Eh, we've had some bigger crushes than that,
              love.

MARGARET: I'll be glad when it's all over.

BEATIE: Nay, Margaret!

MARGARET: I only mean, if we could have the funeral . . .
              without having them all back to the house. I
              think father's had enough to put up with, one
              way and another. So have I, come to that.

BEATIE: *(Rolling up a sock)* There. That's t'last. Wilf's
              easily hurt, for all his manliness. And I will
              say, Gillian's carrying Richard's baby, she's
              a right to be treated as one on t'family.

MARGARET: Well she'll soon find out *that* has its drawbacks, as well as its advantages.

BEATIE: My lot's done nowt but bicker ever since they first opened their mouths, but I don't know as they're any worse for it.

MARGARET: I wouldn't call what Richard and Edgar go in for bickering!

BEATIE: Edgar'll change his tune about Gillian, you mark my words.

(She gets up and goes to put the workbasket away)

MARGARET: It's something more fundamental than whether he does or he doesn't.

BEATIE: When you get to my age and your family's grown up, you get used to them telling you where to get off.

MARGARET: I'm sure I shan't.

BEATIE: Eh, you'll be wanting to get back to them, aren't you?

MARGARET: If it had been for any other reason, I'd have been glad to get away from them!

BEATIE: You're a cut, and no mistake, Margaret. Where did you say Richard and Gillian is?

MARGARET: Gone to see somebody Richard used to go to school with. Laurie Cobb, or somebody.

BEATIE: Oh aye! I know yon one. He's gotten a beard. What do they want to go having beards for? T'isn't natural.

MARGARET: I suppose you could say that not having beards isn't natural either.

BEATIE: My father had a beard. A red one. He were a regular old devil, an' all. He used to sup enough beer on a Friday night to fill a set pot. Mind, fellers *did* have beards in his day. It's these bohemians as gets up my back. *(Clock chimes)* Eh, is that a quarter to ten? They'll be wanting their suppers.

MARGARET: I'll put the kettle on.

BEATIE: Yes love, put t'electric one on.

(Margaret and Beatie go into the kitchen. Margaret fills the kettle. Richard comes in at the back door)

MARGARET: Where's Gillian?

RICHARD: In the fish and chip shop round the corner.

BEATIE: Well didn't you wait for her then? She's just same as I was when I were carrying our Percy. Used to take a fancy to summat and I had to have it there and then. You ought to have waited Richard.

RICHARD: She's only at the fish shop Aunt Beatie, she hasn't entered for the Olympic Games.

BEATIE: You've been in t'knife box and gotten sharp, haven't you!

RICHARD: As a matter of fact she wanted some beer as well. So I went round to the Fox for a couple of bottles. I thought she'd be back by now.
(Takes beer bottles out of his raincoat pocket and takes off coat)
I got you a stout, Aunt Beatie.

BEATIE: Well I wouldn't say no.
(She bustles about preparing for supper)

RICHARD: Would you like it now?

BEATIE: I think I will love. I wouldn't dare with me fish and chips.
(Richard pours the stout)

RICHARD: Edgar back?

BEATIE: Here's luck. *(Drinking)* Nay, I suppose he's still at Mrs. Ramsey's. There's one that's going to miss your mother, an' all. They shared a stall at church bazaar you know.
(Richard goes into livingroom. He sits down and picks up a newspaper. Edgar comes in back door and into the living room)
There you are Edgar. How did she take it then?

EDGAR: She knew already. Heard it from Mrs. Brotherton in town this afternoon.

RICHARD: News travels fast in these parts. They beat it out on the dustbins in the back yards.
(The sound of Wilf and Gillian's voices outside. Wilf is singing 'Why do the nations' from the Messiah. Gillian appears at the kitchen door more or less supporting Wilf)

EDGAR: Dad! What the hell have you—

WILF: *(To Gillian)* What did I tell thee? I told thee he'd be t'first to open his trap.

GILLIAN: Come and sit down.
(Gillian helps him to a chair. She is gentle with him; there is much sympathy now between them. Edgar and Richard watch him closely)

WILF: What are you all gawpin' at then? You're put out, are you? *(Rising and taking off his coat)*

EDGAR: You're drunk!

WILF: Aye lad, I've had a few. What you got to say about that? I've no doubt tha's gotten summat to say.

BEATIE: *(From kitchen door)* Wilf! What have you been doing?

WILF: Nay, don't get thisen worked up Beatie lass. Let him have his say. Then I'll have mine. *(He sits down at the table, turning away)*

EDGAR: I can't trust myself to speak!

WILF: Eh, thy mother's dead and thy father's drunk, poor sod. Poor old sod. *(Shakes his head)* It's noan a reight way to be going on, is it?

EDGAR: What do you think?

WILF: *(Gets up, goes towards Edgar)* Dost know Edgar, I don't know as tha's ever asked me what I think in thy life before.

RICHARD: Don't you think you ought to go up to bed Dad?

WILF: Thee an'all? Nay, one at a time surry.

EDGAR: He's not in a fit condition to reason with.

WILF: *(In front of Edgar)* Now that's nobut an excuse

for not speaking thy mind.

BEATIE: Now he's not going to speak against his father Wilf.

WILF: Isn't he? He's noan barn to speak for him. Are you? Doesn't know enough about me to speak for me. But I know a lot about thee. Funny, isn't it. I nearly brought thee into t'world with my own two hands. Your mother laboured all night, but when it came to t'point tha were born yawling inside twenty minutes. Tha were a raw lump and no mistake. Tha took one look at me and thought daft devil, and tha's thought so ever since! No bigger than that fist. And look at you now. *(Feels Edgar's arm)* We *are* related, tha knows.

EDGAR: *(Moving back, almost recoiling)* Yes, we're related all right!

WILF: *(Turning to Richard)* And thee. Tha were nowt but skin and bone. When they took thee from thy mother, they took her womb, an' all. Now she's dead, isn't she.
(Wilf goes to the window—Richard goes and sits in armchair).
Takes summat to bring families together, doesn't it? I wanted you both to come. It's easy to love a bairn. It's easy tha knows. But when t'bairn's gone.
(Takes Edgar by the shoulders)
I've wiped thee up at both ends. I've powdered thy arse. I've putten food in thy mouth. *(Points at Richard)* Thee an'all. I've rocked you to sleep.
(He sits at the table)
It's nowt but beer talking, is it? Nowt but beer.
(Beatie, Margaret and Gillian come in from the kitchen)

BEATIE: I think it's time I took mesen next door. I'll

	say goodnight to you all. And if you're not too fuddled with ale to take my advice Wilf, you'll do well to get yoursen upstairs.
WILF:	Eh Beatie lass, we shall all live through it tha knows. Stay and have thy fish and a pennorth.
BEATIE:	Thank you very much I know my place. I'll see you all in t'morning. *(Goes out through kitchen door)*
WILF:	Your Auntie Beatie's a good woman.
EDGAR:	*(Coming close to Wilf)* Dad, will you just tell me why this? Why?
WILF:	Why? Why I've gotten in this state with your mother lying dead in t'house? That's a tall order, isn't it lad? But she'd have understood would your mother. Dost think we've been blind, deaf and dumb this last fifteen years? Without feelings? Dost think we noticed *nowt?* Dost think tha can walk into this house t'one time I send for thee and carry on same as tha always has? Both of you? I know tha counts on most on what tha says bouncing off me, like. In at one lugole and out at t'other. Eh, I wonder what I've done. What I've gotten. What you are. What are you? I educated you to get you out on this, did I? Well let me tell you it's a reight home. And it's been a reight home without you. So tha's barking up t'wrong tree there. Aye, I've been weighing form up.
	(He sits at the table and begins rolling a cigarette) Ah've been weighing form up. Dost see.
EDGAR:	I can see you're drunk, and that's about all. I'm surprised you can brazen it out. *(He sits opposite Wilf at the table)*
WILF:	Tha doesn't follow me, Edgar lad. How can I explain to you? Can you . . . can you tell me summat I'm fond on, for a start?

EDGAR: Beer?

WILF: Nay lad, tha mustn't get sarky. Dost know owt
            about me? Tha knows nowt. Except I'm thy
            dad. I'm ignorant. I've putten thee somewhere
            I cannot reach, and tha can't turn back. Even
            if tha wanted to, which I hope and suppose
            tha doesn't. Now, back on t'kitchen window
            there's a bit on a flower bed like. Enough to
            swing a cat, any road. Thy mother used to
            plant a few flowers there. Dost know *what*
            flowers? When t'wind's in t'wrong direction
            tha can't smell them for t'gasworks, but they
            come up year after year. They make a bit of
            colour. In summer we used to take us chairs
            out and enjoy t'sunshine. We never lacked owt
            to talk about your mother and me. We had
            our lads.
            (Finally lights his cigarette clumsily)
            How dost imagine t'sort of life we had? On my
            spiv day we took us dinners out to t'reservoy to
            see a bit of nature, like. One time tha couldn't
            show me a flower or a leaf as I couldn't name.
            We had us pleasures and we'd have given owt
            many a time to have thee both share them. But
            you never settled with each other when you
            did come home. Dost remember how to make
            a fishing rod, Edgar?

EDGAR: This is all beside the point dad.

WILF: I showed thee how to make one when tha
            were ten year old. Dost know when t'haw-
            thorn comes out Richard?

RICHARD: Did I ever? I don't know Dad.

WILF: I told thee. Tha's both forgotten. Tha's gone
            thy own ways. Only I sometimes think as
            t'other things we had to give you, you've left
            them behind. Happen they don't mean nowt.

EDGAR: Oh it sounds fine, the way you put it! But you

forget what you wanted out of us. And if it's gone wrong, well you've just got to make the best of it!

WILF: You say that, do you? I'll tell thee, t'best years on my life was when you were growing up. I could talk to thee both. Show thee things. Put clothes on thy backs and bread in thy hands. Oh, I wanted you to grow up different from me I know. But I got more than I bargained for. I look at you now and think: them's my sons. Reight proud on you both. Only where you've gotten to I don't know. When you chew t'fat about politics and that afore t'war, dost stop to ask *why* I couldn't weigh it all up reight? At eleven year old I were scrattin' coal for me living. What I made were t'difference between eating an' starving in our family. Sixteen year old I were cleaning out boilers. Come home, get washed, drop into bed and start all over t'next morning. And socialism? Tha's reight. I knew nowt, but in them days you didn't have to be brilliant to know which side tha were on. Tha doesn't have to be educated to be a human being tha knows. But in them days I thought I were a man. And that's what I'm noan so sure either on you two is.

EDGAR: It all depends on what you mean by being a man.

WILF: A man's somebody that can hold his head up. He doesn't bury it down into t'ground. He's a feller that won't accept nowt shoddy not if you held a bloody gun to his head. He doesn't give in. An' if y'ask me ... you two's given in. *(He goes to the sideboard drawer and takes out the watch. Holds it to his ear and shakes it gently. Offers it to Gillian)*

Gillian love, take it and give it to t'bairn when it's old enough to appreciate it. Go on love, take it. It'll noan bite thee.

GILLIAN: You know I couldn't.

WILF: And why not?

EDGAR: Put it away Dad. It's yours. You know none of us could take it.

(Wilf hesitates, still holding out the watch and looking at them. Then he puts it back in the drawer)

WILF: Tha mun please thisens. I shall nobut give it to t'bairn mesen if I live to see it grow up.

(Stands with his hands on the drawer, his back to them)

This'll still be your home. I hope you'll come when you want, same as when your mother were alive. Don't get it into your heads I'm barn to leave it and shove mesen on you.

MARGARET: You mustn't take that attitude father. We were going to ask you if you'd like to come to us when you retire.

WILF: That's very kind on you. Both on you. But can you see it Edgar? Can you Margaret? Sort of life I'm used to, and sort of life you're used to. Ah should feel like a fish out of water, same as you feel when you're up here. *(Pause)* We've nowt in common. We're strangers. Talk t'hind leg off a donkey and you won't change that. I've had t'blinkers off since yesterday. When I leave this house I shall leave it in a wooden box, and not before. *(Pause)* Eh, I feel reight dizzy all on a sudden. I mun sit down. Why don't you get your suppers?

(He goes to sofa and sits down. Edgar goes to him and stands over him)

EDGAR: Is it my fault if we've nothing in common? Is it Margaret's? We can do just about as much for you as you did for us . . . *provide* for you!

MARGARET: Edgar!

WILF: Nay let him be. He's nobut letting off steam.

EDGAR: You seem to have gotten a damn sight more out of my childhood than I did! All I remember is the bread and fat and the algebra. You're getting to be a sentimental old man, Dad.

WILF: Is that reight? Dost remember nowt good, Edgar? Has tha nowt to look back on?

(There is a long pause. Edgar sits in the chair by the fire)

EDGAR: I don't see any of it the way you do. *(Pause)* I remember many a day . . . if you want to know . . . when you went to work with meat in your sandwiches; when Richard and me had meat for us dinners, and I know for a fact my mother sat down to potatoes when we'd gone. What about her? She had it rough, God knows. *(Suddenly angry)* Don't ask me to look back on those years through rose coloured spectacles!

WILF: Aye, and all that meat thy mother didn't have . . . tha wore it round thy neck in t'shape on white poplin shirts when tha went to college! Tha didn't refuse t'shirts, Edgar.

EDGAR: Well, people don't have to do things like that any more, do they? Look at your working classes now. Haven't they got it all? But they're not exactly a testament to the highest achievements of the human race, are they?

WILF: They'll never be no different as long as fellers like thee goes over to t'other side!

(Edgar suddenly fetches his coat and puts it on)

What's ta doing now?

EDGAR: I'm going out, and I'm staying out till you've gone to bed. I'll tell you Dad . . . you're no more plausible when you're drunk than you are when you're sober.

WILF: Nay, take thy coat off. I'll get mesen off upstairs.

EDGAR: When you came lurching in here to-night, I was ashamed and embarrassed to look at you. Not so much because you got drunk but because you got drunk when you did. The one thing you had left as far as I was concerned was your dignity—and now you haven't even got that.

RICHARD: *(Going up to Edgar angrily)* For God's sake *go* out then. Get out.

EDGAR: *(With restrained fury)* Don't you talk like that to me.

RICHARD: Are you going? Or not?

(Wilf hurls himself out of his chair at them)

WILF: God damn you. God damn you, stop it! Will you shut up? If you go on I'll not bide you in my house. I'll not have you another night. I'll see you in hell first both on you.

(He goes to the sideboard where there is a framed snapshot of Wilf in his forties, standing by an engine with two small boys—Edgar and Richard. Wilf picks it up and looks at it bitterly)

I wouldn't come and live with either on you not if it were t'last place on earth. I've that much dignity left, any road. I'll not forget this you know. Sitha God damn and sod it I'll noan come to you if I'm crippled! You're noan my sons and why—don't ask me why, noan of you. If it's not class nor education nor growing up, it's past me. Best harm we can do you is to die off and leave you with what you've gotten. For it's nowt to do with us. I grew up t'same road as my father and I've no doubt he grew up t'same as his father, but I'm noan in you two. I'm noan *in* you.

(Still holding the picture he crashes it face down on the table, breaking the glass) I've lost you some road no man should lose his children ever. Summat's done. Summat's finished. Summat's gone. I don't know what it is. My way on seeing things, tha talks about. What's thy way? Tha's summat I never were. Tha's no time. No time for nowt, not even for thisens. There's some folks as is content to live. Gillian—dost know what I mean? A woman with a bairn inside her knows summat on t'sort. Living content. And I don't mean daft content, neither. *(Goes to the window and draws the curtain)* Sitha— t'goodsyard. Work it out for thysen. An average on nigh fifty hour a week for forty year. How much time does that make? I know every siding and signal and permanent way over t'county. I've gotten as far as I can go, and happen I know no more for all that. Canst not think what I wanted for thee two? I'm dumb, but dost think I've never wanted to say owt? My head's gotten nowt in it, but dost think I've never wanted to fill it? And I waited for thee two to grow up and make it reight. *(He looks out)* Eh, when I were a lad we thought it were a marvel to go fifty mile an hour. Now they're barn to t'moon. It's all come about in fifty year, and it'd take a good un to keep up with that. Tha's left us old uns behind reight enough. *(Pause)* I can fire an engine and drive it. I can cop a pike with a spinner. My eyesight's going now, but I could nick a rabbit at twenty yard with yon old catapult, from t'footplate. *(Pause)* But I've gotten that feeling in my bones as summat's finished with thee and me. *(He looks up at the Van Gogh)* Thy mother were bonny. We were

as happy together as t'days were long. If we both had t'same thought in us heads about you two we kept it to us sens. But t'cat's out on t'bag now, isn't it? Happen better so. *(He stands between his two sons, his arms on their shoulders)* It's noan dignity tha misses Edgar lad. It's knowing I've no place in thy world. If tha's ashamed and embarrassed, it's because there's nowt between us. Dost even know what I like to *eat?* What time I get mesen off to work on a morning? They've putten me in t'old men's link. Dost know what that is? Soft jobs for them as time's nearly up. Dost not know *now* why I went on t'beer to-night? *(Pause)* Tha's as far away from me lad as if tha'd gotten off in one of them sputiliks. Tha were fond on thy mother, I know. *(Edgar looks away. His anger has gone and he suddenly appears vulnerable. Wilf looks at Richard)* And thee, lad. I wish tha'd been able to do everything tha wanted to. Nobbut tha's tumbled somewhere between what our Edgar's gotten, an' glory. Haven't you? *(Pause)* Is there nowt left to paint? Nowt left to write about, like? Or what? Tha munt spend thy life doing summat tha cannot bide. Tha *munt! (He looks at Gillian as if appealing to her, nodding over his shoulder at Richard)* He says last night as being a husband and father's all he's capable on, like. *(Pause)* Well, that mun be a start—munt it?

(Gillian looks up at him. Close up of Wilf and Gillian)

END

Credits over Left Book Club photograph.

Music—The Red Flag—*solo treble recorder.*

A CLIMATE OF FEAR

CAST

LEONARD WARING, a nuclear scientist	*John Stratton*
FRIEDA WARING, his wife	*Pauline Letts*
PETER DRIFFIELD, a university lecturer	*Geoffrey Bayldon*
COLIN WARING	*Tony Garnett*
FRANCES WARING	*Sarah Badel*
CLIVE EDGERTON	*Douglas Wilmer*
TOM DRIFFIELD, Peter's father	*Bert Palmer*
GEORGE	*Arch Taylor*
RAY	*William Gaunt*
BRIAN BELL	*Antony Higginson*
POLICEMAN	*Ray Browne*
RAWSON	*Anthony Dawes*
WARDER	*Charles Saynor*
ROSS WYMAN	*Francis Napier*
MRS WYMAN	*Ann Murray*
YOUNG WOMAN	*Brenda Cowling*
OLDER WOMAN	*Winifred Hindle*
MRS RAWSON	*Delia Paton*
SONIA	*Anna Gilcrist*
MAGISTRATE	*George Merrett*
CLERK	*Harold Reese*

GUESTS AT PARTY

Mary Henderson	*John Wilding*
Elizabeth Ellis	*Michael Jackson*
Fran Browne	*Michael Byrne*
Andre Cameron	*Ulton O'Carroll*
Ray Grover	*Alfred Kurti*

Designed by   STEPHEN BUNDY
Produced by   DON TAYLOR
B.B.C. TELEVISION TRANSMISSION: *22nd June, 1962*

Scene 1

Magistrates' Court

Colin Waring, George and Ray are in the dock. The Magistrate and Court Officials are heard but not seen.

CLERK: You are all charged that on the 23rd day of this month at Kensington Palace Gardens, having been made acquainted with the Directions of the Commissioner of the Metropolis dated 23rd made under Section 52 of the Metropolitan Police Act, 1839, for the purpose of keeping order and preventing obstruction in the places, streets, and thoroughfares, and on the occasion specified therein, did wilfully disregard the said directions contrary to Section 54 (9), Metropolitan Police Act, 1839. *(Pause)* Colin Waring—do you plead guilty or not guilty to the charge?

COLIN: Guilty.

CLERK: George William Storey—?

GEORGE: Guilty.

CLERK: Raymond Jennings—?

RAY: Guilty.
  (Pause)

MAGISTRATE: Have you anything to say? Colin Waring—

COLIN: The purpose of the action was a non-violent protest against nuclear weapons and policies. We—

MAGISTRATE: Yes, yes, yes, a matter of conscience. Next—

GEORGE: I would just like to say—

MAGISTRATE: A matter of conscience. Next—

RAY: Our action was justified—

MAGISTRATE: I really must insist that you confine your remarks to the charge and avoid wasting the Court's time on matters which do not concern it. *(Pause)* You are each fined two pounds and bound over to keep the peace for one year in the sum of twenty-five pounds.

COLIN: I refuse to accept binding over. I regard it as nothing more than a legal device to paralyse conscientious protest—and I refuse.

MAGISTRATE: George William Storey?

GEORGE: I refuse an' all. We're prevented from making our case properly in any other way. I say on *this* matter, these courts are an insult to the people—

MAGISTRATE: Raymond Jennings?

RAY: I won't agree to be bound over.

MAGISTRATE: And you are fully acquainted with the possible consequences of refusing?

COLIN: Yes.

GEORGE: Yes.

RAY: Yes.

                (Pause)

MAGISTRATE: You are all sentenced to three months in prison, which can be terminated at any moment on acceptance of the binding over agreement.

Scene 2

Leonard Waring's laboratory. Late afternoon.

Leonard is taking an instrument reading. Brian Bell is making notes at a bench by the ion fraction collector.

LEONARD: You've checked those readings?

BRIAN: Yes.

LEONARD: Well. They don't make sense.

BRIAN: That's what I was trying to tell you last week
            when I—

LEONARD: Look Brian, it's no use blaming the apparatus.

BRIAN: I'm not. I've nothing against the apparatus.
            It's just not suitable for this experiment.

LEONARD: Then for goodness' sake get what you need and
            do it properly.

BRIAN: They won't let me have—
            (Leonard goes to switch off a vacuum pump)

LEONARD: Who left this pump on?

BRIAN: I don't know. Listen Doctor Waring—

LEONARD: *(Turns away irritably. He taps the dial on a gas
            cylinder)* Yes, I know you sent me a written
            report. And your reports are practically un-
            readable. You people may learn science
            nowadays but you don't seem to pick up much
            English.

BRIAN: *(Facetiously)* I must be naïve. I used to think
            money was no object in classified research.
            Well, if they won't get the stuff I ask for —
            let them do the explaining when it all goes to
            cock. I expect their English is good enough.
            *(Clive Edgerton enters the lab unseen by the other
            two)*

LEONARD: All right. So get the stuff you need by any
            methods you like. And if that bunch of mind-
            less idiots over there carp at the expense, you'll
            just have to dodge them. Won't you? The first
            thing you'll learn in government research is
            how to play blind man's buff with the
            administration.

EDGERTON: *(coming forward)* I hope I'm not one of the
            mindless idiots in question—

LEONARD: I thought you'd gone home Clive. No, it's—

BRIAN: I'm off anyway. I'll do what I can. Good

night. 'Night, Doctor Edgerton—
(Removes protective dust covers from his shoes and leaves)

EDGERTON: Have you taken to preaching anarchy, Leonard? That will never do.

LEONARD: Oh, it's the usual thing. Apparatus. Expense. He hasn't been here long enough to pick up the dodges. *(Pause)* He's a bright lad.
(Edgerton takes the stopper from a reagent bottle and bends to sniff at the bottle. He puts the stopper back, absently)

EDGERTON: You're very touchy lately. *(Pause)* Is Colin still in Brixton?

LEONARD: Yes. I think they'll be sending him to an open prison soon.

EDGERTON.   Oh, good.

LEONARD: Well it's hardly your problem, is it? No children. *(Pause)* It would suit Frieda if we had your sort of life. Weekends in London— galleries, theatres. Very nice.

EDGERTON: Well if you will brutalise your wife with rural domesticity!
(Leonard goes to the fume cupboard)

WARING: How would you like it if you had a grown son whose ideas and beliefs you detested?

EDGERTON: It's quite normal, isn't it?

WARING: It's not just something passing, either. Not— what would you call it?—the wayward passions of youth.

EDGERTON: Oh, come now!

WARING: When I was his age I used to go round with my father spouting socialism at street corners—

EDGERTON: One would hardly say your son is labouring under the same disadvantage—

WARING: Very funny.

EDGERTON: At least he isn't a communist.

WARING: No. But he's about as left-wing as you can get
               without leaving the Labour Party altogether.
               (Pause) I suppose he's some sort of Marxist.
EDGERTON: My God! In nineteen .sixty-two? In this
               country? What a hope!
WARING: It isn't a hope, it's a system. Are there any
               other systems kicking around?
EDGERTON: *(Smiling)* I offer up prayers every night for
               having been born into a nation of pragmatists.
WARING: You were born into a family of rich idlers
               living on shares. Who could educate you at
               Oxford and send you to Vienna, and let you
               grow up with the idea that science is a sort of
               exquisite hobby.
EDGERTON: My dear Leonard, you really mustn't bite the
               class that's taken you to its bosom! That's
               terribly old-fashioned.
WARING: Aye. Isn't it. And so is my son.
EDGERTON: Well, speaking as a dyed-in-the-wool hedonist,
               I only came to remind you that you and
               Frieda and Frances are coming to my party
               this evening.
WARING: There's that report—
EDGERTON: *(Coming closer to Leonard)* Aren't you working
               too hard? The secret is to pass the inessentials
               to the *canaille* and do what you are paid to
               do—co-ordinate the research of this section.
               (Pause)
WARING: I used to be happier when I was on the bench.
               The higher you get, the less science you do.
               (Pause) I like to keep well in touch.
EDGERTON: How's that paper of yours coming on?
WARING: I haven't touched it for months. *(Laughs
               sourly)* The original work is obsolete already.
EDGERTON: *(Embarrassed)* Start another one! We shall see
               you tonight then? About nine? *(He goes to the
               door)*

WARING: Oh, yes. Yes.
EDGERTON: Well. *Ciaou—*
WARING: See you.
            (Edgerton leaves. Leonard looks at his watch. He stands at the bench, staring vacantly at a chart on the wall)

Scene 3

The living room of Waring's House. Same afternoon.
Frieda Waring takes a glass of sherry over to Peter Driffield. Frances sits on a stool by the fireplace, reading. Peter is toying with a model of a molecule which stands on the bookcase.

PETER: *(Takes Sherry)* Thanks. Cheers.
FRIEDA: I wish you'd stay to dinner Peter.
PETER: I'd like to. But I've arranged to eat with these people in Oxford. I should be off. *(Pause)* My father was asking after you and Leonard. I wish you'd come up to London for the day some time. *(Pause)* He's very fond of Colin and Frances. Thinks they're a credit to you.
FRANCES: That won't endear him to my father!
FRIEDA: And your truculence doesn't endear you to anyone, darling. I'm surprised you put up with her so often in London, Peter.
PETER: Well, we just have to make the best of it. Can't alienate the lodger's sister.
FRANCES: Can't alienate your unpaid cleaner and general muggins, you mean!
PETER: If you ask me, Colin drags you up to London for all these meetings and students' things in the hope of marrying you off early. That's your fate—you'll marry a fat biochemist and scuttle off to Watford, to breed.

FRANCES: Suppose I learn Spanish and scuttle off to Cuba?

FRIEDA: To breed?

FRANCES: I'd sooner give birth to Cubans than nasty little anglo-saxons—

FRIEDA: You're a credit to the revolution and all that, and we're all frightened to death of you—but why not just concentrate on getting your A level?

                (Frieda stands beside Peter)

                I wish I could believe that this going to prison . . . isn't going to affect Colin at the university. Doesn't anyone object? Well, I suppose if you're his tutor you ought to know.
                (She goes over to the window)

PETER: There are plenty of people who object, all right. But so far there's no sign of anyone taking action. *(Pause)* You mustn't worry about it Frieda— *(Following her to the window. Frances watches them, plainly hostile)*

FRIEDA: And what about Leonard? Are you indifferent to what he feels?

PETER: To what he feels—no! But he's more than what he feels. He's a person living and acting in a society. If his son wants to live and act differently—then the fight's on. *(Pause)* I was surprised Leonard didn't make a fuss about Colin studying sociology under me in the first place.

FRIEDA: Are you closer to my children than I am? *(She goes to Frances)* Is he? *(To Peter)* Frances thinks I'm in a state of mental petrifaction. She doesn't argue with me. She hands me a copy of Simone de Beauvoir and the New Left Review and says: get hip! *(Puts her hand on Frances' shoulder. She goes to refill her glass. Takes the bottle to Peter and fills his)*

PETER: That's because Frances is at a very square age—

FRANCES: Traitor!

FRIEDA: Colin thinks because his father was born in a colliery slum and struggled for comfort and security . . . that his father has betrayed his class . . . and you agree with him, don't you? Of course, you wouldn't put it so crudely!

PETER: How should I put it? Leonard and I were born in the same street. Our fathers worked down the same pit. *(Pause)* I'm sorry, Frieda. We just irritate each other, don't we? We got to this stage years ago. *(Turns to Frances, half smiling)* It must be very depressing to the young.

FRANCES: You think so? I'd call it pathetic. *(Frieda turns to her)*

FRIEDA: I can assure you having no political beliefs is an absolutely painless sacrifice. I keep my respect for people who are human beings first and idealists second.
              (Rather embarrassed, Peter goes to the table and puts his glass down)

PETER: I really must be going.

FRIEDA: And you have . . . no doubts about what you are all doing?

PETER: Of course I have doubts. About the means— not about the ends. *(Frieda looks at him— Frances watching them both)*
              Yes . . . Oh by the way, when they let me see Colin this morning he sent you a message. Keep it up—

FRIEDA: *(Sharply)* keep what up?
              (Frances is confused—looks away)

PETER: *(To Frieda)* Oh, God—I was assuming you knew.

FRANCES: She didn't know. *(To Frieda)* I went on the

sit-down. I was arrested with Colin. Only I was fined the same evening and I was able to get home—and so I kept quiet about it.
(Pause)

FRIEDA: *(Sharply)* That was wrong. Not to tell your father and me.

FRANCES: *(Getting up and going to Frieda)* Yes, you tell me what's right and what's wrong. What'll you be doing when they drop the bomb? Pruning rose trees?

FRIEDA: I'm talking about honesty. We are entitled to your honesty.

FRANCES: I didn't lie—

FRIEDA: Lies don't need words—

FRANCES: What am I supposed to do? Wait till I'm twenty-one? Shall I be alive?
(Pause)

FRIEDA: All the more reason to live decently whilst you still are alive!
(Pause)

FRANCES: Oh, you are smug! *(She goes out of the room noisily. Frieda takes her cigarettes from the table and goes to the mantelpiece for a lighter)*

FRIEDA: You're an old friend, Peter. You might consider whether you should have this sort of influence over our children.

PETER: It isn't my influence. It's the moral, critical rebellion that makes up in the best of their generation for the apathy of the rest. *(Pause)* Maybe if it weren't for Leonard, you might think differently yourself.

FRIEDA: Leonard is a deeply concerned father. Not a cartoon Tory. And I have a mind of my own.

PETER: Have you?

FRIEDA: My children grew in me. They're unformed individuals, not just potential voters or rebels or conformists. *(Turning to him)* Do you think

I'm not baffled about what one ought to do?
Or think? Do you think I wouldn't be grateful
to be passionately involved along with my own
children? But I refuse to accept what they are
doing just because I feel like that.

PETER: *(Preparing to go)* These last twenty years have
killed off a lot in you!

FRIEDA: Twenty years kills off a lot in most people.
What about you? Oh, I can imagine you and
your father together! Dreaming of the days up
north when socialism was socialism.

PETER: I suppose we do that. But what he and
Leonard's father wanted *was* socialism. A
radically different world. When I put my
father in his grave that won't be the end of his
vision. It'll survive through people like Colin.
Not through hawking more and more timid
reforms to fewer and fewer active supporters.
(He goes to the door)

FRIEDA: And where are you in it all? Anyway you've
no children. I have. And I need them. They
are at an age when they need nothing but
themselves—
(Frieda follows him to the door)
I'll leave you to draw your own exotic
conclusions.

Scene 4

Early evening, the same day.

*Frieda and Frances are upstairs, dressing for
Edgerton's party, moving between bathroom and
bedrooms. Frances is filling a tumbler at the bathroom tap. She goes into her bedroom and waters a
plant on the windowsill.*

FRANCES: *(Singing)*
We won't have Yankee bases,
We shall not be moved.
It's like a tree that's standing by the water,
We shall not be moved.
(Frieda comes slowly in through the door. Stands besides Frances, watching her)

FRIEDA: You'll drown it, poor thing.

FRANCES: Shan't. It's a hydromaniac.

FRIEDA: It's getting awfully blotchy.

FRANCES: This here plant has got the will to live. Which is more than I can say for some.
(Frieda goes to the bedside table and picks up a book 'Memoirs of a Dutiful Daughter')

FRIEDA: Frances—

FRANCES: What?

FRIEDA: What are you wearing tonight?

FRANCES: Oh, anything. *(She wanders across to the wardrobe and flings open the door)*
I don't like Clive Edgerton.

FRIEDA: He's a bit smarmy. He's all right, though.
Your father doesn't really like him.

FRANCES: That pseudo-cosmopolitan manner. Have you noticed the way he says '*ciaou*'? Makes me want to kick him.
(She begins to take the dresses out of the wardrobe, throwing them one by one on to her bed)
That one's snazzy. That's the small-talk ensemble. That's my gauche girl listening to big masculine men dress. That's the bosom crusher. A synthetic "you" for every occasion. That's sexy-rexy. Take your pick. All our models supplied with a piece of sticking plaster to stretch over the mouth.

FRIEDA: Oh, Frances—

FRANCES: Well, parties bore me. *(Takes dress she is to wear)* Especially scientists' parties. Conversa-

	tion with them—it's either pi-mesons or disk brakes, with a yawning void in between. If you're a woman you don't get so much of the old pi-mesons, either.
FRIEDA:	You're doing Edgerton an injustice at least. He's very cultured.
FRANCES:	Cultured!
FRIEDA:	You're embarrassingly like I was at your age.
FRANCES:	Oh well, *(Picks up dresses)* I expect when I conceive I shall mutate, and restore the family honour.
FRIEDA:	I wish you wouldn't talk like that—
FRANCES:	Why not? Too sick for you?
FRIEDA:	You can be as sick as you like, darling, but you needn't be cruel. *(She goes out of the door)*
FRANCES:	Oh, mother!
	(She goes on putting the dresses back in the wardrobe)

Scene 5

The hall of the Waring's house. Same evening.

Leonard comes in, slamming the front door. He picks up a letter from the hall table. He reads the letter, his face becoming contorted with anger.

LEONARD:	Frances *(Goes to foot of stairs)* Frances, I want to speak to you . . . *(He starts to go up)*

Scene 6

Waring's house, upstairs. Same evening.
In Leonard and Frieda's bedroom a shirt and dress are laid out on the respective beds. Frieda picks up the dress and goes to the mirror, putting it on. Leonard comes in from bathroom.

LEONARD:	Don't ask me how she found out. She says it

came to her notice. Headmistresses have their informers.

LEONARD: *(He calls from the door to Frances)* The first thing I do tomorrow is write giving her my assurance that you're not going to another sit-down.
(Frances is in the bathroom pulling on a stocking. She pulls a face as he speaks. On the bathroom shelf are a razor in bits, a shaving brush and Frances's mascara)

LEONARD: *(Coming into the bathroom)* I shall stop you. I don't care if you end up loathing the sight of me.

FRANCES: It'll be your loss.
(Her suspender snaps and she goes into her room and rummages in the dressing table drawer. Leonard comes into the doorway of her room)

LEONARD: Yes. It'll be my loss. I wouldn't presume to think it was yours. *(He stamps off back to the bathroom. He turns on the handbasin tap and looks at his razor)*

LEONARD: *(Calling to Frieda, irritably)* You got the wrong razor blades, Frieda. I said red.

FRIEDA: I don't see what difference the colour of the packet makes.
(Frances comes into her parents' room trailing a stocking)

FRANCES: Got a suspender?

FRIEDA: Top right hand drawer—
(Frances goes over to dressing table and pulls open the left hand drawer. Leonard comes in holding up his razor)

LEONARD: They're different blades. Different types of blade. *(Goes to Frances)* What are you doing in my drawer?

FRIEDA: I said right hand, darling.
(Frances slams left drawer and opens right)

LEONARD: You're a minor, remember, a minor.
FRANCES: So what?
             (Fitting suspender into stocking)
LEONARD: Can't you do that somewhere else? There's
             nothing uglier than a woman fiddling with her
             stockings.
FRANCES: Not a woman. A minor.
             *(Leonard crossly picks up his shirt and storms off to
             the bathroom. Frieda crosses to the dressing table.
             begins to put on lipstick)*
FRANCES: That blueish one makes you look ninety.
FRIEDA: You're handling your father very badly.
FRANCES: I'm not handling him at all. I leave all that
             feminine sort of stuff to you.
FRIEDA: There are occasions when tact and restraint—
FRANCES: Nuts. If you'll pardon the expression. *(She goes
             to bathroom. Leonard is lathering his face. Frances
             reaches past him to shelf)*
FRANCES: I left my mascara here somewhere.
LEONARD: You know, you ought to thank your lucky
             stars you're *at* that school. None of this is
             very funny for me you know, Frances.
FRANCES: I've got rights.
LEONARD: With Colin in prison I—
FRANCES: He was trying to assert his rights. That's why
             he's in prison.
LEONARD: Colin's not infallible. Even if he is your
             brother.
FRANCES: I can work out things for myself.
LEONARD: Oh go on. Get out.
             *(Frances goes out. Leonard rinses his face, making
             a lot of noise)*
             (Frances's bedroom)
FRIEDA: Well, my powder suits you at any rate.
FRANCES: Did you know Greek women used to put
             antimony on their eyelids. *(Pulling her eyes to
             slits)* I'm a vestal virgin.

FRIEDA: It's reassuring to know you're any kind of virgin.

(Frances makes a face and Frieda laughs).

Well in my day—people had standards.

(Leonard comes in doing up his shirt)

LEONARD: I think the first thing we'll clamp down on is these weekends in London. We'd never have allowed it in the first place if it hadn't been for Colin.

FRANCES: It's something I believe in, father.

LEONARD: You can believe what you like. It's what you do that I'm concerned about.

FRANCES: How middle-class can you get!

LEONARD: *(Furious)* I *am* middle class. *You* are middle class. Your *mother's* middle class!

FRANCES: You've pushed a lot out of your mind, haven't you?

LEONARD: Such as?

(Pause)

FRANCES: *(Quietly)* My grandad. Old Mr. Driffield. People like them.

LEONARD: I'll tell you something I'm glad my father never lived to see what's become of his precious Labour Party. I'm glad! And don't spout our Colin's sort of nonsense at me. If kids like you had to live in a socialist country you'd wonder what the hell had hit you. What's the matter with you? We've got an account at Barton's, you can buy what you like. You've got a scooter. You go to a good school. We deny you nothing. You live in a country where you can say, write and think anything you like. What the devil's missing? What's missing? *(Pause. Goes close to her)* It may give you some sort of thrill getting in with Colin's left wing pals and all the rest of it, but by God you'd play a different tune if they were running the

country, I'm telling you. So think again.
(He blows his nose. Sniffs and goes across to Frieda, holding out the handkerchief)
This reeks of chlorine, Frieda. I told you they did last week. Can't you stop that woman using bleach? It's a wonder they don't fall to bits.

FRIEDA: She's getting on. She doesn't take much notice of what I say to her.

FRANCES: What do you know about that woman, apart from what she does for you?

LEONARD: I know she has two boys making twenty a week each at Dalton's Light Metals. So spare me the dialectics. How many like them were there on the sit-down? You don't get much support from your working classes, do you? They're on their backsides watching the Black Marias cart you lot off—on the telly!

FRANCES: *(Defensively)* There were four Welsh miners next to Colin and me—

LEONARD: Listen, Frances. I'm not going to argue with you any more. You cut it out, that's all. There'll still be plenty to get worked up about when you're twenty-one—you can vote Labour and sit down then till kingdom come. *(Goes to door)* Though frankly, I sometimes think we'd all be better off if women had been kept out of the whole thing!
(Leonard goes out. Frieda crosses to Frances)

FRANCES: See.
(Frieda quickly follows Leonard into their own bedroom. He is sitting on the bed tying his shoelaces)

FRIEDA: *(In the doorway)* You go too far!

LEONARD: Don't you start. We're late enough as it is.

FRIEDA: *(Coming in)* Do you think you can say something like that and then just pass it off? *(Pause)* You really meant it, didn't you?

LEONARD: Frances—

FRIEDA: Never mind Frances for the moment. Just tell me. That's how your mind really works, isn't it?

LEONARD: Don't *pick* at it Frieda! It was just a remark. She riles me, if you want to know. She gets my back up.

FRIEDA: You don't answer her properly, reasonably. You just order her.

LEONARD: I told her and I'm telling you. I've no more to say.

FRIEDA: There's no one more despicable than a man who blusters his way through an argument by flinging a woman's sex at her. *(Pause)* I won't stand by whilst you browbeat her with that sort of hypocritical cant—
(Pause)

LEONARD: *(Getting up)* Have you finished?
(Frieda takes her handbag from the dressing table, looks inside it and snaps it shut)

FRIEDA: I'm beginning to think I've only just started—
(Leonard stares at her a moment, then stalks out. Frieda goes into Frances's bedroom. Frances is sitting at her dressing table with a top coat slung round her shoulders. Frieda goes to her)

FRIEDA: Are you ready darling?
(Pause)

FRANCES: I suppose he can stop me. Can't he? *(Watching Frieda through the mirror)*

FRIEDA: He may be right to stop you.

FRANCES: Is that what you think?

FRIEDA: I respect you. I can't agree with you. *(Pause)* There were terribly bitter political differences between your father and his father.

FRANCES: Grandad used to put me on his shoulder and sing the Red Flag! *(Pause)* I can remember him telling Colin all about the pit, and the unions. The strikes. *(Pause)* And when they were laid off, some of them used to catch linnets. Put them in cages and sell them in Pontefract on Saturday mornings. *(Pause)* My Grandad said if you watch what men do with animals, you'll know what men do with men. *(Pause)* I can remember my father and he always used to quarrel when we went up to Yorkshire. *(Pause)* They'd end up bitter and quiet, and my grandad would kneel down and play with us. *(Pause)* You know?

(The two women look at each other. Frieda touches her throat).

FRIEDA: I know . . . that children miss nothing.

(Frances fingers an expensive bracelet on her wrist).

FRANCES: I don't get it all from Colin. *(Pause)* I sometimes feel ashamed of the clothes I put on. The food I eat. All the women's magazines selling elegance and perfumed armpits. I read in the paper the other day: diversity is one of our most precious values in the West. And half the people in the world haven't got *one* of anything, never mind a choice! It's all lies and bunk. *(Pause)* I'm ashamed of my father. *(Pause)* They say there's enough bombs already in existence to destroy most of the world. What's he working on the refinements for? To kill an extra few hundred thousand when the time comes?

(She stands. Frieda moves back a little and they look each other up and down. They both make a move to leave, both look in the mirror again)

FRIEDA: We ought to be going down. He's waiting for us. *(Pause. She smiles)* It's no use trying to convert me!

FRANCES: It's something, if you'll listen.

FRIEDA: Have I ever refused to listen? To you or Colin?

FRANCES: No. You haven't—
              (She goes to the door)
FRIEDA: Anyway, scientists were among the first to
              protest—weren't they?

Scene 7

Clive Edgerton's House.

*Edgerton's house is furnished with ostentatious good
taste—period furniture, a grand piano, contemporary
paintings. There are several small groups of people
in the room. Edgerton is pouring a drink for Wyman,
an American visiting scientist. Edgerton at home,
entertaining, is even more suave than in his
laboratory.*

WYMAN: Fools?
EDGERTON: Yes. Most scientists are fools outside their own
              subject. It's an occupational hazard. In this
              country, it's endemic. When I was in Germany
              and central Europe as a young chap, their
              people could switch from neutrons to Aes-
              chylus without batting an eyelid.
              (Pause. He speaks sardonically)
              No doubt they learned to hide the fact when
              they got to America later on—
WYMAN: Now I don't think that's quite fair, Doctor
              Edgerton—
EDGERTON: Of course it's not fair. Being unfair is more
              human and it's more fun.
WYMAN: I guess Einstein—
EDGERTON: Ah yes—well if they're too clever they're just
              a bloody nuisance. What's that remark of his
              they quote nowadays? 'If I had known I would
              have been a locksmith!' Makes you wonder
              which is really most dangerous—ignorance or

innocence. I leave the ethics of my work to the politicians. They're bigger fools than scientists, of course, but it's supposed to be a democracy. People get the sort of government they deserve, and all that. Are you interested in art? I bought a Reg Butler the other day—

(*He leads Wyman away to the other side of the room. In another part of the room, the youngish wife of a scientist and a country-looking elderly lady are sipping Martinis*)

YOUNG
WOMAN: I had to get round Bobby—the mortgage is crippling us—but then I heard about this riding school. I told her: when you kneel to say your prayers you want to thank Him for a daddy who can let you have all these things. (*As she speaks, she is peering round the room to see who is present and who isn't*)

Bobby's in for an S.S.O. at Aldermaston. Is there any riding there?

OLDER
WOMAN: My father always kept horses. Before the war. And my husband. We haven't been able to afford them for years.

YOUNG
WOMAN: I meant riding schools really. After we've bought the jodhpurs and everything, then if we have to move . . .

OLDER
WOMAN: I used to ride to hounds myself. I must say on looking back, we led a rather silly sort of existence. Mediocrity and tittle-tattle. (*With a certain slyness*) I'm sure you young people are *much* more functional. My father said in nineteen-forty-five, let's winkle out the fellers on the other side with ambition and make the best of it.

(*Mrs. Rawson, trying to light her cigarette, flicks her lighter as she speaks*)

MRS.
RAWSON: I caught her standing over Nina's milk with a cigarette in her mouth this morning. We had a

blazing row but her English is appalling. You know I'm sure she's pregnant. She has an Indian—

(Someone lights her cigarette).

CUT TO:

(Edgerton stubbing his cigarette in ashtray on piano. He takes a drink to Frieda. Frances and Leonard are with Mrs. Wyman and Brian Bell. Frances watches them contemptuously)

MRS. WYMAN: I just can't keep warm here. You know? I'm just shivering all the time.

BRIAN: *(Grinning)* This is nothing! It's mild, really.

MRS. WYMAN: Mild! If this is mild!

LEONARD: Which part of the States do you come from, Mrs. Wyman?

MRS. WYMAN: Florida.

BRIAN: I suppose it's very warm there—

FRANCES: Sub-tropical. Just right for hatching counter revolutions.

MRS. WYMAN: Young lady, if you had a communist country ninety miles off your coastline—

FRANCES: You must all be trembling in your shoes!

MRS. WYMAN: There's too many gone soft on Castro over here. Do you know that guy's still shooting people?

BRIAN: I know. It's terrible. May I just introduce you to — *(They move away towards the other groups)*

LEONARD: Can't you give it a rest? Just for once?

FRANCES: These people don't care about anything—

LEONARD: This is a party, not a political slanging match. There's a time and a place—

CUT TO:

(Frieda, talking to the country-looking woman)

OLDER
WOMAN:
Some of them are quite prepared to see the village hall rot under their noses—

CUT TO:

(Wyman talking to a colleague)

WYMAN:
Well now, if we can accelerate these particles —though I admit there's a whole lot of problems—

CUT TO:

(Mrs. Rawson still with a cigarette in her mouth.)

MRS.
RAWSON:
Do you know I caught her standing with a cigarette in her mouth over Nina's milk to-day?

CUT TO:

(Frances and Leonard)

FRANCES:
What's the use of having beliefs if you don't, if you never—

(Edgerton has noticed that Leonard and Frances are becoming openly hostile with each other. He comes up to them).

LEONARD:
Save it for the sixth form debating society, will you?

EDGERTON:
(Taking Frances's arm) No one ever talks to me at my own parties. Frances, you haven't got a drink. Come and let me tempt you to something soft but potent. Leonard?

LEONARD:
I'm all right, thanks.

(He turns away abruptly. Edgerton steers Frances to the drinks)

EDGERTON:
The true, the blushful Hippocrene. Whisky? Or one of those puritanical cola things?

FRANCES:
Bitter lemon please.

EDGERTON: *(Pouring and handing her the glass)* There. Your poor father doesn't understand the misplaced energies of youth.

FRANCES: Do you?

EDGERTON: I don't understand. I tolerate. Come and meet some extraordinarily boring people—

CUT TO:

(Mrs. Wyman)

MRS. WYMAN: I'm glad you told me. If I had a son in the better red than dead set, and a daughter like her—why I'd blow my head off! It just couldn't happen, back home. I'm sorry, because Ross and Doctor Waring took to each other right away—

YOUNG WOMAN: Yes indeed. Would you like another drink—

CUT TO:

(Another group—Rawson and his wife, Brian, Sonia and Frances, who is still truculent)

RAWSON: No, we didn't stop at Belgrade. All I wanted was to drive through the damn country and get to Greece.

MRS. RAWSON: I don't think we were once spoken to civilly, anywhere in Yugoslavia. The food's appalling, the roads are terrible. The cities give you the willies.

FRANCES: Why?

MRS. RAWSON: They're so dreary! Nothing in the shops, everybody dressed alike—it's like a graveyard after ten at night.

SONIA: Shades of England under the Labour government!

MRS. Much worse, darling! Do you know, they

RAWSON: don't even have labels on their tinned foods? Talk about the joyless society!

FRANCES: Well they haven't—they, have they had a chance yet? The war, and—

RAWSON: And throwing all their best people into prison!

FRANCES: *(Becoming agitated)* They started *off* poor. They've got to—well, to start with the basic things.

BRIAN: Time they got past the basic stage after fifteen years, isn't it? What about West Germany? It sticks out a mile what you can do with free enterprise.

RAWSON: I was sympathetic to Labour for years, give and take a few of their howlers. But if Yugoslavia's got socialism, they can keep it. Give me the Tories.

FRANCES: Oh, you needn't even bother to change. You won't get socialism from the Labour Party!

RAWSON: *(Coldly)* Oh? It rather depends what you mean by socialism, doesn't it?

FRANCES: It certainly does!

BRIAN: *(Smiling patronisingly)* What do *you* mean then?

FRANCES: *(Immediately on her guard)* You know perfectly well there isn't a simple answer, just like that—

RAWSON: Oh, come! Are you backing out?

FRANCES: No, I'm not.

BRIAN: Well, then—

CUT TO:

(Leonard and Frieda, watching. Leonard starts to go to Frances)

FRIEDA: *(Catching hold of his arm)* Leonard!

CUT BACK TO:

(Frances)

FRANCES: You're only baiting me—
BRIAN: No. Go on. You started it.
FRANCES: I didn't make the snide remarks about Yugoslavia, did I?

CUT TO:

(Young woman, talking to Wyman)

YOUNG   Yes, Frances Waring. That's her mother over
WOMAN: there. I've always found her a teeny bit stand-
          offish. And Dr. Waring must be out of his
          mind with the boy in prison—
FRANCES: *(Flustered)* It's to—you've got to—try to
          change the relationships between people.
          Make them social, not economic ones. *(Pause)*
          And the land, everything a country has—it
          should belong to everyone. *(More firmly)* A
          society that isn't based on acquisition and
          greed—
RAWSON: How naïve can you get!
BRIAN: There's such a thing as human nature you
          know.
          (They move away a little)

CUT TO:

(Frieda, who puts her hands to her cheeks)
(Frances makes one more effort and faces Rawson)
FRANCES: One thing I do know. You're so full of sneers,
          but I do know—the communist countries
          have been cynical and cruel in the past—
BRIAN: The past! What about Djilas then?
FRANCES: —But you. People like you are just full of hate
          really—
RAWSON: The communists aren't, of course?

FRANCES: —All hate and death—

RAWSON: Oh, we've an absolute monopoly—

FRANCES: And if there hadn't been evil in the com-
              munist system, then men like you would still
              have invented it . . .

BRIAN: We didn't invent the N.K.V.D.!

FRANCES: —You won't face what's in yourself, so you—
              you put it outside—

RAWSON: Rather! Where it belongs—

FRANCES: *(Suddenly almost hysterical, shouting to be heard over
              their laughter)*—That's what the cold war's
              about on both sides, isn't it?
              *(She throws her glass to the floor. Brian and Rawson
              stop laughing and walk away from Frances leaving
              her isolated. Leonard and Frieda have been watching.
              Frieda goes across to Frances who turns away from
              her and goes slowly out the door, Edgerton following
              her. Leonard moves to follow too but Frieda restrains
              him)*

Scene 8

The cloakroom in Edgerton's house.

*Edgerton is helping Frances on with her coat. She
is strained and defiant, near to tears.*

EDGERTON: Well, that was one in the eye for Rawson.
              He's rather an inoffensive man, as a matter of
              fact. It's his ghastly wife I can't stand.

FRANCES: You don't have to smooth it all over for me!

EDGERTON: My dear Frances! *Chacun à son métier.* Cheer
              up. I'll go in and reassure them all that you're
              a sound democrat at heart—

FRANCES: I won't apologise for what I said to him. But
              I'm sorry I mucked up your party. I really am.

EDGERTON: Nonsense. It'll give us all something to gossip
              about for weeks.
FRANCES: You're treating me like a child. Patronising
              me—
EDGERTON: Yes. Patronising. Decadent. Hedonistic. *(Puts
              his hands to his eyes in mocking despair)* Uncom-
              mitted. I shall be one of the first to be shot,
              when the revolution comes—
              (Frances is laughing, unwillingly)
EDGERTON: And your father will be cool with me all next
              week. He won't be able to forgive me for
              having witnessed—if you see what I mean?
FRANCES: I'm sorry.
EDGERTON: You'd better wait for them outside.
              *(They get out. She down the hall and he back to
              the party)*

Scene 9

*Leonard and Frieda's bedroom. Later the same night.
Twin beds. Leonard and Frieda are lying awake
in the darkness.*

FRIEDA: I don't want to judge my children. I want to
              understand them.
LEONARD: Do you think I don't?
FRIEDA: But you're—so full of anger. Anger runs under
              everything you say to them. What have you
              missed, Leonard?
LEONARD: Missed? Aren't you getting a bit fanciful?
FRIEDA: Frances was crying when I left her.
LEONARD: And more power to her tear-ducts!
              (Pause)
FRIEDA: I wonder if Colin is asleep—
LEONARD: It's one o'clock. *(Pause)* It's Brixton he's in,
              you know—not the Lubianka. *(Reaches out of
              bed)* I forgot to wind my watch. *(Begins to wind it)*

FRIEDA: If you and I fought, if we clashed—even that
            would be better than this. A puny relation-
            ship, now. *(Pause)* If you were to die or be
            killed, I'd cry . . . I'd be wretched with grief.
            And what would I be mourning? Or if I died,
            what would you mourn? *(Pause)* Human loss,
            but what is it? When we can touch neither our
            own children nor each other. *(Pause)* If there's
            a failure, who has failed? Why? I feel bleak,
            but there's fury somewhere. Hunger. And
            rage. For nothing. Because I can't even
            imagine how it could be different.
            *(Leonard turns in bed. Peers through the darkness
            towards her)*

LEONARD: Do you think it's only you who feel anything?
            (Pause) Are you like Colin and Frances, living
            in comfort and despising the circumstances
            that make it possible? *(Pause)* That's too easy.

FRIEDA: There's more to it—

LEONARD: What?   *(Pause)*

FRIEDA: We live, but we have no real connections with
            life. What are we afraid of? Fire? Burglars?
            Burst pipes? Accidents? Human beings should
            have more dignified fears! *(Pause)* Why do we
            find it so easy to live with the idea of extinction
            when our children find it so hard? We don't
            believe it. They do. *(Pause)* A lot of people
            believe it. *(Pause)* When you and I were young,
            we had no doubts about the Nazis. But what
            did my father say? A solid citizen—a respect-
            able lawyer. Remember what he said?

LEONARD: Your father was a decent man who tried to
            face the fact that the world was changing. And
            by his standards, for the worse. That didn't
            make him a fascist.

FRIEDA: Oh no, it didn't. He loathed the Nazis all
            right. He really detested them for confronting

professional men with a choice between the party or ruin! There was agony for you.

LEONARD: Well. It's true.

FRIEDA: And inside that truth, a kind of damnation. *(Pause)*

LEONARD: I'm going to sleep. I don't know why you're raking all this up.

FRIEDA: We turned our backs on it—a long time ago.

LEONARD: Is that what I did? In Normandy? On the Rhine? *(Pause)* Didn't I just turn my back!

FRIEDA: There were no doubts during the war. But after—

LEONARD: Look, do you mind? I'm tired.

FRIEDA: My father once came out with another 'truth' that disturbed me. He said: 'At least the Nazis left some things alone. The communists leave nothing alone'.

LEONARD: And thank God we don't have to be either Nazis or communists and I'm off to sleep. *(Frieda turns over)*

FRIEDA: How I wished in those days I'd been born into a family like yours. *(Pause)* We had a room each, and icy contact at mealtimes. *(Pause)* You all lived, ate, cooked—battled— all in that one small living room. Bedrooms were for bed, and that was an end of it.

LEONARD: Idyllic. Mine had fungus growing through the wallpaper, bare lino and a jerry you could have launched the Queen Mary in.

FRIEDA: At least you lived close enough for everything to be open between you. For something to exist.

LEONARD: That's right. When my father came in tanked up he could spit into the fire from the back door. Very intimate. *(Frieda sits up in bed and turns to Leonard)*

FRIEDA: Leonard—won't you try to understand? We're

shallow and unreal to our children. In some ways, contemptible. *(Pause)* You've often said how your father expected you to be like him. Do you expect that of Colin? And Frances?

LEONARD: I'd be a pretty frustrated man by now, if I did!

FRIEDA: Don't you see, you've no power? Nor have I. This extends to—everything. *(Pause)* When I was Frances' age, I didn't know a thing. Freud, and Wells and Lawrence had thoroughly undermined my father's world. He didn't know it, or he wouldn't face it. There was I, all sweet and—dim, and accepting— well, for example, that I ought to be a virgin when I got married. I accepted a moral sanction. *(Pause)* But if I were to try and impose that on Frances, she'd simply say: 'Why?' For her it's not a moral problem. It's a matter of choice, of discovering who she is in terms of what she wants to do—

(Leonard lurches up in bed, startled and angry)

LEONARD: I've never heard such bloody nonsense in all my life! Do you really mean to say she—

FRIEDA: As a matter of fact she's completely inexperienced. Pure enough to satisfy even a bigot like you. But what if she wasn't? If you condemned her, what would be your authority? *(Pause)* They don't accept an authority that rests on abstractions. Not any more.

LEONARD: Grand. Marvellous. Bless you, my children. Have you got everything you'll need in your cell? Will you remember your old dad, when we ban the bomb and the Russians walk in and they make you a commissar? *(Pause. He settles down in bed)* For God's sake, all I want is for my children to be honest, decent, dignified human beings. And allow others to be the same. *(Pause)*

FRIEDA: We're a family. We ought to know where we belong to each other and where we don't— where the love and the hatred are.

LEONARD: Hatred?

FRIEDA: Aren't we hateful? Whenever our self-deceptions cause us to deceive?

LEONARD: I'm not aware of having deceived you.

FRIEDA: No! Because for some peculiar reason your picture of yourself doesn't disturb you.

LEONARD: I don't think I'm abnormally satisfied with myself—

FRIEDA: Oh, you're a paragon of normality. Britain's new man on the decline. The brainy working class kid who puts his head down and swots. And looks up one day to find himself created in his own absence. Who made him? What is he? A bit of a Christian, a bit of a Tory. Doubtful about trades unions and the United Nations, living harmlessly. Whose creation is it? Didn't know it was happening. Whilst the world goes to pieces over his bewildered head. *(Pause)* Nuts, as our dear daughter would say. *(Leonard gets up. Goes wearily over to dressing-table and opens drawer. He takes out a box of pills and moves over to the bedside table with water and glass on it. He swallows the pill)* You needn't take those. I'll shut up. *(Pause)*

LEONARD: I've taken them. *(The sound of owls outside. Pause)*

FRIEDA: You love me? *(Pause)* Leonard? *(Pause)*

LEONARD: Yes. *(Goes to the window)* Is that an owl? *(Pause)* I bloody hate nature, really. Trees, and grass, and—things buzzing. *(Pause)* I dropped biology in my second year. I met you that summer. *(Pause)* Do you know, it's hard to

remember what I was like before I met you.
(Pause) I feel as if I've never been a young
man.
*(Leonard gets back into bed, pulling the sheet up
under his chin)*
You've got my number all right, I suppose.
(Pause) I don't think I ever heard an owl, when
I was a kid. The pit donkey engine at nights.
Shunting trucks. Peter Driffield stayed with
us once, when his mother died. He cried,
under the bedclothes. I always thought he was
a bit soft. *(Pause)* In form four we had one
of those right bitter schoolmasters. If he caught
Peter up to any mischief he used to say:
'Driffield, you're naught but a dead leaf on the
tree of your dad!'

FRIEDA: And what did he say to you?

LEONARD: What? Who?

FRIEDA: The schoolmaster—

LEONARD: He used to tell me I'd—I'd got the brains
to get out of that hole. He never let up on that.
(Pause. Laughs) Peter used to say he was going
to be a Labour prime minister! *(Pause)* I think
teaching in a university rots some people.
*(Frieda turns restlessly under the bed clothes. There
is the sound of a big aeroplane passing low over the
house. A shuddering, throbbing gush of sound)*

FRIEDA: That sound makes my stomach shrink. Sometimes I can't understand why people aren't
running mad in the streets. *(Pause)* Why are
we so ashamed of fear?

LEONARD: It's a passenger plane. Britannia by the sound
of it. *(Pause)* Next thing, the damned birds 'll
be twittering and then we've had it. Are we
never going to sleep?
(Pause)

FRIEDA: What should we be doing? Saying? *(Pause)*

Saying to our children? I don't even know what to think. *(Pause)* When I was carrying them, I felt possessed by them. It seemed an outrage. And then it was too late to protest. One morning a few weeks before Colin was born I lay in bed feeling him kicking. And I shouted. I swore. *(Pause)* I'm a person, I said. A person. And that was the end of me, for nearly twenty years. But if it was too late then, aren't I past redemption now?

LEONARD: Redemption! *(Mocking)* Why don't you try nembutal?

FRIEDA: You love me—and inside love, I'm starved. I have a nice house—and inside the house I'm frightened. We have friends—neighbours—and among them I'm appalled by them. I love you—and inside *that* love there's hysteria because I want to live before I die. I want love to nourish life. But it doesn't. *(Pause. Speaks suddenly and sharply)* It makes a cow out of a woman!

(Leonard inhales a long and long-suffering yawn and turns on to his back)

LEONARD: I don't think I've met anybody with so much going on inside and so little to show for it as you. *(Pause)* I sometimes think you ought to have married Peter Driffield. He's just the same as you. *(Yawns)* Give me women about me that are fat, and sleep o' nights.

FRIEDA: Are you so secure?

LEONARD: I know my head's going like a hammer. My eyes are burning. You natter on and natter on. *(Pause. Leonard turns over, facing away from Frieda. He has his eyes closed)*

FRIEDA: *(Quietly)* I've so much time now. To be whatever I want. And I can't become anything. Look after this house. Clean it. Warm it.

Bring other women in. Chatter. Play readings.
Or go out. Bicker on committees for the suffering and the unwanted. *(Pause)* People who
do those things really do them for themselves.
(Pause) I want to enter the world.

CUT TO:

*(Leonard. He is sleeping soundly. His hand is lying
on the top of the sheet)*
I have this . . . baffled respect for our
children. For anybody who believes, acts—
who isn't—what is it?—determined. Caused.
Who isn't just shaped by what lies outside
them. You hear me Leonard?

CUT TO:

*(Leonard's face. His tongue moves between his lips
but he is still asleep. He stirs a little, pressing his
face deeper into the pillow)*
Our lives, the world we make and allow to be
made—it seems to me one long, sustained
insult to ourselves. We're insulted. We invite
menace, and death. We yield. We're numb.
(Pause) Leonard? And it isn't just passive.
We insult. We do. Leonard?
*(She puts her hand out across the space between the
beds. She grips the sheet of Leonard's bed, then
lets it go. Her hand gropes in the darkness. Slowly,
she withdraws it)*

Scene 10

A Prison Cell

*Colin is sitting on a top bunk. Ray sits reading on
the lower bunk. George is also sitting on his bed
at the other side of the cell.*

GEORGE: So I says to the screw, you've got another thing comin' kiddah, afore I call ye sir. I call nobody sir. Not even the wife. *(He laughs)*

RAY: *(Getting up, speaking to Colin)* Do you call him 'sir'?

COLIN: I call him 'you'.
(Pause)

GEORGE: Aye. I'm lossin' three pound a day, in here. *(Looks from Colin to Ray)* Aye. Well, it's only money. *(Sits up. Drums his fingers on his knees)* I wonder if the Queen visits these places? *(Pause)* I cannot make out what royalty's for, meself. Can ye? Colin? What's royalty for?

COLIN: A symbol, my friends, a symbol. A link with the past—a noble image.
(George gets up and goes to the table)

GEORGE: I'm a republican, meself. *(Pause)* Well, what does a man need but four walls and a roof? *(Gestures at the cell)* I live in a place no better than this in Newcastle. Byker. Do you know Byker? *(Pause)* To tell the truth, I haven't got a wife. She run off wi' another feller. A brickie. One of them that cannot stop talking. Cannot hold their peace. I've niver been able to keep a woman, not at any time in my life. My mother left us when I was fourteen. That seemed to set the pattern, like.
(Sings)
Whisht lads, had yor gobs
I'll tell y'all an awful story,
Whisht lads had yor gobs,
I'll tell y'aboot the worm.
(George goes back and sits on his bed)

COLIN: My father's coming to visit me.

GEORGE: Aye? He'll be proud of ye.

COLIN: He won't. Just the opposite.

RAY: Well, at least, you haven't a job to lose.

GEORGE: What we want now is strikes, man. Industrial action. But the workin' man to-day—an' I'm a workin' man meself—he doesn't give a damn aboot nothing. Not even obliteration. You see? You educated fellers that's workin' for the cause, you'll get nowhere wi' the workin' man.

RAY: What about you, then?

GEORGE: Aye, hinny! But nobody had to set about convincing me. They hadn't. I can see through them that runs this country like I can see through a pane of glass. *(Rather smugly)* Why no! The working man is dreaming in his avarice.

COLIN: I wish you'd shut up George.

RAY: You shouldn't speak to him like that.

GEORGE: You shouldn't speak to me like that, kiddah. I'm old enough to be your father.
(George comes down and taps Colin's shoulder. Then stands with back to the two-tier bunks. Colin rises and turns to face him)

COLIN: What can you see for yourself, George? Nothing. For instance, that brickie your wife ran off with's a mute compared to you.

RAY: Leave him alone. What's the matter with you? *(Pause)*

GEORGE: *(Airily)* I suppose you can expect to meet all sorts in these places.

RAY: *(To Colin)* You're getting touchy. You can't afford to, not in here. *(Pause)*

COLIN: I'm sorry George.

GEORGE: We'll say no more about it. It's nerves. They try to take away a man's dignity in these places. *(Pause)* They say our ancestors lived in trees. I wonder what they'd make of this lot? Give me a treetop any day of the week. *(Pause)*

RAY: *(To Colin)* What's your father like?
COLIN: *(Hesitating)* I'm ... very fond of him.
RAY: That doesn't say what he's like!
          (Pause)
COLIN: He won't just come here to see me. He'll come
          for the satisfaction of knowing that he acted
          magnanimously. He won't be a father. I won't
          be a son. We're trapped, him and me.
          (Suddenly disgusted with himself) There's nothing
          like prison for creating an atmosphere of
          phoney intimacy, is there? This has nothing
          to do with you.
          (Colin turns away from them)
GEORGE: You're old enough to make peace with your
          dad. I never did meself. Mine was a coward,
          and a blackleg. Fellers used to come to our
          house and go upstairs with my mother. He'd
          grin at them. I've seen him gan past the
          pickets with the same grin. Aye. She left us.
          Then I left him. He's still alive. He's a
          shuffling, starin' old man in a looney bin. I
          could make it up with him now. But he's gone.
          He's not there in his own body. *(Pause)* You
          want to watch it, kiddah! Here, have a tab.
          *(George brings his hand up closed. Makes the magic
          pass and opens it to reveal three cigarette ends. He
          lights them, then goes to give one to Ray)*
GEORGE: Me giving tabs away—it's like giving blood.
RAY: *(Ironically)* I must say, you two make me feel
          depressingly uncomplicated.
GEORGE: *(Giving Colin a cigarette end)* It's bad enough
          when father and son hate each other as men.
          It's worse when they could love one another
          but for where they stand in the world.
RAY: *(Laughing)* Bring on the incubators and state
          nurseries!
          (A warder comes to the judas hole)

WARDER: Waring—
COLIN: *(Going to door)* Yes?
WARDER: Visitor.
             *(The warder unlocks the cell door. Colin looks back
             at George. Then Ray. Ray mockingly salutes him.
             George gives the thumbs up sign)*
GEORGE: *(Shyly)* Tell him you're doing fine, kiddah—
             *(Colin smiles. The warder opens the door and Colin
             goes out)*

Scene 11

Prison Visiting Room.

*Leonard sits in a bare, small room, at a table.
Colin is brought in and sits down opposite his
father.*

COLIN: I never expected to see you here.
LEONARD: They tell me you can come out if you change
             your mind. If you agree to be bound over.
COLIN: I won't.   *(Pause)*
LEONARD: Are you all right?
COLIN: Yes.
LEONARD: Do you want anything?
COLIN: No thanks. I'm fine. It's not bad.
LEONARD: I've always suspected people who suffer for
             causes. They get something out of it.
COLIN: *(Smiling)* This isn't suffering. It's incon-
             venience.
LEONARD: I wonder if you'd be in here if you had a wife
             and kids.
COLIN: I can't answer that. I don't know. I hope I'd
             still be here.
LEONARD: You want to get yourself out of here. Give it
             up.

COLIN: I could say the same to you. About your work.
            We both have the choice.
LEONARD: I don't know what comes between you and
            me. Do you know? I'm damned if I do. I
            won't accept that it's what brought you here.
COLIN: Why not?
LEONARD: There is such a thing as feeling. You're my
            son. I don't stop to ask myself whether we
            have the same opinions, beliefs, when I think
            of you as my son. *(Pause)* Would I have come
            to see you otherwise?
COLIN: Will you come to see me again?
LEONARD: I want you to promise me you'll come out—
            and get on with your life. *(Pause)* What you
            people are doing—it's not going to make any
            difference. You should be studying—enjoy-
            ing yourself. College is the last chance you'll
            get!
COLIN: If we do nothing, that certainly won't make
            any difference. We have to try. It's no use
            telling me to get on with my life as if that was
            something separate, something apart from
            political issues. It shouldn't be. That's how
            you live. That's what disgusts me about how
            you live. All of you.
LEONARD: All?
COLIN: All your generation that were born working
            class, and 'got on' as my grandad called it—
            and betrayed all those tired and disillusioned
            old men that put you in your mother's bellies!
LEONARD: Betrayed? What comes next? Fascist hyena?
            Capitalist jackal?
            (Pause)
COLIN: If my grandad was alive, do you think he'd be
            with you—or with me?
LEONARD: Oh, he'd certainly have had his backside to
            the pavement!

COLIN: Yes, and why?

LEONARD: Because being sent to prison would have fitted
              in very nicely with his antiquated socialist
              mythology. He'd have loved it. They wouldn't
              have been able to get him out!
              (Pause)

COLIN: There's not much point in going on with this.
              Is there?
              (Pause)

LEONARD: Your grandad could have been a bigoted
              drunken Tory. Plenty of colliers were. If there
              was anything special about him, it was him—
              not his work, or his politics, or his class.

COLIN: I believe just the opposite. I believe his work
              and his politics and his class *were* him. And
              what you are, you make cruel nonsense of his
              best hopes. You do, because you use what he
              gave you only for yourself. If that isn't
              betrayal, I don't know what is.

LEONARD: I used the chance he gave me to give you and
              your sister a life that I couldn't—couldn't
              have dreamed of, when I was a kid. *(Pause)*
              I don't know why we've never discussed these
              things—

COLIN: *(Sharply)* I've never been to prison before. I
              expect it was a jolt, even to somebody as
              complacent as you. No doubt it's embarrassing
              to have a political prisoner in the family!

LEONARD: Political prisoner be damned! You broke the
              law.

COLIN: For certain reasons—

LEONARD: You can't expect a magistrate to take your
              reasons into account. You broke the law.

COLIN: And that's self-evidently wrong?

LEONARD: Yes.

COLIN: Any law?

LEONARD: Yes.

COLIN: You think apartheid laws are right?

LEONARD: I'm not going to sit here and listen to sophistry. This isn't South Africa. We have perfectly legal ways of expressing opposition in this country.

COLIN: The legal ways haven't been very effective. And time's short.

LEONARD: In a democracy, you must accept it if you can't persuade the others.

COLIN: And if the others aren't properly informed about the issue? *(Pause)* Oh, let's stop it. Let's just say I'm against democratic suicide for whole nations.

LEONARD: *(Quickly butting in)* Do you know where the mystery is for me? Where all this started with you?

COLIN: There's no mystery. It's precisely the things you stand for that I can't value. What have you done? Built a house and put a wife and children in it—put your gifts as a scientist into weapons of mass murder—isn't there something inconsistent there? Brick on brick and seeds in the garden and your children growing into a man and a woman. What for? To burn? To incinerate? Is *that* your example?

LEONARD: I hope one day you'll build a house. Put a wife in it. And children. But you won't know what for, any more than I do. As for the great gift of socialism from your grandfather— you're not in here because you're a socialist. What's that got to do with it? Your views aren't even accepted in your own party, let alone mine!

COLIN: Let's not be ironic! What did you do with the great gift of socialism? You grew up with it, from the time you were no higher than his pit boots! *(Pause)*

LEONARD: (*Awkwardly*) Colin, your—your grandad—if you could understand it—what I am is what he wanted me to be. Never mind what he said about politics. He really only understood success in terms of money. Position. He never respected me till I had both. Underneath his talk, I've never known such a bloody old reactionary in all my life. It's true. It was hard for me when I was your age. One of the things that drove me on was knowing I'd be free of him. That one day I'd have him respecting me for things that were the lie to all he said he believed in. If my father lost me, it was his own fault. At bottom of him he was phoney. He was ignorant and frustrated. He was a union man because he saw the workers could get more by collective blackmail than they'd ever get as individuals on their own. He was labour because he saw labour as nothing but an extension of the unions and hence people like himself. (*Leaning towards Colin over the table*) It's time you caught on, Colin. In the end he was like everybody else— out for himself. As for being against the bomb, aren't we all? Isn't everybody? Scared out of our wits. And that's why we're still alive and still free, because we've *got* it!

COLIN: Free for what? To turn into what you've turned into? Is it worth it? Free to wait until it's too late? Free to twist the meaning of that dedicated old man? You make me want to throw up. You make me ashamed to be your son. (*Pause*) What is there to love in you? The brute fact that you got me? I wish you never had, because I'd sooner not have existed than exist through you. Believe me. (*He gets up and goes to the door, then turns back to his father*) It's

tragic, isn't it? Men like your father and Peter
Driffield's father. They thought you were
going to take over and bring in the millenium!
Of course, some of you have taken over.
Sleek technocrats and executives in the old
firm. (*Pause*) My grandad didn't lose you. You
lost yourself, father. You belong to the people
he fought and hated all his life. They didn't
buy you. You didn't sell. It just happened—
didn't it?

(*A prison officer opens the door and Colin goes out.
Door closes behind him. Leonard slowly gets up from
the table*)

Scene 12

*Peter Driffield's flat in Camden Town. Some
months later.*

*Tom Driffield is sitting in the living room peeling
potatoes. He has a bowl in front of him on the table,
on a spread-out newspaper. Open on a pan of milk
boiling over in the small kitchen off the living room.
Cut to Tom.*

TOM: (*Singing*) They say that this England's a
            wonderful place,
            With the workers mixed up in the bourgeois
            rat-race.
            (*Peter comes in with a carrier bag of groceries. He
            yells* 'Burning' *and dashes straight through to the
            kitchen. Takes the milk off. Reappears in doorway*)
PETER: You've done it again! Where's Colin?
TOM: Getting bathed.
PETER: Couldn't you smell it? What did you want
            milk for?
TOM: I can smell it now. I couldn't afore. I were
            going to make mesen a cup of cocoa.

PETER: If you'd peeled the potatoes in the kitchen you'd have sm—

TOM: Nay, I can't get used to these little kitchens. Typical Southerner's kitchen yon one is.

PETER: *(Smiling affectionately)* You prejudiced old devil!

TOM: I don't know why I come to live wi' thee in the first place. Nowt's same once you get south of Bawtry.

PETFR: Did you take the chicken out of the fridge?

TOM: Aye. If tha can call it a chicken. Nowt but a bag of skin and bones wi' an I.O.U. inside.

PETER: A southern chicken! *(Peter goes out to Hall to hang up his coat)*

TOM: *(Unruffled)* That's about top an' bottom on it. A Bradford sparrer, your mam would have called it. *(Pause. Jabs at a potato)* Aye, when the revolution comes, it'll noan—

PETER: *(With Tom)* Start south on Bawtry.
          (They both laugh)

PETER: You're getting a bit doctrinaire in your old age, aren't you?

TOM: Tha what? With a reactionary government and a reformist opposition? Tha wants to get thy buttons sewn on!
          (Peter hangs his coat up. Then comes back into the living room with a sheaf of pamphlets in his hands)

TOM: I went to t'House of Commons this afternoon. You should have seen them. That isn't what *I* call government. They're nowt but a gang of dummies tarted up with self-importance.

PETER: How was our old dummy from up north?

TOM: Fast asleep with a grin on his face like a pig in a barrel of stout. I bet they have to give yon one injections to get him on his feet!

PETER: *(Putting the pamphlets on the table)* I got confirmations of your bookings. There's a few pamphlets and things. If you don't break your

	journey in Warsaw, you'll be in Moscow on the second of June.
TOM:	I noan care, so long as I get there.
PETER:	I think you're out of your mind.

(Tom gets his glasses from a case on the table, puts them on and eagerly takes the brochures from the envelope. They advertise holidays in the U.S.S.R.)

TOM:	Your mam and me went to Cleethorpes year in year out for nigh on thirty year. Now then. I've told you. I've got my savings and I'm barn to Russia. I want to set eyes on it once afore I go.
PETER:	What if you fall ill, or something?
TOM:	Nay lad, if I die they mun bury me in t'Soviet Union. *(Slyly)* It'll save thee a quid or two.

(He looks at one of the brochures—pictures of Moscow. Peter takes the bowl into the kitchen and comes back)

PETER:	You're too old for it, dad. You're stubborn!

(Tom is looking closely at a picture of the Winter Palace in Leningrad)

TOM:	I come home from t'pit one afternoon—1905 it was. I must have been fourteen. My dad were sittin' by the fire. Soon as I'd got myself through the door he takes hold on me by the shoulders and looks me straight in the eyes. He were crying—crying and same road nearly laughin' an' all. He grabs hold of my ears and pulls them. He says: 'Tom—the people has marched on the Winter Palace! That's in St. Petersburg, in Russia,' he says. 'That's just the beginning'.
PETER:	*(Almost as if his father's excitement exasperates as well as moves him)* Dad—
TOM:	*(Still absorbed in his reminiscence)* I'd been on a shift with Surry Waring, that day. Leonard's dad. They called him Surry because he always

called everybody else Surry! *(Pause)* It comes from sirrah, tha knows. It's a right old word.

PETER: And you're the one that, when the lads from the Communist Party came to the house during a strike—you're the one that used to say: nay, come and twist my arm when I'm in work. I'll let thee know then! *(Pause)*

TOM: *(Quieter)* Being a communist or not being a communist had nowt to do with it for fellers like me. All I know is, there come a time in 1917 when soldiers looked at the people marching on—and lowered their rifles.
(He puts his glasses back into their case and goes to the mantelpiece for his pipe)
Colin must be drowning himself. Don't they give them baths in prison, then?
(Peter gathers up the brochures and puts them on the sideboard)

PETER: Did he tell you Leonard had been to see him?

TOM: Aye. *(Sitting on sofa filling his pipe. Colin comes to the sitting room door. He is buttoning a clean shirt. He hears Peter talking and stops at the door)*

PETER: I sometimes think we should never have let Colin come here to live.

TOM: Dost think he'd have been any better on his own? Any different?

PETER: I don't mean that. *(Pause)* I know Leonard. All he can feel is—he has a right to his son.

TOM: Have you stopped him, then?

PETER: *(Slowly)* Leonard knows I'm a parody of what I ought to be.
(Colin comes forward into the room, tucking his shirt into his trousers)

COLIN: *(Sourly)* You're a parody of what you never were. My father thinks there's some kind of contest going on. But he doesn't care what I am at all. He only cares about my allegiance.

Blood's thicker than ideology—that's his real line. *(Pause. To Peter)* And you, with your diffidence and your anxiety and your scruples! You're nearly as sterile as he is! So he's a reactionary nit, and you're a jaded left winger and all that jazz—and what is it? Categories, man. Categories!

PETER: What the hell's come over you?

COLIN: I'm traumatised by my old man, man. Traumatised.

(His manner changes. He becomes tired, sincere)

You should have been able to stand in that doorway and hear yourself talking. You want to be careful. *(Turns mockingly to Tom)* You left your Russian grammar in the lav. *(Stands behind the sofa holding up the grammar)* Gospodin —archaic usage meaning lord, sir, gentleman. Gospodin Driffield, as a canonised member of the old guard, Yorkshire division, what do you think, old shock worker?

TOM: *(Looking up at him, puzzled)* I think tha's gone barmy. Out of thy mind.

(Colin carefully places and leaves the grammar on Tom's bald head and crosses to Peter)

COLIN: Here I am, a passionate socialist. Which is a very difficult thing to be at this time etcetera etcetera. And you go grubbing under the surface looking for dadda complexes. It's not white. Not nice. Where's the cooking sherry, men? We're in this socialist vacuum together.

PETER: Sherry's in the sideboard. *(Colin goes to sideboard)*

COLIN: I'm going to get me a nice chick with a leather raincoat, a cosy bed-sitter done out in Victorian, no landlady—and move in.

(He pours out glasses of sherry and takes one to Peter and Tom)

A toast, a very special toast. (*Drinking*)
Here's to Her Majesty's prisons. (*To Tom*)
Dad, yours was the hip generation. What's he
got? (*Pointing to Peter*) Memories of the Peace
Ballot, doubts about democracy, and psycho-
somatic catarrh.

TOM: Aye? And what's tha got?

COLIN: Me? I've got my worries, man. (*Points at Peter*)
I worry about his worries. And he worries
about my dad's worries. When Freud comes
in through the window, comrades, Marx goes
out through the door. (*Again he relaxes the pose*)
Come off it, chums. Give us a break.

TOM: I'm barn to put dinner on. I thought we were
supposed to be celebrating thee coming out on
prison? There's a reight morbid atmosphere
round here to-day—(*Goes into the kitchen*)

PETER: (*Looking at Colin*) Well. Why so rattled?

COLIN: There's a soft, too reasonable centre in you.
Caught a glimpse of it just now. You're just as
dug in as my father is. Your tutorials, and your
books—your articles and meetings, all the
slaver about the new left defining itself. You're
dusty. You need a beating. The way you
blather on about fathers and sons. Man,
you're way out.
(*Colin flops down on the sofa*)

PETER: Your mother thinks I've influenced you. And
Frances.

COLIN: My mother mistakes your ineffectualness for
depth.
(*Pause. They sit looking at each other*)

PETER: I wonder why you do stay on here, man!
(*Pause*)

COLIN: I suppose I dig the old Gospodin in the
kitchen. But not sentimentally, like you.
You're really bucked to think you have your

old miner dad alive and kicking in your flat. Have the forty-ish cats along now and then to yes Mr. Driffield him, and no Mr. Driffield him, and isn't Peter marvellous with his father! And isn't his father marvellous anyway! Isn't he wonderful? Going to Moscow all on his own at his age? Ole!

PETER: You must have been doing some profound thinking in prison.

COLIN: It's true, Peter. All true.

(Peter looks at his watch. Takes a cloth from the sideboard, and cutlery. Begins to set the table)

PETER: Your sister'll be here soon—

COLIN: Don't be offended. It's my sorting out week. Very brash and arrogant of me. Maybe it's revenge. I came out of jail feeling it had been absolutely useless to go in—and knowing I'll most likely be in again after the demonstration on Sunday. I'm still with it, but I feel bitchy. Want to take somebody apart.

(Pause)

PETER: You're partly right about me. But you see, when my father retired and I asked him to come down here—I felt the right thing had happened at last. When he came, he brought everything with him that I—that I'd felt the loss of since I came to London as a young man.

COLIN: And what did you give him? Your destructive insights about the futility of the Labour Party? Your fantasies of a left-wing revival? Or the other side of it. Disillusioned intellectual and all that jazz. Gods that bloody failed.

(Pause)

PETER: Why haven't you said any of this before?

COLIN: I don't know. I'm like the bloke in the sexual assault case. I don't know what came over me. *(Pause)* Well. What's the gospodin, after all?

Nothing but a primitive, that's what. The old codger.

(Tom appears in the kitchen doorway wearing a butcher's apron)

TOM: If tha's goin' to talk about me behind my back, make sure this door's shut.

(Comes into the room. Speaks to Colin)

What's up then?

(Goes to sideboard drawer, takes out carving knife and steel. Sharpens knife)

You're a pair, you two is. *(Sings)*

> Merry Dick you soon would know,
> If you lived in Jackson's Row.

(Pause) Man is born to suffer. Cheer up. You make me feel like a member on a dying species. *(Sings)*

> Our Democracy sure is a wonderful thing.
> It lets Labour exist, but it pulls out its sting.

(Sharpens knife furiously on steel)

Citizen Driffield, we hereby appoint you Commissar of Potter's Bar.

(Tom goes to Colin)

When I get to Moscow I'm off to see Kruschev, I'll say: Nikita—Nikita lad, what's up wi' the British Left? He'll look back, a bit old-fashioned, like, and he'll say: Tom, the British Left is like a kipper. Two faced and no guts. *(Disappears into kitchen)*

(Peter and Colin look at each other, smiling. They begin to laugh. Tom is humming and banging about in the kitchen)

PETER: Have you ever heard him on about my Auntie Rose? His sister? She nearly always came for her tea on a Sunday, and whenever he got on about politics she'd sit down at the piano and bang out a hymn.

> *(Peter sits at the old upright piano and begins to play*
> *'We plough the fields and scatter'. Tom comes in)*

TOM: Your Auntie Rose!

PETER: I was just telling Colin.

TOM: The old maniac. She had a face like a plate
             o' chitterlings!
             (Peter strikes up the hymn again. Tom and Colin
             join in)

TOGETHER: We plough the fields and scatter
             The good seed on the land.
             And it is fed and watered
             By God's almighty hand.
             (During the last line the doorbell rings)

COLIN: That'll be Frances—
             (Colin goes to let in Frances. She is accompanied by
             Frieda. Colin hugs Frances warmly and turns to his
             mother)

FRANCES: Hello, jailbird.

COLIN: *(To Frieda)* I didn't know you were coming—
             (She goes to him and he puts his arms round her)

FRIEDA: *(Anxiously)* Are you all right?

FRANCES: Did they beat you up?

COLIN: *(Laughing)* No. Disappointed?

FRIEDA: We've just been seeing your father off at the
             station. I mustn't stay. I'm meeting a woman
             who was in my year at college. Is there a
             Bergmann film on anywhere? We thought
             we'd—

FRANCES: They're on a culture kick.

COLIN: Where's he off to?

FRIEDA: Your father? Windscale—for two days.
             Frances, I'll pick you up when? Elevenish?
             (She follows Colin and Frances into the sitting room)

FRANCES: Peter—hello! Hello, Mr. Driffield—

TOM: Now then, lass. And it's Frieda an' all. Nay,
             come in. Come in.
             (Frieda shakes hands with Tom)

FRIEDA:	How are you? *(To Tom and Peter)* How's the celebration dinner coming on?
PETER:	Won't you stay? Have some with us?
COLIN:	You'd better!
FRANCES:	You're not meeting Rosa till eight. You can stay a bit, anyway—
FRIEDA:	Well, I—I was really just giving Frances a lift. I don't know whether I—ought to.
TOM:	We're having roast albatross. Yon one that's been flying over the ship of state for the past ten year. You mun stop and have a bit, lass! *(They all laugh. Frieda still hesitates. Colin slips her coat off her shoulders)*
FRIEDA:	*(Shyly)* It is nice to be with you all. *(To Colin)* You've lost weight—
COLIN:	*(Laughing)* I've put some on. I've been eating the screws.
FRIEDA:	Screws?
COLIN:	Warders. *(He goes into the hall with Frieda's coat. Frances follows)*
FRANCES:	I'll bet they starved you. *(Gives him her coat. They go back into the sitting room)* Were you with anybody interesting?
COLIN:	On and off. At first I was with a geordie steelworker and a schoolteacher.
FRANCES:	Miss Carson's threatening to kick me out if I go on another sit-down.
TOM:	Some on these women that runs schools, they get more kick out of malice than other folk gets out of sex!
PETER:	But didn't you say you saw a girl from your school at the last one? What about her?
FRANCES:	Iris Mellor. She's given in. Father's putting the pressure on me, as well.
PETER:	Goodness, the chicken! *(He goes quickly out to the kitchen)*
TOM:	What's your mother got to say about it, then?

FRIEDA: If Leonard insists that she mustn't go—I don't
            know.
            (Tom sits down and picks up a book)
COLIN: What can be done? Lock her up for the week-
            end? God, I wish I could break a leg or some-
            thing. I don't want to go through it all again.
PETER: *(From kitchen door)* Frieda, I left its guts inside.
            In the polythene bag, and everything. It's
            been cooking for twenty minutes—
            (Frieda laughs and hurries out to the kitchen)
TOM: By, tha's a reight un!
FRANCES: *(To Colin)* But you are going on Sunday?
            Aren't you?
COLIN: I'm going all right. But I don't have to be
            enthusiastic, do I? You won't be so starry-
            eyed about it if they get you in, either!
FRANCES: *(Deflated)* I'm not starry-eyed. You needn't
            feel so superior. I don't know why people think
            if you're young you're—invalid, somehow. As
            if your age affects the truth of your case.
COLIN: I didn't mean that.
FRANCES: Well, then—
COLIN: I didn't mind jail. I'll go as often as I have to.
            But—I never realised before how a prison is
            . . . our society in action. I knew it, but I
            hadn't felt it. You feel like a fly in a man's fist.
            And behind the fist there's the arm . . . the
            shoulder . . . his total strength. *(Pause)* A
            prison doesn't make you doubt your moral
            position, it makes you doubt men. It's a system
            resting mostly on humiliation and degrada-
            tion . . . on power. I know there are people
            devoting their lives to changing the prisons—
            all that. But as a human invention, as a
            necessary social creation—it makes you want
            to turn your face to the wall. To withdraw
            your complicity from all life.

(Puts a cigarette in his mouth, takes it out to speak again. Frieda appears in the kitchen doorway).
And be damned.
(Lights the cigarette)
I forgot everything, except that I felt like a rat.
(Frieda comes into the room)

FRIEDA: You say that? You?

COLIN: I don't think I'm either a banner-waving extrovert, or a crank.

FRIEDA: What do you mean?

COLIN: Mother, I've as much despair and hopelessness in me as anybody has.

FRIEDA: And your sister . . . people like Frances . . . where do they fit into it? Should they be chanting your slogans? Acting for life? Isn't it their blood shouting? Apparently not. It—sickens me, to think you might be hollow. Shrivelled. *(Pause)* Because—isn't that what I'm supposed to be? Aren't I supposed to cherish the absence of it in you?
(Colin goes to her, puts his hands to her cheeks. Speaks tenderly, using a Yorkshire inflection)

COLIN: Nay, mother! *(Pause)* You don't know whether you want me in it or out of it. Do you?
(Cut to Frances sitting at the table with a box of matches. Takes them out. Builds a house of matches, slowly).

FRIEDA: *(With difficulty)* There's part of me that would . . . would almost welcome death. An end. *(Pause)* I don't necessarily mean war, either. Not physical dying. There are other ways. Bovine tranquillity. Failing to be outraged by the little you've made of life. *(Pause)* Colin, love, you . . . and Frances . . . you . . . I can only put it in an absurd way. You make me weep—
(Pause)

TOM: *(Going to the kitchen)* I think I'd best take mesen in yonder.

FRIEDA: No. *(Pause)* Have I upset you? Can't I speak directly?
(Looking at Colin and Frances)
To them?
(She faces them gently and surely)
One becomes impatient, you know—with frightened, cautious ways of putting things. I have recently.

TOM: I don't know as I follow you. That's all. And it's between you and them—isn't it?

FRIEDA: *(To Colin)* You talk about prison. I think you are trying to say it crushes the love in you. *(Pause)* But me? The prisons are *in* me. The bars are in my bones. The locks in my own doors. *(Pause. She lowers her head)* I am embarrassing myself, and you both want to connect it with your father, but you mustn't.
(She raises her head)
Oh, I came in and found you three men . . . together . . .
(To Colin) And your father going north in that train with a heart like a stone. He knew I would see you.

PETER: *(From kitchen)* Dad. Dad—come and give me a hand with this, will you?
(Colin sits at the piano. Tom goes to Frieda)

TOM: And Leonard's father? Yon was a man with a *right* heart. *(Pause)* Yon was a man that put Leonard on the table when he was nobut a bairn, in front of some of the pit lads. He runs his hand through Leonard's hair and says: I shall make him speak with tongues. The bairn looked up at him. Surry says: The tongue of dignity, the tongue of community, the tongue that the illiterate man who fathered him to his

mother never had. *(Pause)* Surry's heart isn't
stone. Surry's heart's rotting in a flooded seam
under Broughton Colliery this many a long
year. It's gotten t'worms in. *(Pause)* And so has
your Leonard's!

*(Tom goes out to kitchen. Frieda stands for a
moment. Colin sits silent at the piano. Frances goes
on building her match house. Frieda sits down)*

FRIEDA: Your other grandfather . . . my father . . .
tried to marry me off to his partner's son when
I was just over seventeen. *(Pause)* He was a
nice boy. My father did everything he could
to stop me going to university . . . short of
actually refusing to let me. I sometimes wish
he'd had the courage of his aberrations.

(Pause. She looks at Colin and Frances)

I'd sooner not have lived than not borne you
two. But now you see it all. And there's no
real substance in what I say. One imagines
tensions. What would it be, to be twitched into
some sense of life now? At my age. Galvanised
into life by a what is it? A final spasm of loss?
(Laughs at herself) Of hysteria? *(Sneering)* Of
nothing.

*(Frances places the last match on her pile. Sits back
with her hands on her knees. Sings, with an almost
vulgar tone of mockery)*

FRANCES: Men and women, stand together
Do not heed the men of war.
Make your minds up now or never,
Ban the bomb—for ever more.

COLIN: *(Violently)* Shut up!   *(Pause)*

FRANCES: *(Coldly)* I'm immune, mother.

FRIEDA: To what?

FRANCES: Colin doesn't know you very well in one of
your sensitive moods. As you say, they're
quite recent. But I do.

FRIEDA: Meaning?

FRANCES: You're getting to be great at self-contemplat-
              ion. But you don't change. Even my father's
              more consistent than you are. He thinks like
              a puppet and lives like one. You live like one
              . . . and indulge yourself by thinking like a
              human being where it's no challenge . . . inside
              your own head. *(Pause)* You're not honest . . .
              you're simply—inventive. *(Laughs harshly)* Or
              maybe, an invention!

FRIEDA: And who, or what, invented me?

FRANCES: *(Airily)* Oh, what shall we say? The past? Will
              that do? It invents most people.

COLIN: Hadn't you better stop reading, and digest for
              about six months?

FRANCES: But I mean it. You close your eyes. Recall the
              past. *(Closes her eyes)* Jab a pin into it.
              (Makes a jabbing motion with her hand)
              And something's there. What about: *(Standing
              up)* How Peter Driffield went to war?

FRIEDA: I haven't the faintest idea what you're getting
              at.

FRANCES: I think you and I have never found each other
              so tolerable as when Colin was in prison. It's
              really funny.

FRIEDA: I'm sorry. This is too deep for me!

FRANCES: No. Sometimes I can feel you *in* me mother.
              There are moments *(facetiously)* of rapport!
              You're morbidly at your best when you're cut
              off. Isolated.
              (Pause. She smiles wryly)
              Provided of course you survive in those outside
              the quarantine as . . . someone loved . . .
              needed . . . all that jazz.

FRIEDA: I see. And Peter?
              *(Frances turns to the bookshelves and runs her fingers
              along the spines of the books)*

FRANCES: I've read a lot of these. I borrowed one the last time I was here, the day Colin was arrested.

    (She looks round for her handbag. Takes out a tattered paper-bound French edition)

    This one. The poems of Louis Aragon—I opened it for the first time this afternoon. *(She puts the book down on the desk, opens it and reads from the flyleaf, in a clear, hard voice)* Perpignan, July 1937. My dear Frieda, your letter reached me here. Yes, Leonard is a splendid, fine man. I am glad for you both. Forgive me for writing in this book—I hate people who do it. Only a book will be a little harder for you to throw away than a letter.

    (Frances picks up the book and turns to face Frieda and Colin. Frieda is bewildered, Colin stony. Frances goes on reading)

    I got to the Spanish border. I could have got across. We rested in a gully from the sun. It was bare—rubble, jagged rocks, a pitiless place. I thought of you and Leonard. Read your letter again and again. I got up and left the others without a word. Came back to Perpignan. Their war . . . it is hard to say this . . . notice how I say "their war" not mine, yours, ours . . . I was going into it despicably. I could weep with self-hatred to think that I brought my wretched passion into their struggle. So that . . . so that . . . a woman might reassess me as, don't laugh, heroic—dedicated.

COLIN: *(Goes to Frances and snatches the book from her)* Stop this! Stop!

FRIEDA: No. She must finish—

    (Colin and Frances stand facing each other. Colin holds the book and Frances has to take it from him.

*She is a little unnerved but, having started feels
compelled to go on. As she reads she becomes more
and more subdued)*

FRANCES: *(Reads on)* I know you are innocent of all this.
But I am certainly guilty. If I had gone in, if
I had been killed even—there would only have
been a trivial confusion of my weakness with
their expiring strength. Well, I am coming
home. You see what I am like. I even pro-
tected myself by telling you all I was going on
holiday in France. Only my father knew.
When he saw me off at Doncaster, he gave me
a savage-looking clasp knife and hugged me
like a Spanish comrade. My poor father. He
wanted to tell Surry and the others at the pit—
how glad I am that I didn't let him. Regards,
and congratulations to Leonard. Love to you.
Peter.

(Frances closes the book and watches Frieda)

FRIEDA: *(Dazed)* I never received it—

*(Colin looks at Frances bitterly. He sits down with
his back to them, withdrawn. Peter comes bustling
in)*

PETER: Dinner won't be long. You're all looking very
solemn. *(Goes to the piano)* What about another
hymn? Wait till you see my dad's Yorkshire
pudding. It'd win a prize.

*(Plays a few chords on the piano; turns the pages
of the hymn book)*

I always used to like this one. When I was a
kid it made me think of stooked corn and
windfall apples.

*(He plays, and sings softly. The others watch and
listen helplessly)*

Come ye thankful people come,
Raise the song of harvest home.
All is safely gathered in,

Free from want and free from sin.

(Peter stops singing, aware that something is wrong. He looks at them, puzzled. Frances throws the book on to the coffee table. Peter gets up and goes to the coffee table. Picks up the book and looks at the fly leaf. He looks at Frances with an expression of pain)

PETER: Frances—?
           (Pause)

FRANCES: I—I thought she knew about it. I thought she must have given it back to you, long ago.

PETER: But why did you? Why?   *(Pause)*

FRANCES: I wanted to hurt. *(Pause)* But not you—

FRIEDA: *(Harshly)* Oh, there's certainly a moral there!

FRANCES: What are we to you? We mean so much to you. All love, and affection and insight, aren't you! I just think you're a—an emotional parasite.

FRIEDA: I couldn't agree more. What shall I do? Blow my brains out? Or sit tight and pray for the menopause to finish me off in a less spectacular way?
           (A long pause)

PETER: As soon as I'd written this I knew that it was irrelevant. I know I should have gone into Spain whether I had dubious motives or not. *(Pause)* I *(selfconsciously)* was a crafty enough Marxist in those days. I knew the difference between what was historical and . . . what belonged only to me. *(Pause)* It's fairly simple. I was frightened. Scared stiff. *(He sits down at the desk)*

FRANCES: Do you think my mother cares a damn?
           (Pause)

PETER: Yes. I do.
           (Frances crosses the room and sits on the coffee table)

FRANCES: *(To Frieda)* If that had ever reached you, you'd really have been rather flattered— wouldn't you?

FRIEDA: I was in love with your father. I don't know
            what you're after, what you want to drag out.
            There's nothing.

FRANCES: You loved my father? And you shut yourself
            up in him? And that was an end of all doubt!
            What a perfect alibi!

FRIEDA: So—you want to point me out in a certain
            way! As preferring what? Weakness to
            strength? Confusion to certainty? Caution to
            extravagance? *(Half smiles)* You can't bear to
            have me love you without being on your side.

FRANCES: And what's wrong with that?
            (Pause)

FRIEDA: Franco won, didn't he? Hitler got to power.
            In countries where far more people opposed
            them than go on your demonstrations! *(Pause)*
            You tire me out, Frances. You make me pity
            you. *(Pause)* I think I'd better go.
            (She gets up and goes over to Peter).
            What can I say? It's too long ago. I really do
            believe you're all wasting your time. *(Pause)*
            If people were determined to live, then they
            would insist on it . . . demand it . . . but they
            accept the possibility of annihilation already.
            And they're learning to live with the certainty.
            (Pause) What's the use of saying they're lied
            to? Or mislead? Or ill-informed about the
            alternatives? They *know* the facts. There's only
            one conclusion. Death must be less of a strain
            on us than our humanity! *(Pause)* I see your
            beliefs as an emotional trap. I don't reject
            them—I've no energy left for them. No hope.
            I feel as if my life has—flickered out. *(Pause)*
            Can I have my coat Peter?
            *(Peter gets up and goes into the hall. He returns with
            her coat and helps her on with it)*

PETER: And do you think I feel very much differently

from you? For weak and doubting people it's painful to act. For me it began then and there. I've had over twenty years of it. I'm a passive man . . . but in a climate of fear—who profits? Only those with a greater fear than mine. The fear . . . of what the people could do, if they knew they could do it. Still there. Unchanged. Quite simple.

FRIEDA: Well, they've got you all where they want, haven't they? All they have to do is put you in court—where legal judgments count, not moral ones. Are you going to this next demonstration? *(Looks at Colin)*

COLIN: Yes.

FRIEDA: And you Frances?

FRANCES: Yes.

(Tom comes in from the kitchen)

TOM: Aye, and the place for parents is down on yon pavement next to their bairns.

FRIEDA: I hope your cause is worthy of more valid reasons for joining it than mine would be. I don't like wild gestures.

FRANCES: Is that how you've lived with my father? With it all inside you? Maybe you got a kick out of watching him turn into somebody you could despise.

FRIEDA: But I don't despise Leonard. I love him. I've no doubt he feels as much bewildered pity for me as I feel for him. It's a sour consolation for my middle age—but it's a consolation.

(Frieda goes out into the hall. The outer door slams. Peter goes to the desk and picks up book, knocking down the match house)

PETER: *(To Frances)* I'll make you a present of that. In memoriam.

(He throws the book at her feet)

Scene 13

The Waring's Living Room. The following Sunday Morning.

Leonard's brief case is on the sofa. Leonard in Sunday morning clothes comes in and reaches for his papers. Searches for glasses then crosses to mantelpiece and finds them. He sits on the sofa and settles down to read typewritten notes. Frieda comes in with coffee on a tray.

FRIEDA: The bathroom window's jammed again.

LEONARD: You know sometimes when I look round at the things I own, I want to bloody kick them. You buy a new house—in three years it's practically falling to bits. A new car—it's full of bugs. How many times have we sent the telly back? Three? I feel like the bloke in that Greek myth, rolling his stone up the hill. Who is it?

FRIEDA: Sisyphus.

LEONARD: That's him.

FRIEDA: King of Corinth—

LEONARD: And I, as my grandma used to say, am lord of all I survey!

FRIEDA: He didn't have to do it until he was dead.

LEONARD: Yes. We've come along way since then, haven't we?

(Pause)

FRIEDA: Maybe you should have taken that university job you were offered in Ghana—

LEONARD: Oh, yes! That would have taken care of our Colin. They'd soon have had him in preventive detention.

FRIEDA: Did you see the papers? They're moving extra police into London for this afternoon.

LEONARD: I don't know why they waste the coppers' time. They should hose them into the gutters. *(Pause. Sips his coffee)* I had the Security people on my back yesterday.

FRIEDA: They're not serious, surely.

LEONARD: I hate those bastards as much as my dad hated the means test people. *(Pause)* Wanted to know if Colin was a communist. They always take the shortest line between two points. They think: I wonder if X is a communist? Let's go and ask his dad.

FRIEDA: *(Smiling)* Do they think you might pass on a few nuclear secrets?

LEONARD: These people don't think at all.

FRIEDA: You could get out of classified work, couldn't you?

LEONARD: Don't you start!
(Leafs through his papers)
I've left half the stuff I'm working on in the lab. What about a drive this afternoon?

FRIEDA: The Morleys are coming to tea.

LEONARD: So they are.

FRIEDA: You asked them.

LEONARD: Don't you like Jim Morley?

FRIEDA: I think they're both fascinating. Especially Myra. I don't know any other woman who can expand the woman's page of the Times into a monologue lasting nearly three hours.

LEONARD: Well, I know she's not very intellectual. A bit limited.

FRIEDA: Yes. I don't know how she keeps up with Jim.

LEONARD: I wouldn't have said Jim was very bright. The only book he's read in years is the Kon Tiki Expedition.
(Pause)

FRIEDA: Exactly.

LEONARD: Oh. Sarky.

FRIEDA: Yes.

LEONARD: What time's dinner?

FRIEDA: One o'clock. *(Rises and goes to window)*

LEONARD: I said I might have a drink with Clive about half twelve. *(Pause)* Jim Morley's a good scientist, anyway.

FRIEDA: Oh, yes. Good scientist. Good gardener. Good do-it-yourself man. Good little man. Good little pygmy.
             (Leonard glances up at her, says nothing, holding his temper. Pause)

FRIEDA: What if Frances gets arrested to-day?
             (Leonard explodes in temper)

LEONARD: I'm damn well past caring. I hope they give her six months. I hope they give them all six months. As of now, I don't want to talk about it. I'm sick of it. I wish to God my father had sent me down the pit and I'd married a mill girl and had thick kids and sent *them* down the pit. Why did I bother? What's it brought me? You want to know? *(He goes over to her)* Loneliness and boredom and nostalgia. Years of it. Years and years and bloody years. *(Pause)* When I think. I used to have fantasies about marrying somebody posh, when I was a lad. Imagine that. And you were what I thought 'posh'. Well, I fettled myself didn't I? Pulled myself out of the working class by my own bootstrings and then hanged myself with them. What is there in you? Nowt warm. There's nothing warm. I've never known warmth since I was a kid. You come from a rotten, remote, alien class. Cold as death. And you know what I am? I'm a jumped up imitation of you and your lot. So are my kids, only gone one stage further. You get me? Lonely, because at bottom I've nothing to do with wife or children. Bored

because I've not one living lust for anything. Nostalgic, *(Subsiding)* because—when it comes to it, I loved what I had when I was a kid. Never wanted it to change. *(Pause)* Do you think I damn well don't *know?*
(He turns away towards the window. Frieda is very moved) *(Pause)*

FRIEDA: Aren't those . . . some of the things your father used to say about you? *(Pause)*

LEONARD: It was anger talking. Nonsense. *(Pause)* You grin and bear it for years, and when you finally open your mouth—you come out with a lot of drivel. It was precisely because my dad held those views about you and me that I hated his guts!

FRIEDA: I didn't hate his guts—

LEONARD: I didn't know I was full of such muck. It is muck. It's not true—
(The front doorbell rings. They stand looking at each other. The doorbell rings again. Frieda goes to answer it).

RAWSON: *(In the hall)* Hello Mrs. Waring. I'm sorry to disturb you.

FRIEDA: Not at all. Do you want to see Leonard?

RAWSON: Well, if it's not too much trouble—

FRIEDA: *(Calling)* Leonard—
(They come into the sitting room)

RAWSON: Leonard—sorry to butt in on you like this.
(Leonard switches with disturbing facility to a 'social' manner)

LEONARD: Are you wanting the roller back? I've finished with it—
(Rawson seems uncomfortable. He hesitates. Leonard goes over to him)

RAWSON: I just wondered if I could have a word with you. For a minute.
(Frieda watches them both closely)

LEONARD: What is it? I was just clearing up. Can't get off the launching pad this morning, somehow.

RAWSON: I don't know how to put it. It's Joan who asked me to come round.

LEONARD: What's the matter, then?

RAWSON: It's Frances's scooter. *(Pause)* You know how we usually get to bed early. Well Frances does *tend*, you know, to come roaring in a bit late sometimes.

(Frieda sits on the sofa, her back to the men)

LEONARD: I doubt if Frances is ever out much after half past ten.

RAWSON: That's what I'm saying. We like to go up at about ten, and I don't know what it is, Frances seems to accelerate up the road. You know what it sounds like, these two strokes. And Joan, well many a time it's woken her up. Then she can't get back. She gets a headache just like that.

(Frieda pours herself a cup of coffee)

LEONARD: I'm very sorry she's been disturbed—

RAWSON: It isn't that we want to make a fuss, Leonard—

LEONARD: Not at all. No trouble. I'll tell Frances to cut her motor out at the corner and wheel the bike in. After all it's only twenty yards from the corner. You should have mentioned it before.

RAWSON: We were both in a quandary, as a matter of fact. Well you know, live and let live. I'm really sorry about this Leonard—

LEONARD: Well, and I'm sorry about Joan. I can't say I've noticed the bike myself, but—

RAWSON: Of course, I know you and Frieda get to bed a bit later than we do. I don't know, two strokes are so insistent aren't they?

LEONARD: I suppose Frances is a bit careless, at times.

RAWSON: I wouldn't say careless. After all, she didn't know—did she?

(Frieda sits gripping her cup in both hands, listening. Now that the complaint has been settled both men are anxious to deny that there has been anything wrong)

LEONARD: Look, I'm just off for a drink with Edgerton. Feel like one?

RAWSON: I wouldn't say no—

LEONARD: Shall I just come in and have a word with Joan?

RAWSON: I'm sure she'd appreciate it—

LEONARD: Frankly, I loathe scooters myself.

RAWSON: Are you sure you don't mind my mentioning it?

LEONARD: Of course not. You did right.

RAWSON: Really, when you've done something like that —you almost wish you'd never said anything. It seems niggling really.

LEONARD: Better than keeping quiet and festering away there—

RAWSON: Well I always think it's better to—

(Frieda, her face tense, clashes her cup down in the saucer)

LEONARD: I can't stand being on bad terms with people next door. By the way, have you seen what Morley's dog's done to my young currant bushes? The little beggar's got in and rooted half of them up. I must say they want to—

(Frieda gets up and hurries over to Leonard. She is obviously distressed)

FRIEDA: Would you give me the car keys please—

LEONARD: But—what for?

FRIEDA: I want to use the car—if you don't mind.

(Leonard feels in the pocket of his jacket)

LEONARD: But—

(He remembers Rawson and hands over the keys. Frieda goes into the hall)

LEONARD: Where are you going?

(Frieda takes her handbag from the hall table and puts on her coat and gloves)

FRIEDA: To London—

(She goes out and slams the door)

LEONARD: Frieda—

CUT INTO TELECINE:

(Same day. Afternoon)

B.B.C. newsreel film of a Committee of 100 demonstration in Trafalgar Square. The square is packed, Bertrand Russell is speaking.

I doubt if many of those here present to-day realise the very considerable likelihood of a nuclear war within the next few months. I would say deliberately if any of you here present are alive a year hence you will be lucky—

CUT INTO TELECINE *of onlookers on a traffic island. Frieda appears behind them, trying to see into the square.* CUT BACK TO NEWSREEL OF THE DEMONSTRATORS MARCHING INTO WHITEHALL BEHIND A LARGE BLACK BANNER. CUT BACK INTO TELECINE: *Frieda is walking on the pavement down Whitehall, anxiously looking at the people si.ting in the road. A row of policemen in the gutter. Frieda sees Colin, Frances, Peter and Tom Driffield sitting silently in the crowd. She pushes through the police cordon and goes up to them. Colin and Frances look at her without speaking. Frieda hesitates, then sits down beside them, selfconsciously.* CUT INTO NEWSREEL FILM: *Demonstrators are being carried into police vans.*

(John Tidmarsh interviews George Clark).

TIDMARSH: Would you say that this demonstration has been a failure?

CLARK: No. As far as the demonstrators were concerned—an absolute triumph—as far as the organisation is concerned, very, very good indeed.

TIDMARSH:	Have you any idea how many of the people arrested are going to refuse to pay the fine?
CLARK:	I would think about a third.

Scene 14

Inside a Black Maria. Same afternoon.

There are grills in the doors of the cubicles on either side of the narrow central corridor of the van. The engine starts and the van moves off, jolting. Frieda sits huddled in her cubicle, staring at some writing scratched into the wood: 'If you think this is bad——man, wait till you're back in the world there isn't anybody cares about you'.

FRIEDA:	*(Calling)* Colin?
COLIN:	*(In a similar cubicle)* Mother?
FRIEDA:	Are you near me?
COLIN:	*(Calmly)* I think I'm in the next one. *(Pause)*
FRIEDA:	*(Calling)* Frances? *(Pause)* Frances? *(She is very frightened, shaking—her hands on her cheeks)*
COLIN:	I believe they took her in another van.
FRIEDA:	They offered to let me out on bail—
COLIN:	Well, you'll be up before the magistrate to-morrow. Only one night.
FRIEDA:	And you? *(Pause)*
COLIN:	Back to the calaboose to-morrow, I suppose.
FRIEDA:	No one should be put in these things. Not thieves . . . murderers . . . no one.
COLIN:	You're just an old liberal, mother—
FRIEDA:	Are there things written in yours?
COLIN:	There always are.
FRIEDA:	You know why I came? *(Pause)*

	You know why I came?
COLIN:	I heard you. You tell me.
	(Pause)
FRIEDA:	I don't know whether it's right. I don't know. One can't know. *(Pause)* It's like a coffin in here. What people must have sat in here. There must be better ways—
COLIN:	Don't be afraid. It's funny, isn't it? These vans? Imagine somebody actually designing them.
FRIEDA:	I'm trying to imagine the people who are using them—
COLIN:	They are people. You once forget that, and they've won.
FRIEDA:	I'm still quibbling. Quibbling in my mind. *(Pause)* A democracy—
COLIN:	*Our* democracy includes this, mother.
FRIEDA:	But it has to.
COLIN:	Yes. It has to.
FRIEDA:	I *am* afraid. I know it's silly.
COLIN:	Then *be* afraid. And remember it.
	(Pause)
FRIEDA:	Those who are against us are equally sincere. Equally convinced.
	(Pause)
COLIN:	You just said 'us'—
FRIEDA:	What?
COLIN:	Before, you used to say 'you'. Now you say 'us'.
FRIEDA:	Don't count on that meaning very much.
COLIN:	Somebody's written in mine: the man who gave me five years cut himself shaving this morning . . . and bled blood.
FRIEDA:	My stomach's churning.
COLIN:	It's only men, all the way up from the Station Sergeant to the Government.
FRIEDA:	Without the law—
COLIN:	Who wants to abolish the law?

FRIEDA: Aren't we holding it in contempt?

COLIN: Not the law.

FRIEDA: No?

COLIN: You are here, mother. You were more or less free.
            (Pause)

FRIEDA: I shan't stop at this, either.

COLIN: Wait till you come to the doubletalk—both sides are right, according to their values. And supposing we don't choose to die for any of the bastards.

FRIEDA: I'm feeling sick. There isn't even room to be sick, in this—

COLIN: Close your eyes.

FRIEDA: I did. It made me dizzy. I wish I could see you. I feel wretched.

COLIN: This is what it is. They say there must be a stand against anarchy. They are right. But is it? A middle class woman with a curdling stomach and a conscience—shut like a rat in a cage, for what you did to-day. Was it anarchy?

FRIEDA: I don't know what it was. *(Pause)* But rather this than anything else. I'm sure of that. No one should leave it to someone else.

COLIN: They'll say you're a muddler, that you haven't properly considered what you are about. Pseudo-martyr, red beast, idealist, crank, neurotic, beatnik, emotional—a fine selection of labels. Failing those, the point may be that you don't understand tactics, strategy, the necessary risks taken in defence of freedom. You don't *understand* mother, you don't understand the fine things those men who decide are doing for you. In good faith. How dare you assert?

FRIEDA: You are too bitter—

COLIN: And you?

FRIEDA: I'm here.
               (*The van stops. A policeman unlocks Colin's cubicle.
               The policeman hesitates*)
POLICEMAN: (*Consulting list*) Waring?
COLIN: Yes.
               (*Colin goes into corridor*)
POLICEMAN: Same Waring as this Waring?
COLIN: Yes.
POLICEMAN: Your mother, is it?
COLIN: Yes.
POLICEMAN: Say goodnight to her then—
               (*Colin goes to the grill in Frieda's door*)
COLIN: Don't worry, they're taking you on somewhere
               else. Goodnight.
FRIEDA: (*Calmer*) Goodnight darling—
COLIN: Goodnight mother—
               (*Colin goes with policeman*)
               (*Captions over close-up of Frieda, her whole body
               shaking, jolted by the movement of the van*)

END

THE BIRTH OF A PRIVATE MAN

CAST

COLIN WARING	*Tony Garnett*
FRIEDA WARING	*Pauline Letts*
FRANCES WARING	*Jane Merrow*
PETER DRIFFIELD	*Michael Gwynn*
AUNT BELLA	*Kitty Attwood*
LINDA	*Anna Cropper*
CHRISTINE	*Elizabeth Proud*
MOORE	*Edward Evans*
DART	*Donald Oliver*
HARRY	*Ivor Salter*
COUNTER HAND	*Jeanine Garrard*
JACK	*Derek Newark*
ALAN	*Peter Thomas*
JUREK STYPULKOWSKI	*Vladek Sheybal*
KRYSTYNA	*Irena Marr*
JUREK'S MOTHER	*Iola Korian*
WANDA	*Joanna Royce*
GIRL SINGER	*Rhoda Lewis*
GUNTHER	*Paul Hansard*

Members of Lofthouse Colliery Band, Wakefield.

Designed by RICHARD WILMOT
Produced by DON TAYLOR
B.B.C. TELEVISION TRANSMISSION: *1st February, 1963.*

A cemetery on the outskirts of an industrial town in Yorkshire. Winter. A coffin lies in its open grave. Beyond the cemetery are rows of terrace houses and the power station cooling towers. A few yards to the side of the grave a small section of the colliery brass band is playing 'Jesu Lover of my Soul'. The men are dressed in coarse serge band uniforms. Around the grave, people are unconsciously grouped—four miners in their best raincoats and standing slightly apart, the visiting Londoners: Peter Driffield, Frieda Waring and her two grown up children, Colin and Frances. Colin stands close to the grave, looking down.

After the short ceremony and the throwing of earth on to the coffin, Peter turns from the grave and walks away towards the path. Frieda hesitates a moment, looking at Colin, then follows Peter with Frances behind her. The four miners leave together. Colin is still looking down into the grave, his face a bony marblelike mask of deadness.

As Peter reaches the path, the group of miners hesitate, then one of them comes towards him. They face each other a few steps apart. The miner looks at Peter as one might compassionately look at a stranger, hesitating, wondering whether to speak. Finally he puts his hand out. Peter takes it and they clasp hands without shaking.

MINER: You've brought your dad home, then—

Peter doesn't speak but nods his head. The miner squeezes his hand and walks away. Frieda and Frances walk off down the path with Peter. They stop and turn, looking for Colin.

Colin is seen from inside the grave, looking down into it, his hands thrust deep into the pockets of his reefer jacket. He looks round, straightening his shoulders. Suddenly he squats down on his heels, peering hard into the grave. He takes a chrysanthemum from a wreath and throws it gently into the grave, then throws a handful of earth on to the white flower. His eyes close. Then he stands up, waves almost cheerfully at the coffin and hurries away.

Scene 1

Aunt Bella's kitchen and yard. Later the same day.

The kitchen door opens on to a small back yard with coalhouse and lavatory. On an old kitchen table is a roughly-made rabbit hutch. Colin and Frances stand by the hutch, each holding a rabbit.

CUT TO:

The kitchen. The room is rather dark, old-fashioned. A heavy sideboard and table, a plush cover round the mantelpiece with tassels, a sink in one corner, a hard couch. It is a poor-looking but clean room. There are one or two framed sepia Victorian photographs on the wall.

Bella, Peter's aunt, sits in a rocking chair by the range. She is a stringy, rheumatic old woman, with a kind of arrogant, beady, ignorant intelligence.

Frieda and Peter sit on the couch, rather awkwardly. They are deferential to the old lady, but numb in themselves—wanting to get away, not because of Bella but simply the strain of facing someone after the funeral . . . particularly someone who is everything that Peter left behind him over twenty years ago.

BELLA: I'm sorry you're not stopping to your teas.

PETER: We've got to get this train, Aunt Bella. I just wanted to see you.

BELLA: If I could get out on this chair a bit easier, I'd have been down there at the funeral.
(Pause)

PETER: I'm glad you're not on your own.

BELLA: Well, I took in this lass, it'll be eight year this summer. *(Laughs)* She's one on them that left home and went down the North Road, going wi' lorry drivers. Come back wi' a bairn and a bit of sense knocked into her. Them's her lad's rabbits that your two's laking wi', Mrs. Waring. She's good to me. Your father was good to me, Peter. A good brother. He made me laugh.

CUT TO:

Frances, in the yard. She holds the rabbit up close to her face, nuzzling it. Colin holds his rabbit in the crook of his arm. He is stroking its ears flat over its back.

FRANCES: I don't care what you say, it's dishonest giving the old man a chapel funeral—

COLIN: It's what he wanted. It was in his will—

FRANCES: Tom Driffield wasn't chapel. He wasn't anything.

COLIN: His wife was. *(Puts the rabbit gently back into the hutch)* And now he's next to her. *(He strokes the rabbit Frances is holding)* I wish you were more of a rabbit. They're gentle. Timid.

FRANCES: Soft, I'd say! Real victims.

CUT BACK TO:

Kitchen, where Bella is showing Frieda a picture of herself and Tom.

BELLA: That's Tom and me at the Miners' Picnic at Durham. Eh, we had some times. I had a glass of beer that day. And a tongue sandwich. I can remember that beer now . . . *(Smiling)* I was quite sweet on your Leonard's father, Mrs. Waring. But them men!

(Frieda puts the photograph on the table)

FRIEDA: Did you know my husband, then?

BELLA: Only when he were a little lad. They go away, don't they? Yours is two grand young people. Your Frances has got a straight back. I like young ladies to have a straight back.

PETER: *(Half smiling)* And what about young men, Aunt Bella?

BELLA: Young men's all buggeroos, no matter what shape they are. Colliers was more rough in my day than they are now. Aye—all laughing and little presents and kiss me quick. Till they got us married. Then it was back to their men's life, and us left with the bairns and the baking. But that's only men, int it?

(Peter gets up, puts his glasses on and takes the photograph from the table)

PETER: He was handsome, wasn't he? And you were pretty.

(Bella holds out her skinny hand, which is shaking slightly)

BELLA: Pretty—aye! That hand's slapped a few faces, I can tell you. People thought I was forward *(she laughs a little crazily)*, but I wasn't—I was just the soul of curiosity!

FRIEDA: Perhaps some girl ought to slap Colin's face. They put up with awful things from him.

CUT BACK TO:

The yard. Both rabbits are back in the hutch and Frances is teasing one with a bit of straw.

FRANCES: How's Linda?

COLIN: All right.

FRANCES: Mother's funny. I'm sure she's proud of the way you get girls to live with you. It makes her feel modern.

COLIN: I don't *get* girls to live with me.

FRANCES: It just happens—

COLIN: Twice. It's happened twice.

FRANCES: I expect you'll grow up eventually. You're just not a whole person, dad.

COLIN: No, dad, I'm not.

FRANCES: Have you noticed what a gloomy mess mother and Peter are drifting into? They do irritate me.

            (Colin turns his back on her. Frances taps him on the shoulder)

FRANCES: I said they do irritate me.

COLIN: *(Slowly)* Haven't you a grain of compassion in you?

FRANCES: For what? The mutual inadequacies of middle age? The faded intellectual bachelor and the pathetic *divorcée*?

            (Pause)

COLIN: Why do you hate her, Frances?

FRANCES: Why do you love her?

            (Colin goes to the hutch. He tickles one of the rabbits with his finger through the wire mesh)

COLIN: She has courage.

CUT BACK TO:

Kitchen, where Frieda is speaking to Bella.

FRIEDA: No, it's my daughter who's the tough one, Aunt Bella.

            (Frieda goes to the window which overlooks the yard. Colin is standing in a corner of the yard with hunched shoulders, kicking absently at the wall.

Frances goes up to him from behind, puts her fingers under his ribs and tickles him. Colin turns quickly, laughing. Frances puts her fingers to her nose and dashes into the house. Colin's laughter subsides immediately. He stands rubbing at his eyes with his knuckles, then drops his hands slackly by his sides. Seeing his mother looking through the window he goes to her and presses his face to the glass, exactly in front of her. Frances is now in the room and Bella turns to her)

BELLA: Your mother says you're a tough lass.

FRANCES: Does she?

(Frieda turns back towards Frances. Colin goes back to the hutch and starts shadow boxing the rabbits)

BELLA: Well, there's nowt wrong with that. *(Turns to Peter)* Yon man that you've laid to rest to-day, and my man as well . . . there were too many like them, round here. They were all that busy talking about changing the world, their bairns and their women grew old nearly behind their backs. For all they were good men, I have to say that. *(Reaches out her hand to Frances, who takes it)* Yes, my love. You mun be hard when it suits. Because nowt has changed. Nowt does change, for the women-folk—nobut one day on the next, and one season on the back on another. Now help me to my feet, young lady, for I say goodbye to nobody sitting down.

(There is a sudden grace and deference in Frances, and some correspondence between the old woman and the girl. Once Bella is on her feet, she puts her arms out to Peter. He goes to her and gently embraces her. She holds him, leaning back to speak)

BELLA: Well, son—grieve your father then leave him be. Happen I shall grieve him longer, but that's because I shall soon be following on. *(She grips his arm)* You were a tender boy.

You've made a tender feller, haven't you! He sent me his book on nationalisation you know, Mrs. Waring. But I'm a poor one at reading. Now, where's yon lad? *(As Colin comes in)* He looks as if he eats nowt but chalk. *(Colin goes to her)* We're getting the goodbyes over with. Our Peter tells me you're clever and you've been to prison—

PETER: *(Laughing)* I didn't put it quite like that—

BELLA: *(Taking Colin's arm)* You're a pinched looking mongrel to me. Why, he's shaking! *(She puts her hand over his)* Hast never seen inside on a grave afore, lad? Is that it? *(Looks at him closely)*
(Pause)

COLIN: I don't know.

BELLA: But I know. Take me out into the street. I want to see you all off.
(She puts her hand on Colin's shoulder. They go to the door, followed by the others)

CUT TO CLOSE SHOT OF:

Bella and Tom at the miners' picnic.

Scene 2

Colin's bedsitter in Pimlico. Same day.

On one wall of the room is a great collage of Italian film stars, portraits of Russian writers and revolutionaries, jazzmen, Lord Russell, Castro, posters etc. The other walls are white. There are a few shabby armchairs, a big deal table covered with files, books, a jug and coffee cups, pages of notes. A Victorian sofa by the gas fire. A sink and draining board with piles of dishes, and a gas stove stand behind a folding screen. Above the sink is a mirror and a shelf with a mug containing toothbrushes. A typewriter stands on a coffee table, and a duplicating machine on a small table. On the double bed, the floor, the chairs and shelves are books.

Linda is sitting on the bed, her shoulders straight, her hands in her lap. Christine, a second girl, is working the duplicating machine. Two plainclothes men are in the room, one idly looking at the books on the plank shelves, the other standing near the fire lighting a cigarette.

MOORE: Well, if you don't know where he is, there's nothing to keep us here. *(Goes to duplicator and picks up one of the freshly rolled-off sheets)* Speaking for myself, I'm not unsympathetic to what your movement stands for—it's your methods. We can't ignore people deliberately breaking the law. Where would it lead to?

DART: *(Squatting by the bookshelves)* Quite an intellectual, your Colin. Lenin, Marx, Bakunin, Kropotkin—

LINDA: If you look on that bottom shelf you'll find one on Jesus Christ. There's Mein Kampf, as well.

MOORE: Now, now, Linda.

LINDA: Use my surname.
(Pause)

MOORE: You probably don't realise the sort of chap you're involved with—

CHRISTINE: Oh yes she does! He's a Nazi-Christian-Anarchist-Marxist—
(Moore stares at her quite neutrally, then places the sheet on the pile and turns to Linda)

MOORE: If we could talk to your young man, we might be able to save him—what shall I say? Some

	embarrassment. After all, I don't suppose he wants to be taken in on an incitement charge—
LINDA:	It's no use talking to me about it.
MOORE:	*(Sighing)* Is it worth it? Maybe fifteen months in jail? And for a cause that's on its last legs anyway—
CHRISTINE:	That's what you want everybody to think, isn't it?
MOORE:	*(Wearily)* I don't want anybody to think anything. I'm doing my job. That's all there is to it.
CHRISTINE:	That's more or less what Eichmann said. He was hanged for *not* breaking the law!
MOORE:	*(Waving irritably at Dart)* Oh come on. Come on. Let's get out of it. *(They go to the door)* We shall very likely be back. Tell him that, will you?
	(They go out. Christine stops the machine and looks at Linda with hostility)
CHRISTINE:	It's no use just shutting up like a clam. You've got to talk back to them.
LINDA:	Have I? I can't.
CHRISTINE:	It's not easy—but everybody's got to try.
LINDA:	*(Stands facing her with clenched fists)* If I'm dumb, I'm bloody dumb.
CHRISTINE:	There's no need to be offensive, Linda—
LINDA:	I get sick of you all. Coming here night and day—you don't seem to know the difference. *(Goes to Christine)* I'm trying to live in this room. To *live* in it. With Colin. I'm tired of making coffee for you. Listening to you. Clearing up after you—
CHRISTINE:	It isn't much, compared with what some of our people have gone through!
	(Linda turns away. She is sad, baffled and angry all at once)

LINDA: I try to make a bit of a life for him. He'll never make one for hisself.

CHRISTINE: It depends what you mean by a life. *(Dryly)* Perhaps we have different priorities—

LINDA: *(Sharply)* You want Colin yourself, don't you?

CHRISTINE: *(Smiling)* Do I?

LINDA: You can't understand what he sees in me! I'm not his sort. Not your sort. *(She looks round)* I sometimes wonder what I'm doing here.

             (Christine pulls on her coat, takes the pile of duplicated sheets and goes to the door)

CHRISTINE: I think Colin's quite capable of making a life for himself. Goodnight—

             (She goes to the door and leaves. Linda stands at the sink, looking at the pile of cups and saucers. Stacks them in the dish and turns the tap on)

Scene 3

Station Waiting Room. Evening of Same Day.

The station is on a branch line connecting with the main London trains at Doncaster.
It is a poky, dirty room—a leftover from the last century. There is a stove and high-backed wooden seats and a big table. The window looks out over the tracks and the town beyond. The room is poorly lit. It is in the process of being redecorated and there are ladders and pots of paint in one corner.

Colin sits at the table, scribbling on a piece of writing paper. Frieda is looking out of the window and Frances, sitting by the stove, is looking through a folder of photos of Warsaw. Peter comes in.

PETER: We've got eight minutes at Doncaster to get the London train.

(Nobody reacts. Peter sits near Frances. She passes one of the snaps to him)

FRANCES: That's Jurek's flat. I wonder what it'll be like, living in Warsaw . . .

PETER: Got the willies? *(Looking at the snap)*

FRANCES: I've got something. *(She passes him more pictures)* That's the same street in 1945. We don't really know what it is, to be European. Do we? That's the Old Town. It's been rebuilt just as it was before the war.

PETER: Will you be able to go on with your studies?

FRANCES: I hope so. Got to learn Polish first. That one's Jurek and the editor of the journal he writes for. *(She hesitates, then fumbles in her bag and takes out a battered and yellowing sheet of paper)* Have you ever seen one of these? It's a list of people under death sentence during the occupation—

(Peter takes the paper and looks at it)

FRANCES: Jurek's name is on it. He got away. They caught him again a long time afterwards and sent him to a camp.

PETER: And you carry it round with you—

FRANCES: I asked him to let me keep it. I never want to forget it. *(Puts it carefully back in her bag)*

PETER: *(Dryly)* For political reasons? Or personal ones?

FRANCES: Simply because he once lived under such conditions. They all did. And I never did . . . Anyway I'm marrying a man, not an ideology.

PETER: I hope so.

(Frieda goes to Colin. She puts her hand on the nape of his neck. Still writing, he reaches up and grasps her wrist, rubbing it with his thumb)

FRIEDA: What are you writing?

COLIN: A letter. Draft for one, anyway.

FRIEDA: You're getting shortsighted.

COLIN: It's the light.
(Frieda moves to his side, half leaning, half sitting on the table)

FRIEDA: You're very depressed, since the funeral.
(Colin stops writing and rests his hands flat, palms down on the table)

COLIN: Those miners at the graveside—we weren't just strangers to them. We were alien. My grandfather was a friend of Peter's dad. Both men worked with those miners. Boozed . . . sweated . . . got families. What am I then? Where's the human link between me and them? Who could be more isolated nowadays than a man who still believes passionately in the things they once passionately wanted? *(Gestures irritably)* I believe it's called refusing to come to terms with modern conditions.

FRIEDA: *(Going to the window)* That's what it's called. That's what it *is*. Well, Tom's dead. Your grandad lost his life in the pit. Soon they'll all be dead. *(Harshly)* And there'll be no grand old men of socialism left to bother anybody's conscience.
(Colin turns and stares at her, stares her out and she turns back to the window)

FRANCES: The train's late. I hate waiting. *(She gets up)* I'm going to ask somebody. *(Goes to door)*

PETER: Hang on. I'll come with you. *(Goes to door, sniffing)* Phew—that stove! *(He follows Frances out)*
(Colin is leaning back from the table, his face vacant, almost slack. He stares in front of him with an intensity that is almost inward, as if looking into some invisible mirror which shows him his own image. Frieda moves round the table. She must sense the growing strangeness in him, not madness in any straightforward clinical sense, but a stretching and torsion of the personality)

FRIEDA: I shouldn't have said what I did. I try to understand you. *(She half smiles)* Aren't I always breathlessly arriving at positions you've just abandoned?
            (Colin doesn't respond to the joke. He sits fiddling with his pen)

COLIN: Do I make sense, mother?

FRIEDA: What do you mean?

COLIN: You know—sense. Connected meanings.
            (Pause)

FRIEDA: I'm sorry, love—I'm not with you—
            (Colin spins the sheet of paper across the table. She picks it up and reads)

FRIEDA: You're resigning from the Committee of 100?

COLIN: *(Aridly)* Coming at a time when you've plunged into it right up to your neck—very ironic! *(Takes the letter, holding it between thumb and forefinger, waving it up and down)* But this is only part of it really. *(Puts his other thumb and forefinger about one quarter of an inch apart)* A fairly small part.

FRIEDA: *(Rather coldly)* Oh?
            (Colin gets up and goes to the window, standing with his back to her)

COLIN: I suspect I'm about to become the sort of person I've always described as a . . . private man.

FRIEDA: Whatever that is.
            (Colin flings up the window frame as a goods train goes down the line with a string of rattling trucks. The engine hoots and noisily blows off steam)

COLIN: Ah, you're a bit shocked! *(He turns to face her)* But all I mean is—*(He pulls down the window and turns back to her sharply)* You see, Linda wants—

FRIEDA: Well?

COLIN: All she wants is babies and peace. Not peace

movement peace. Peace in a room with a child on the floor. It would be strange, wouldn't it? To stop agitating. Turn your back on everything. Watch your wife grow pregnant, take a job, furnish a flat, keep your head well down . . . in a world you believe the *public* men will destroy.

FRIEDA: You'd only be doing what everyone else is doing.

COLIN: That's not really my point. Very few people believe in their sudden and violent extinction. I do.

(The door bangs open. A porter comes in carrying two large suitcases. He is followed by a prosperous looking man in his fifties)

PORTER: You'd better get yoursens used to the idea on a long wait. There's all hell let loose down the line.

(Peter and Frances come in)

FRIEDA: What's happened?

PORTER: A feller well nigh cut in two, that's what's happened. Drunk—or trying to take his own life, you know. They do . . . you'd be surprised how many does. Gettin' London train at Doncaster, are you? There's one forty minutes after, if you miss that.

FRIEDA: Is he . . . is he alive?

PORTER: Won't last the night.

MAN: But I must catch that London train—

PORTER: Sorry mister, you've had it. *(He goes to the door. Speaks in an unpleasantly confidential tone to Peter.)* Don't let on I told you owt. He weren't drunk. It's as clear as owt he meant to do it. *(He goes out)*

FADE ON CLOSE-UP OF *Colin*.

Scene 4

Colin's Bedsitter. Same Evening

Linda is sitting at the table, her face cupped in her hands. She is bored. She looks idly round the room then goes to the window, opens it and looks out, leaning over the window sill. A radio begins to play somewhere outside. Linda moves back and does a few steps of the twist. Closes the window and walks round the room looking for something to do.

She goes to the collage on the wall. Gives Castro the clenched fist salute. She puts on a Bessie Smith record and lies face down on the floor, sees something on the other side of the bed, picks it up and finds it is a pair of Colin's trousers. She stands up, folds them and puts them on a chair back. She goes to a tall mirror on the wall. Stands looking at her figure sideways; puts her hands under her stomach. Then she gets a cushion from the bed and puts it under her skirt; looks at herself in the mirror again. Marches round the room holding the cushion in position.

Scene 5

The Station Waiting Room. Same Evening.

Colin is wandering round the room aimlessly. The business man is reading his paper, occasionally glancing covertly at the others. Frieda sits at the table, upset and withdrawn.

COLIN: *(Going up to Frieda)* Well, mother—don't sit there looking all Greek and tragic because some unknown man had the guts to put his face to the track and blow —

PETER: *(Coming to Colin, interrupting him)* What's twisting you lately? You're becoming insufferable.

FRIEDA: He's becoming a private man. That's what he calls it.

COLIN: That's right. He's being born. *(Puts his face close to Peter's)* Do you know what a private man is? Oh yes you do.
              (Peter shrugs and half turns away, speaking with baffled affection)

PETER: Oh, you're a lunatic—*(He stands with his back to the stove)*

COLIN: Something in that! Yes man. Lunacy is absolute privacy. What were you thinking about when they swung your dad down into his pit to-day?
              (Peter swings round sharply, away from Colin)

COLIN: Another one gone? Did you think that? Were you sentimental? And will you go back to that empty flat in Camden Town and add a paragraph to your paper on the attrition of socialism since Keir Hardie?

FRIEDA: I've never known cruelty in you before.

COLIN: Like my sister says, I can grow up if given a chance!

FRIEDA: You two have been quarrelling?

FRANCES: Not really. But my God, when the colliery band chimed in this afternoon with Jesu Lover of My Soul! I ask you—

PETER: *(Quietly)* He was brought up a Methodist. *(He goes to Colin)* Maybe I should tell you what I was thinking in the cemetery. I was thinking how much I shall miss him. I loved him very much. And I thought . . . no doubt rather pompous of me . . . if only history had gone his way.

COLIN: *(He gets up, faces Peter and raises his arms in a kind of loving exasperation, banging his hands down on Peter's shoulders)* Peter! *(He steps back. His face slackens again, staring vacantly, mask-like. He shivers, then stands with his hands on the edge of the table. He speaks flatly)* I wish I were a mindless, shambling idiot. I wish I was that poor sod whoever he was, spattered over the rails in the darkness.

(Frieda goes up to him, touches his arm)

FRIEDA: Colin!

COLIN: *(Ignoring her, and speaking to Peter)* I've marched. I've been on sit-downs. I've been arrested a dozen times and in prison twice. I've worked in the Labour Party and the New Left till I couldn't stomach the one and the other disintegrated. I've hovered on the brink of joining the Communist Party—like a virgin waiting for the act of defloration—couldn't bring myself to do it. I've read and argued and talked . . . factories, dockyards . . . turned my home into a bloody office . . . refused to give my girl a child, which is what she wants more than me even. I've dropped my Ph.D. I live on handouts from the people who are 'sympathetic' to the movement . . . I'm poor, and tired, and rapidly turning nihilistic. You talk about history? All I want to do is to crawl away and laugh.

(There is complete silence. After a moment, Peter turns away. Frieda sits fiddling neurotically with her handbag clasp. Frances, who has been watching and listening to Colin with cold intensity, comes to him, looks him up and down. He is staring in front of him and she waves her hand in front of his eyes. She stands watching him, tapping her teeth with her fingernail)

FRANCES: Oh, brother! *(She walks out of the door, laughing. Slams it behind her)*

PETER: You reek of self-pity.

(Colin shrugs. Goes to Frieda)

COLIN: I'm not coming back to London with you.

FRIEDA: What are you going to do?

COLIN: I don't know. I'll come back in a day or two.

FRIEDA: And Linda? Waiting for you . . . I don't understand you.

PORTER: *(Putting his head round door)* Doncaster train coming in now—

FRIEDA: Have you any money?

COLIN: A bit. Enough.

PETER: *(Embarrassed and a little agitated)* You're ill . . . aren't you?

(Colin stares at him, expressionless. The train roars into the station. Peter looks at Frieda, at Colin, then goes to the door)

PETER: I think you'd better come to see me in college, when you get back. *(He hesitates, then goes out)*

FRIEDA: *(Opens her bag and takes a £5 note from her purse. She holds it out to Colin)* Please take it, Colin. Take it. I don't need it.

(Colin shakes his head. She pushes the note into his pocket)

FRIEDA: I've got to go. Darling—I've got to go. You make me afraid. You do.

COLIN: I'm afraid. The grave. The old man in his wooden box. The smell of gas and cinders blowing across there. I feel isolated. I feel as if my mind's going to burst . . . disgorge . . . and there'll be nothing.

(Frances appears in the doorway)

FRANCES: Mother—come on.

(She waits. Frieda looks at Colin)

FRIEDA: Come with us—

FRANCES: Come *on* mother—

(Colin shakes his head. He puts his arm round Frieda's shoulders and leads her to the door)

TELECINE:

A few days later. Colin is walking up the hill out of town, along the main road. In the valley behind him there is a sombre, winter panorama of factory chimneys, a power station, the thick white plume of a shunting engine. He looks back and thumbs a lorry, which pulls in. He opens the cab door and climbs in. As the lorry draws away he curls up on the seat beside the driver.

Scene 6

Transport Cafe. Same Day, evening.

Two or three drivers are sitting at a long trestle table. Colin comes in with Harry, the driver who gave him a lift. Harry goes straight to the counter. Colin stands looking around him. He is hunched up, vacant. He pulls out a chair at the long table and sits down, staring in front of him. Harry turns from the counter and calls to Colin.

HARRY:	What you want then, Colin? Bacon sandwich?
COLIN:	Anything, thanks.
HARRY:	(*To woman behind the counter*) Two bacon sandwiches and two teas—
	(*Harry leans with his back to the counter, resting on his elbows. He is a burly, good-natured man, with a protective instinct*)
HARRY:	Cheer up, mate—
	(*Colin is shy, embarrassed. He looks at the other men, who have turned to look at him. Jack, one of them, goes to the counter with his mug. Harry turns to greet him.*)
JACK:	What you got there, then?
HARRY:	Picked him up this side of Wakefield. He doesn't say much. Going to London—
JACK:	He looks barmy to me.

(The woman pushes two teas towards Harry. He takes them, waiting for a moment)

HARRY: What do you mean—barmy?

JACK: Looks like he was stillborn, to me—

HARRY: *(Moving closer to Jack)* What do you mean barmy?
         (Jack stares at him then quickly pushes his mug across the counter)

JACK: Another tea, please.
         (Harry hesitates, then carries the tea over to Colin. He sits down and they both drink)

HARRY: How long you been on the road, then?

COLIN: Nearly a week.

HARRY: Looking for a job?
         (Colin shakes his head, holding his cup in front of his face)

HARRY: I thought you were about done in when I picked you up. You all right?

COLIN: Yes. I'm all right.

WOMAN: *(Calling from counter)* Two bacon sandwiches—
         (Harry goes to the counter as Jack is leaving with his tea)

JACK: I've told you before. You're bloody soft, you are, Harry. *(He goes back to the table and sits down)*

HARRY: *(Bringing the sandwiches to the table)* I don't usually ask questions. *(He looks up at Colin)* I don't know what the hell I'm apologising for myself for. *(He notices Colin's CND badge and points to it)* I didn't notice that before—you one of that anti-bomb lot, then?
         (Pause. Colin unpins the badge and puts it in his pocket)

COLIN: In principle—but not in practice. Not any more.

HARRY: My girl goes to Aldermaston.

COLIN: Do you?

HARRY: Not me, mate. They'll either blow us up or
                they won't. Nothing we can do about it.
                Anybody thinks different, he don't know his
                arse from the back of his hand.

COLIN: That's more or less what I've come to think.
                (Smiles) I think!

HARRY: My trouble is, I don't bloody care.

COLIN: Don't you?
                (The other drivers are listening now)

HARRY: What do I live for—I ask you! Driving?
                Eating? My old woman? You can blow us up
                to-morrow, mate! *(Laughs)*
                *(Harry is pulling Colin's leg but there is an undertone
                of seriousness. Jack leans across the table and
                touches Colin's arm)*

JACK: They call him Charity Harry—

HARRY: Come off it—

JACK: He don't go for the birds at all. Won't have
                a bird in his cab. You a student? Very fond of
                students is Harry. Likes to buy them meals and
                play the big feller—

HARRY: *(Leaning across the table, very genial and tough)* It
                ain't like you to look for trouble, Jack.
                *(There is a moment of tension which slackens when
                Harry laughs and thumps the table with his
                clenched fist. Jack leans towards Colin)*

JACK: I don't go for your sort, that's all.

COLIN: What's my sort?
                *(Jack turns to the others. He is a clever mimic and
                has a reputation for it. Speaks in a 'posh' voice)*

JACK: If the workers of this country was to get up on
                their little hind legs and boycott nuclear
                weapons, there wouldn't be no nuclear war.
                *(The others find this extremely funny and laugh,
                drowning a protest by Harry)*

ALAN: *(Another driver)* The workers! What are you
                then? You ain't done a stroke in your life,
                mate. What's the betting?

HARRY: Aw, lay off him.
                (Colin stands up, looks round at them. A long pause.
                He picks up the half-eaten sandwich from his plate
                and walks out. In the passage from the café to the
                door there is a telephone. He stands in the passage;
                bites at the sandwich. After a moment he feels in his
                pocket for coins, puts money in the box and dials)

Scene 7

Frieda's Flat in London

CUT TO:

Frieda picking up telephone.

FRIEDA: Hello? Colin? Where are you? When will you
                be back then? What, darling? Didn't you
                write to Linda? *(Pause)* Yes, but—don't you
                care? Care about *her?*

Scene 8

Transport Café

CUT TO:

Colin on phone.

COLIN: Yes, I do care. For Linda. For you. *(Pause)*
                Yes, of course I'm all right. Coming home.
                Going to be a father. I want a child. She does.
                I do. Yes, man—we'll make one. What's that?
                No. Listen. The most incorrigible . . . now
                listen, mother. The most incorrigible force in
                the human personality is destruction. Yes.
                What? Isn't it? I am not drunk. What? Why

have a child then? I believe in spitting in the face of the executioner.
(Frieda's receiver is slammed down. Colin gently replaces his. He goes to the door of the cafe and looks in. Harry and the others are in heated argument. Colin turns and goes out, turning up the collar of his reefer jacket)

Scene 9

Colin's Bedsitter

Linda is in slip and skirt, ironing the collar of her blouse. She holds it up, looks at it and puts it on. Colin comes in carrying some letters. He throws them on the table then sits on the bed, watching her put away the ironing board.

COLIN: I've told you why I didn't come straight back after the funeral. I wanted a few days on my own.
(Linda stares at him a moment. She goes to him and pulls away a skirt that he is sitting on, and packs it in her suitcase, open on the floor)

LINDA: You don't think I'm leaving you just because you took yourself off for a week, do you?
(She goes to the mantelpiece and takes down a tin box. Puts a thin wad of pound notes from the box on to the table and counts them into two piles. Colin stretches out on the bed)

COLIN: Have you ever heard about the voles? *(He waits for some reaction but she takes no notice and goes on folding clothes)* The vole is a two-inch mouse. It lives respectably in communities. What with natural enemies and so on, voles have a stable population. But if some factors change and the population rises unchecked, the voles begin to die. Spontaneously.

	(He gets up and pours himself a cup of tea) I think that's very sad and clever of them. What do you make of it?
LINDA:	*(Quietly and harshly)* You come home in the middle of the night . . . never say where you've been or what you've been doing. You're unhappy. You make love to me. It never entered your head I might have the guts to walk out on this mess. Did it?
COLIN:	I noticed you waited until after I'd made love to you, to tell me you were going—
LINDA:	Do you think I could ever turn my back on you? Do you think I don't want you any more? It isn't that. It's your sort of life I'm leaving —not you. I want to live *now*. *(She puts half of the money back into the tin)* Why ever did you want me? I'm ignorant. I don't care about politics like you do. Who does? Well, I suppose there's always that little Christine that sits in the front row whenever you're speaking at a meeting and shows her knees!
COLIN:	They're knobbly.
LINDA:	What?
COLIN:	I said they're knobbly. Christine's knees.
LINDA:	She's a bitch.
COLIN:	She knows a thing or two about Plekhanov—
LINDA:	I don't care if she can recite the Bible backwards. She's still a bitch.
COLIN:	*(Going up to her)* Don't go, Linda— *(She moves away. Takes her toothbrush, comb and shampoo from the shelf behind the screen and packs them in suitcase)*
LINDA:	There's been too much against it with you and me. From the start. I must have been daft . . . Well, I know one thing—I can't live with a cross between the labour movement and the Committee of 100. It isn't a woman you

want—it's a Gestetner with a sex life! Do you remember the first time I came round here? You'd been setting up that hand press. You were that tired—and you looked like a starved cat . . . You went to sleep when I was telling you I'd never been with nobody else.

COLIN: It was just a pose. I was playing the frail intellectual. That's how I get women into my clutches—

LINDA: Well, you can try it on somebody else—
(Linda takes a pair of nylons down from a line. Colin puts on a record of a Mozart Horn Concerto. He sprawls on the bed, idly leafing through a book without looking at the pages)

COLIN: Have you given in your notice at the canteen?

LINDA: Yes. That's one place I shall be glad to see the last of. No more bloody students. *(Rolls up the stockings and puts them into a polythene bag which she tucks into the case)* My Aunty May says they're taking packers on at a warehouse near where she works.

COLIN: I've never been attracted to Brighouse, somehow. I don't know why it is—

LINDA: *(Suddenly turning on him angrily)* Go on—bloody sneer! It's just where I was born and grew up. That's all! You and your Frances—when she was doing her 'O' Level I had three years in a factory behind me. *(Turns away)* Eleven plus failures of the world unite!
(Colin goes to her and they stand looking at each other. Linda is the first to look away)

COLIN: I do love you . . . I want to keep you. *(He switches off the record player)* But I suppose you're right. Your instincts are right. It's impossible —I mean, what could I do? I've been submerged in all this for so long . . . I'm not used to having life take meaning from the things it really consists of. *(He goes to the window. Linda sits on the bed, her hands in her lap, her head down)* You are. You live. You live when you're feeding the cat, washing your face . . . shoving dinners across the counter in college. You live . . . on your back in bed, in your hands when you touch. *(Pulls the curtain back)* And millions out there are busy living, more or less . . . And I want to say, I *do* say: they are cheated, conned, manipulated. I exhort them to reclaim their society . . . strike, swarm on to air bases, into the streets. To choke the politicians and owners and bishops and generals . . . and all the rest—to choke them not with bare hands but human need and right for something different.

(Long pause. He stands in the middle of the room, staring) That's what I've exhorted them to do. But they don't. And they won't. And I give up. When *how* to live has ceased to be an issue, political differences lose meaning. So why can't I have you, at least? Why can't I simply lie doggo? *(Sits huddled on the edge of a chair)* People are doing it all the time.

(They sit in silence. Somewhere in the house, a radio blares. Linda gets up and starts to shut and strap her suitcase. She kneels on the floor)

COLIN: I shall miss you—

LINDA: If I really thought anything would change here, I'd stay.

COLIN: I meant what I said. I've jagged it all in.

LINDA: I expect you've made some kind of a decision. For me it would nearly be worse to watch what it'll do to you, than it was before.

COLIN: So you think it'll do something to me?

(He crouches down beside her. Puts his hand next to hers on the floor. She puts her hand over his)

COLIN: You're a great one for the self-preservation, aren't you?

(She forces his hand into hers and grips it tightly. They kneel side by side. Slowly he pulls her round to face him. He takes her other hand and kisses her. At first she tries to avoid him, then she kisses him. She becomes more intense and sharply breaks away)

LINDA: No! You'll not keep me with that! *(She stands up, looking down at him)* You wear me out, you do! If I don't go this time, I'll never get away from you.

COLIN: Why must you get away from me, then?

LINDA: I wish you could choose the people you love. I've stopped wanting to love you! There's so much about you I'm tired on. Tired of hearing about your bloody old grandad and that Tom Driffield . . . and what bloody marvellous socialists they all were before the war . . . *(Sharply)* when they hadn't two shillings to rub together. I *come* from that background, you know. You don't. Fellers like you might be talking Chinese for all it means to people nowadays. You do right to give up. It's about time. Any road, it's too late . . . for me. *(She puts the notes into her purse)* I expect I really need somebody a bit stupid. *(Shuts her purse)* I'm taking half the money. That all right? *(Puts on her outdoor coat)* That money you gave me for Frances's wedding present—I bought some Swedish knives and forks. In a box under the bed. *(Picks up the case and a straw basket)* And I brought some tinned stuff in this morning. And there's a loaf. I wrote my aunty's address in your desk diary—in case there's any letters.

COLIN: You can't carry that case. I'll come with you to the station—

LINDA: No, I don't want you to. I don't want you to

come out of this room with me.
(They stand looking at each other. Linda looks round for the cat)

LINDA: There's the cat.

COLIN: I'll ask my mother to take it.

LINDA: *(Quietly)* I like your mother. You'll tell her my side of this, won't you?

COLIN: Yes, I will.
(Linda fumbles with the door catch. She takes the case on to the landing and comes back into the doorway)

LINDA: Well, then. Are you going to kiss me?
(Colin hesitates then goes to her and kisses her quickly)

LINDA: I'll be off, then.
(Linda leaves)

COLIN: This is wrong. *(She looks back at him then goes on)* It's wrong. It's pointless. *(Shouts after her)* It's bloody idiotic.
(He slams the door shut, and leans his cheek against it, his hands splayed out either side of his face. He feels underneath the bed and brings out the box of Swedish cutlery. Restarts the Mozart record then unwraps the parcel, looks at the contents and throws it on the bed. Stands staring at the door)

Scene 10

Frieda's Flat in Earls Court. The same evening.

The flat is neat and comfortable. In the sitting room there is a sewing machine on the table with material and paper patterns spread about. Frieda sits at the table, studying the pattern. Frances is taking from its tissue paper wrappings an elegant glass jug, a wedding present. She is wearing a suit jacket which is partly sewn and partly pinned together. Peter

Driffield sits in a low armchair, typing with two fingers. The typewriter stands on a low coffee table littered with leaflets and letters with CND symbols on the printed heading. Jurek Stypulowsky, Frances's future husband, is crouched in a chair by the electric fire, reading. He is a thin, tired-looking man in his early forties—nervous, intellectual, rather sardonic.

FRIEDA: *(To Frances)* I haven't gone wrong after all. *(She puts the pattern down and takes pins from a pincushion)* Just a minute, darling, then you can take it off.
(Frances stands in front of her, still holding the jug)

FRIEDA: Now how can I do this when you—

FRANCES: *(Puts the jug on the table and stands passively for Frieda to put pins in the jacket)* Do you like it, Jurek? Jurek?

FRIEDA: Do stand still, Frances.

JUREK: Do I like what?

FRANCES: The jug. That glass thing on the table.

JUREK: It's very nice. *(He goes on reading)*

PETER: I hate concocting these leaflets.

FRIEDA: Oh, Peter—leave it. I shouldn't have pushed it on to you. Frances, *please* darling! There. You can take it off now. Do you think you'll like it?

FRANCES: It's a bit voguery-poguery.

FRIEDA: Warsaw fashions are supposed to be quite smart. I don't think you'll look too much of the bourgeois siren!

FRANCES: Fashions!

FRIEDA: Don't be such a puritan. *(She slips the jacket into the sewing machine and begins to sew. Frances drifts round the room looking bored. Bends over Peter's shoulder)*

FRANCES: You've spelt 'diffusion' wrong.
(Peter looks up at her, screws back the roller and

alters the word. Frances goes to Jurek and pulls his nose. He takes this with a kind of amiable bewilderment)

FRANCES: *(Looking at his book)* I wish I could read Russian.

PETER: You will, Oscar, you will.

FRANCES: *(Standing behind Jurek, she flings her arms round his neck and speaks with a heavy Slavonic accent)* I shall marry you and take you to my collective farm—

JUREK: God forbid!

FRANCES: Do you think our English policemen are wonderful?

JUREK: Oh, charming!

FRIEDA: Damn! *(She peers closely at her work)* You'll be getting married in something off the peg if I go on like this—

FRANCES: I don't care. *(Takes Jurek by the ears and rocks his head)* Do you care, Jurek? I don't.

JUREK: I've always been addicted to smart women.

FRANCES: Well, *I'm* not smart.

JUREK: So I've noticed.

FRIEDA: The thread's all twisted.

PETER: Why don't we all go out and get drunk?
(Frieda pushes her chair away from the table and rubs her face)

FRIEDA: I'm so *tired.*

JUREK: Why not let Frances do it? You and Peter and I will go out and get drunk—and Frances will stay and sew.

FRANCES: Very central European!

FRIEDA: I'm tempted to go round to Colin and Linda's room and wait for him there. *Surely* he's back by now. He was supposed to come last night. I wish he'd marry Linda. She's a very sweet girl. She's very insecure. Do ring them, Frances.

(Frances goes to the phone, dials and holds up the receiver for them to hear the ringing tone. There is no answer. Frances puts the phone down. She spreads material on the floor and begins to place pattern pieces on it. Frieda gets up wearily, lights a cigarette and stands beside Jurek at the fire. Jurek looks up at her)

FRIEDA: Are there young men like Colin in Poland?

JUREK: Of course. In Warsaw, Prague, Moscow. In New York, Rome, everywhere—one is relieved to observe the fact.

FRIEDA: *(Cynically)* Relieved! What do you do with yours?

JUREK: Well, of course, they express themselves differently. The official . . . the official attitude is . . . it varies. Sometimes a pat on the head. Sometimes a rap over the knuckles. They have as little obvious impact on our system as your rebellious young people have on yours.

FRIEDA: *(Edgily)* And what about your personal attitude—as distinct from the official attitude?

FRANCES: Stop *grilling* him, mother!

(Jurek puts his book down. He kneels beside Frances on the floor. Frieda sits on the arm of the chair)

JUREK: You find it almost preposterous, don't you? That Frances should marry me. *(He smoothes down a corner of the pattern)* Well, I agree. It is. *(He stands up and faces Frieda)* Would you like me to—what is it? Defect? And live in London? Join the little community of bitter *émigrés*? Dream of another Poland? An extremely *unlikely* Poland—

FRIEDA: I didn't mean to offend you.

(Jurek is sombre, abstracted. He wants to reach Frieda, but the sheer extent of the division between them is crushing)

JUREK: *(Speaking quietly, slowly)* In the concentration camp where I was held for—not long really—a year. There was a line some distance from the fence. If anyone crossed that line, they were shot. Many people chose to cross it. *(He goes to the coffee table where Peter is working and absently picks up a leaflet, holding it but not looking at it)* To those people, it was the only answer to what was intolerable. I've been a communist since I was a boy in my teens. My passion was to be a writer—and my . . . if you can call it . . . social passion was for revolution, justice—all the things most cruelly perverted or lost after nineteen forty-eight. Soon after the revolution, I found myself looking for the equivalent of that line in front of the fence in the camp. I wanted to take some irrevocable step. And be obliterated. *(He smiles)* It was easy . . . All one had to do was go round insisting on the truth about the . . . forgive me . . . murdering bastards who'd found their way to power. *(Goes to Frieda)* I've evaded this talk with you for a long time, Mrs. Waring. I suppose I have too much pride. I don't want to concede an account of myself. Well—they didn't kill me. They did some interesting and painful things to me, but I survived. I was released early one morning in Warsaw—the city was lovely that morning . . . My mother nursed me. I grew strong again. I saw and heard of a lot of changes. I began to write—and they published my work. I compelled myself to understand again that it is men who destroy ideas, and not the other way round. I still believe in the essential humanism of communism. I do. I can't say more. Except perhaps, the problem of our young men and

women is to try to understand men like me . . .
not to isolate themselves. Not to be defeated.
(Frieda goes to him, takes the leaflet from his hand)

FRIEDA: You know what this is, don't you?

JUREK: I haven't looked.

FRIEDA: Well, *look! (She holds it up in front of his face. It is a CND leaflet showing a baby born deformed in Hiroshima due to radiation)* Does the 'workers' bomb' somehow avoid causing such things? Is there some kind of metaphysical difference between your radiation and ours? What the hell am I bothering about in my middle age? What the hell am I doing, in your opinion? Contributing to the internal collapse of capitalism? Is that what makes my efforts correct and similar efforts on your side incorrect? Of course, there aren't any similar efforts on your side—are there?

JUREK: *(Raising his hands, partly in resignation, partly as if fending her off)* Really, I'm tired of this English pride in freedom of speech and freedom of action. You will be ruled exactly as your government wishes to rule you—whatever you say in protest and wherever you say it. Certainly you can push one lot out and another lot in every few years, but I can assure you from the other side of the Oder-Neisse they all look very much the same. And in between elections—your parliament is a charade, your democratic movements are irrelevant to what is actually done, your freedom is useless because it has no real function in your society! Now I *am* going out for a drink, and I apologise for not providing you with a more tractable future son-in-law.
(Jurek goes into the hall for his coat. Frances goes to Frieda)

FRANCES: You've mucked up your own life—now I suppose you want to spoil mine!

FRIEDA: Is that what I've done?

FRANCES: Well, when you still lived with my father, at least you had some kind of identity. And what are you now? Lonely. Nervy. *(Takes Frieda's hand)* Nicotine-stained fingers. *(Drops her hand. Rubs her palm on Frieda's shoulder)* Dandruff! You're pathetic, mother. And you know I love him so you *go* for him.
            (Frieda stands staring at Frances for a long moment, then she goes to Jurek at the door and touches his arm. She speaks with compelling dignity)

FRIEDA: I wonder if you can imagine what a relief it is to hear my daughter say she loves *anybody*. And I love you too, Jurek. I . . . care for what you are as a man, and that's all that really matters to me.

FRANCES: That's convenient, mother. Isn't it?
            (Jurek hesitates, looking at Frieda, his coat hung over his shoulder. Then he goes to her and kisses her quickly on both cheeks. Goes to the door)

JUREK: Come on, Frances.
            (Frances puts her clenched fists to her mouth, looking at her mother and Jurek. Then they both go out. Frieda stands over the material spread on the floor where Frances has been pinning on the pattern. She puts her hands to her face. Peter is watching her. He hesitates, then goes to her. She turns away and bends down to pick up the material and pattern)

PETER: She's a bitch—your Frances!

FRIEDA: You don't understand her—

PETER: God knows how you've managed to share a flat with her—

FRIEDA: When we're alone, we get on quite well. It's when we're with other people she feels she has to attack me. Leonard was the same. He

never wanted me to *be* anything in public.
(Pause)

PETER: Shall I make some coffee?

FRIEDA: Would you? *(She tidies up the material on the table)* I'm leaving this till to-morrow.

(Peter goes into the kitchen. Frieda closes up the machine. She notices her nicotine-stained fingers and rubs at them with the fingers of her other hand. Peter comes in and stands at the door watching her. She looks up and sees him)

FRIEDA: I'm getting tatty. She's right. *(Goes to mirror)* Middle-aged tat! When I was a girl, I thought I'd be terrific in my forties. *(Smiles at him)* All soignée and well-preserved.

PETER: Frieda, I've been offered a job in Oxford. I've been waiting all evening to tell you . . . I—

(The kettle whistle blows. Peter goes into the kitchen, turns the gas down and spoons instant coffee into two cups. Frieda comes to the door)

FRIEDA: You didn't even tell me you were applying—

PETER: *(Pouring the water into the cups)* What I said just now wasn't entirely honest—the job's semi-engineered. I detest Oxford, of course—but it's a marvellous place to petrify.

FRIEDA: Is it in sociology?

PETER: *(Setting the cups on a tray with milk and sugar)* Political philosophy—

FRIEDA: But . . .

PETER: Look—the academic details are very boring— *(Going to the door with the tray. Frieda pulls a small table up to the fire. Peter sits down opposite her)*

FRIEDA: Well, if you detest Oxford! Now *I'm* being dishonest . . . I do know why. I don't want you to go away.

PETER: Which is both selfish and perverse.

FRIEDA: Yes.

PETER: You won't marry me. You won't live with me.

You won't even sleep with me. We have a
chronically aborted loving relationship . . .
which wears me out. I prescribe Oxford for
me . . . isolation for you when Frances goes to
Poland . . . and we'll see whose nerve gives
first. More trivially—I can't stand the flat
since my father died. I'm sick and tired of
London—and I haven't the energy for a more
dramatic change than this one.

FRIEDA: *(She puts her hands out to him across the table. He
            takes them)* Something prevents me having you.
            Something . . . I feel *(She laughs nervously)*
            doomed. I care for you. I do want to sleep
            with you. Sometimes the last twenty years are
            just—blotted out. For a while. I put my coat
            on. I get on the bus to come to you. And I
            always come back without seeing you. What
            stops me is a kind of pitiless clarity. I seem
            obscene to myself. And I feel as if the children
            are watching me. *(She releases his hands and leans
            back, closing her eyes)* I feel . . . *haunted* by Colin
            —sometimes.

PETER: Only Colin?

FRIEDA: Frances wouldn't care.

PETER: Why should Colin care?

FRIEDA: *(Smiles)* Colin's always put the basilisk eye on
            me! When he was a child, I'd be doing house-
            work, anything . . . and I'd look up and find
            him standing near me. Watching. Serious.
            Curious. His eyes like black stones. *(She
            shudders slightly)*

PETER: Are you cold?

FRIEDA: Cold? No. I—a goose walked over my grave.

PETER: Lucky Colin. My mother was just a huge
            warm bundle that smelled of carbolic and new
            bread. *(He grins)* I didn't experience these
            complex middle-class responses. *(Frieda laughs.*

There is a pause. Peter sighs) You have an amazing talent for depressing me! I must be a masochist. I hang round you too much. I have my chances, you know. If you aren't careful I shall marry an adoring eighteen-year-old student with social mobility problems.

FRIEDA: I wish you would. No, I don't. I wonder if I do?

PETER: Anything rather than come between mother and son!

FRIEDA: Oh, Peter!

PETER: One of the causes of my failure to get what I want from people has always been my paralyzing ability to understand why they wouldn't give it to me. I should be more predatory. You behave more like Colin's daughter than his mother half the time. You know you can have me—yet there's still some break with him that you haven't made. You prefer the fantasy that he's all you have. If he needs anything, I should say it's psychiatric help—he can do without your complications.

FRIEDA: *(Tense, almost haughty)* Colin is *not* ill. What are you trying to say? *(She gets up for her cigarettes. Lights one, her hands restless and jerky)*

PETER: Don't misunderstand me. Well, for God's sake—you told me the way he talked to you on the phone yesterday! Aren't *you* uneasy? Oh, *look*, Frieda—I'm not trying to say he's going out of his mind.

FRIEDA: You're getting damn close to it!

PETER: It took me half a lifetime to go through the stages he's gone through. To be a shagged-out revolutionary in your early forties is regrettable—but human, I suppose. At twenty-five or whatever Colin is it's preposterous. Not because there's hope for socialism, but because the political imagination should be more sturdy. And because to opt out is to threaten the . . . the moral coherence of your life. Frieda, I'm sorry but I don't want to talk about Colin now. *(Goes to her, putting his hands on her arms)* I feel selfish . . . demanding. *(Sharply)* If you can tolerate the future you're letting yourself in for, I'm damned if I can!

FRIEDA: I'd sooner cut my throat than go to Oxford, I can tell you that much.

PETER: So would I.

(They laugh at each other and sit down again)

FRIEDA: When I was eighteen, I used to dream of having a flat in London. There was a desk with a typewriter, the walls were lined with books. People drifted in and out, discussing Sartre. *(Shrugs, looks round the room)* Well, I've finally got the flat, anyway. I can't believe I've put Leonard and the rest of that life behind me. Oh, we're hopeless, Peter. I mean—it would be absurd, you and me. I don't think in terms of a future. I live in each day as if the following morning I shall wake up beside Leonard. I think I love you—but I don't *need* you, Peter. I think I want for the first time in my life to exist in my own right. To *be* someone on my . . . on my own.

PETER: This is an evasion.

FRIEDA: It isn't. It's honesty. I want—*(The doorbell rings. She gets up quickly)* If that's Colin, Peter be gentle with him. Please.

(She goes to the front door. Colin is waiting outside. It is raining and he is soaked. He has the cat under his reefer. Frieda kisses him. They move apart and they stand looking at each other for a moment)

FRIEDA: I was worried about you. Where's Linda? I thought she'd come round with you.

COLIN: *(Pointing at his wet coat)* Can I just take this off
            first? *(Follows her into the sitting room)*

FRIEDA: Peter's here. *(To Peter)* He's soaked through.
            Take your coat off, darling. Would you like a
            whisky?

COLIN: *(Stands motionless)* Where's Frances?

FRIEDA: Gone to the corner pub with Jurek. I'll get you
            a towel. *Do* get that coat off—
            *(Frieda goes to get him the towel. Colin and Peter
            look at each other. Colin seems tired and withdrawn.
            There is an embarrassment between them)*

PETER: What have you been doing with yourself, then
            —this last week?

COLIN: *(Still motionless, holding the bulge of the cat under
            his coat)* Nothing.
            *(Frieda comes back with the towel. Colin unbuttons
            his jacket and holds out the cat)*

COLIN: Will you look after this? It's Linda's. *(He puts
            the cat on the floor and takes off his jacket. Rubs his
            hair with the towel)*

FRIEDA: But why should she—

COLIN: She's left me.
            *(Frieda hesitates, opens her mouth to speak but
            changes her mind. Colin kneels down in front of the
            fire, drying himself)*

COLIN: Do you like cats? I can't remember.

FRIEDA: Why has she left you?

COLIN: Can I have that whisky?

PETER: *(Getting up and going to sideboard)* I'll get it.

FRIEDA: She loves you—doesn't she? It wasn't a . . .
            temporary thing?

COLIN: Oh yes. She loves me. And she's gone back to
            Brighouse. The police searched our place
            while I was away. They're getting out a
            warrant for my arrest. I'm not sure which
            item's uppermost in my mind, at the moment.
            Can you put me up for the night?

FRIEDA: Frances can come in with me. You can have
             her room. But I don't see how the police can—
COLIN: I held a briefing meeting for the last sit-down.
             Which makes me guilty of incitement.
FRIEDA: Do the police know you've resigned from the
             Committee?
COLIN: I don't know what the police know. I don't
             really care.
FRIEDA: You'd better have a lawyer—
COLIN: Don't talk about lawyers, mother. These are
             political trials masquerading as issues of law.
             *(Frieda is bewildered and inadequate. In silence she
             goes back to the kitchen, makes Colin a cup of coffee
             and brings it to him)*
FRIEDA: What are you going to do, then? What should
             he do, Peter?
COLIN: There's nothing *to* do, mother!

CUT TO:

*Hall. Frances and Jurek are coming in. They are
very happy and kiss each other before they begin to
take their coats off. Frances listens at the sitting room
door.*

FRANCES: *(Whispering)* Colin's here—
             *(She goes to her bedroom door and beckons Jurek
             after her. She kneels to light the fire whilst Jurek
             takes his coat off. The room is rather austere. A
             narrow bed, easy chairs, desk and books. There is a
             photo of Colin on the desk. A chart of wild bird
             drawings is stuck on the wall. Frances sits by the fire)*
JUREK: Don't you want to see your brother?
FRANCES: We'll go in in a minute.
JUREK: I shall have to go.
FRANCES: This time next week we shall be married. We'll
             be on the train to Warsaw.

JUREK: And your mother will be alone.

FRANCES: I wish to goodness she'd marry Peter Driffield and stop vacillating. Or shack up with him even—

JUREK: Shack up?

FRANCES: Live with him. *(Turns to fire)* No other society in the world could have produced my mother. Liberally educated, provincially sub-cultured and morally confused. She has the Lady Almoner approach to life—

JUREK: You are very hard on her—

(Frances slips off her chair, on to her knees in front of him. Beats his knees with her fists)

FRANCES: You're stuffy, you are. A stuffy commy!

JUREK: *(Teasing)* When we get to Warsaw, I shall tell everybody—I shall say: Frances, you know, is a social democrat.

FRANCES: Just you dare—

JUREK: Or suppose I say: this is my wife, poor dear, a communist without a party! *(Frances laughs)* And they will raise their eyebrows and look very Polish and sophisticated, and tell you: but who would join the *English* communist party?

(Frances stands up laughing. Holds her arms out)

FRANCES: Teach me the polka—

JUREK: That's very old hat, nowadays—

FRANCES: How do you say get knotted in Polish?

JUREK: I don't think we have anything quite—

FRANCES: *(Interrupting)* Do you love me? *(Puts her arms round him)* Shall we be all right? Lots of kids?

JUREK: *(Stands up. Speaks deadpan)* Comrades—we must all have many babies. The bureaucracy is expanding every day!

(They laugh and put their arms round each other. As they stand swaying together, Colin comes in in his shirtsleeves with a towel over his shoulder. They break apart)

COLIN: I'm sorry. I didn't know you were back. *(Puts his hand out to Jurek)* Hello Jurek—

FRANCES: What did you want in here?
            (Colin stands awkwardly for a moment)

COLIN: I'm staying the night. My mother thought you might let me have your room—

JUREK: I'm just going away.

FRANCES: But—why? Is there something wrong?
            (Jurek goes to her. Kisses her cheek)

JUREK: Look, I'm going. I'll ring you to-morrow. *(Goes to door. His eyes and Colin's meet)* See you Colin—
            (Jurek goes out. Frances goes into the hall, but the outer door is already closing behind him. She comes back into her room. Colin is sitting on the bed. She goes to him sympathetically)

FRANCES: What's the matter.

COLIN: I think I'm going to be arrested on an incitement charge. I've half decided to go to France. Somewhere. Anywhere.
            (Frances turns away)

FRANCES: *(Turning back)* Is Peter still here?

COLIN: Yes.

FRANCES: Have you discussed it with him? And mother?

COLIN: There's not much to discuss.

FRANCES: And what's Linda got to say about it?

COLIN: Linda's gone. Gone back north. *(Gets up. Crouches by fire)* I don't seem to have the knack of convincing her that I need her.
            (Colin now sits by the fire. Frances sits on the bed)

FRANCES: I wonder why I ever thought you were strong—

COLIN: I suppose it was a useful thought. Till you met Jurek. *(His face becomes set and stony)* What is it to be strong? *(Pause)* I know exactly what I am, you know. *(Goes to desk. Sees his photo. Runs his finger absently over the image of himself)* There are people in every generation who act out some of its hopes and needs. The subjective reasons for their actions hardly matter. In some way they define a generation to itself. *(Pause)* In times of violent or radical change such people, either as individuals or a group, can be decisive. *(Laughs)* In times of stagnation what are they? Articulate phantoms? The self-elected conscience of the nation? *(Pause)* They're so much weaker than the forces they oppose.

FRANCES: Aren't you inflating your own importance?

COLIN: No. I'm not referring to myself precisely. I'm judging the social meaning of what people like me have been doing.

FRANCES: As if that's the end of it!

COLIN: Well isn't it? When the very word 'protest' makes a nation yawn? *(Pause)* The middle classes are bored by it, the working class is suspicious of it—and the writers have grown fat on it! Bloody hell, when a society—*(He stops suddenly. His violence subsides. He goes to Frances and takes her face between his hands)* Stop me. Shut me up. You've come through it all with me. *(Turns away)* Do you understand though Frances? Do you?

FRANCES: All too well!

COLIN: That sounds very accusatory—

FRANCES: Are you surprised? Did you expect me to soothe you? You'll get an overdose of that from my mother. *(Quite gently)* I can't help making comparisons, that's all. Jurek has to fight too, you know. For truth, and honesty. For what communism *should* mean. He's been doing it all his life. *(Pause)* He's tired. But he goes on. *(Pause)* What stops you, except your own preoccupation with your sense of defeat? You can't afford it. It's a luxury.

(They stand staring at each other. Colin shrugs.
Frances pulls the cover back on her bed and takes her
pyjamas from under the pillow)

FRANCES: I want to change into my pyjamas—
(Colin goes out, closing the door behind him, and into
the living room. Frieda is sitting alone by the fire)

COLIN: Peter gone?

FRIEDA: Yes.

COLIN: *(Wanders round the room)* Isn't it about time you
two got married?

FRIEDA: I don't think so. *(Pause)* He's left you the
phone number of a lawyer he knows.

COLIN: He must have gone off in a bloody hurry—

FRIEDA: You and he don't seem to get on as well as you
used to. *(Pause)* I believe he thought you were
irritated to find him here.

COLIN: I wasn't. *(Goes up to her. Laughs gently)* I like
him to come here. It discourages my tendency
to feel responsible for you.

FRIEDA: That's almost insulting Colin!

COLIN: Is it? *(Flops into a chair)* If I'd been different, I
think you would have too.

FRIEDA: You mean I'd never have grown angry with
my life? Never left your father? Perhaps you
flatter yourself.

COLIN: *(Sharply)* Oh, don't put it on that silly level
mother!

FRIEDA: *(Quietly)* And don't you be so arrogant.

COLIN: *(Quietly)* No, it's resentment. I resent you for
having made your gesture too late. *(Looks round*
the room) For having come to this in . . . in
middle life, with no resources. *(Pause)* What
was admirable was the act of leaving him. But
what remains? How do you live now?
(Frieda stands, facing him)

FRIEDA: You make a very unnerving inquisitor. Oh
yes, you have ruthless insights don't you?

	(Turns away) I'd almost prefer Frances's crude dislike to your subtleties—
COLIN:	*(Half smiling)* Frances is only crude because she *fears* what is complex. She needs to be simple. To believe this, like that, hate something else. She daren't hesitate. It would be a strain for her to love you, for example.
FRIEDA:	*(Turning to him almost pathetically)* Why?
	(Colin laughs harshly. Leans back in his chair laughing, with his eyes closed)
COLIN:	Ah, mother! She dislikes what you stand for politically so much, that loving you would be a kind of disloyalty to herself.
FRIEDA:	*(As if to herself)* I . . . I don't know what I *do* stand for in that way.
COLIN:	*(Stands, shouting)* Exactly!
	(Frances enters unseen by them)
COLIN:	Like all good communists she knows where she is with a conservative, but liberals bring her out in spots—
FRANCES:	*(Goes to Colin)* That was a remark you'd have despised in anybody else's mouth—
	(Frieda sits down, upset and confused at being apparently under attack from Colin. Frances, who is now in pyjamas and dressing gown, goes to her mother, hesitates, touches Frieda's arm)
FRANCES:	What's all this? What's going on?
	(A long pause. Frieda would really like to move away from the clash, yet she is too honest to evade Frances)
FRIEDA:	How do I live, Frances? *(Pause)* Can you tell him how I live?
FRANCES:	*(Suddenly tired, moving away)* It's going to be a relief to get away from both of you.
	(Pause. Colin sits down. Frieda goes to the mantelpiece for cigarettes. Lights one. Stands in front of the fire)

FRIEDA: When I get tired of the office at the hospital, I go round the wards. Amongst the children. *(Pause)* I like the very young ones. *(Pause)* Children used to embarrass me a bit. Even you two when you were small. *(Pause)* They don't now. *(Pause)* I feel quite detached from them. I'm not impressed when they smile, or put off when they are angry. *(Pause)* What I feel is a kind of gratitude for their exuberance, their craziness. *(Pause)* Children speak and behave improbably. And one responds. *(Pause)* I'm tired of knowing what adults *are*.
(She is slightly embarrassed at having exposed herself. Turns away, tapping her ash into an ashtray on the mantelpiece)
(Turning back) What can I do for you Colin? How can I help you? *(Pause)*

COLIN: Nothing. I'll be away to-morrow. I'm damned if I'll hang round waiting to be arrested.

FRANCES: Once the police know you've finished with the committee, they'll drop the whole thing. After all, by running out you've done their job for them. Haven't you?

COLIN: You can choose to see it that way.

FRANCES: *(Going to him)* I do. *(Pause)* To me your explanations are a waste of breath. Do you remember your final row with my father about the sit-downs? You said: I have to judge you. It doesn't help to understand you. You said anyone must be judged who allows to be done what should not be done. *(Pause)* There's no escape from that, Colin. *(Pause)* I'm going to bed.
(Frances goes out. Frieda goes to Colin. Puts her hand on his cheek)

FRIEDA: What will you do with yourself? *(Pause. Turns away)* Peter thinks you could have a brilliant

COLIN: academic career. If you wanted. *(Sits down)*
                      You never know. I might even come round to
                      that. *(Pause)* He's managed to cocoon himself
                      nicely in that way. Shoves out a venomous
                      article every now and then, attacking the right
                      wing of the Labour Party. Life goes on. There
                      are even people saying: by God, Driffield's got
                      that Frognal bunch by the scrotum!

FRIEDA: *(Stung, but controlling herself)* If you turn me
                      away with your bitterness, you'll have no one
                      left. *(Pause)* I can't believe you really tried to
                      keep Linda. *(Pause)* What have you become?

COLIN: I told you in Yorkshire. A private man.
                      (Pause)

FRIEDA: I thought I understood what you meant. But
                      you're much too young to be feeling what you
                      seem to feel. *(Pause)* Look, go to France or
                      wherever you like till we know what the police
                      intend. If they do drop the charge, you can
                      come back here. Live here. *(Pause)* Frances
                      will be in Poland—

COLIN: *(Smiling)* You accept my evasion of the law
                      very easily—

FRIEDA: I don't accept *this* use of the law against you,
                      any more than you do. *(Pause)*

COLIN: You're going to miss Frances. *(Pause)* Miss
                      that rancid integrity around the place!

FRIEDA: It's fatal to be educated by your own children.
                      You take from them what's needed to begin
                      life, when what you really need is the means
                      to face middle age with dignity and purpose.
                      You discipline yourself to cling to nothing,
                      only to find yourself still human and greedy
                      for warmth. *(She laughs)* The other women at
                      the hospital terrify me. They seem so well
                      adjusted. And then I remind myself that
                      they're adjusted because they seem to accept

all the things I reject now. They're no less human than I am, but it's as if they've been morally put to sleep by the drone of lies and false attitudes all round them. *(Goes to Colin)* I'm sorry darling. This doesn't help you very much, does it. *(She puts her hand out. Colin takes it. Puts his cheek to hers. Moves quickly away to the fireplace)*

COLIN: I'm grateful . . . that you are what you are. I'd rather have you suffer than not notice that there's cause for pain, and anger, and opposition. It helps me to feel that we really are separate. Related more as people. Not too compromised by the fact that I was once *(smiling)* a bundle of cells nesting in your belly!

FRIEDA: *(Laughing)* I refuse to be shocked—

COLIN: Well. I've got the single fare to Paris. And five quid. Don't offer me more money because I'd rather go like this. I want to be exposed. To whatever else there is besides obsessions about politics and nuclear genocide. Do you know I haven't been to the pictures for months? Haven't read a novel, walked in the park, indulged in a friendship. *(Pause)* Linda was the only route I had to a more balanced existence, and I could hardly forgive her for the absolute normality of her interests. I wish it . . . I wish it had worked out with us.

FRIEDA: Couldn't you, when you come back, go to see her?

COLIN: I could. I will. I'll do everything I can do, when I come back mother—

FRIEDA: You won't be here to see Frances and Jurek married—

COLIN: I don't think she'll shed any tears. *(Pause)* I'm glad it's Jurek.
(Pause)

FRIEDA: I must go to bed, love. I'm going in to the hospital early to-morrow. *(Getting up)* I'll come in and see you before I leave in the morning—

COLIN: I'm off to bed anyway. I'm tired out.

(They look at each other. He goes to her. They kiss)

COLIN: Goodnight—

FRIEDA: Goodnight, love—

(Colin goes out. Frieda stands quite still for a moment. She crosses the room, picks up the cover for the pattern of Frances's costume. Puts it down. Catches a glimpse of herself in the mirror. Goes to the mirror. Looks at herself. Looks at her shoulders. Brushes at them with her hand)

Scene 11

Jurek's Flat in Warsaw. A week later.

Present are: Jurek and his mother, his sister Krystyna and Frances. Open on Jurek's mother: A sturdy old woman of peasant origin—her face worn and wrinkled. A strong woman who has suffered a great deal but is now calm and gentle. Devoted to Jurek and Krystyna.

Krystyna is in her late thirties. Her personality was destroyed by her experiences in a concentration camp. She is in a condition of almost total withdrawal. Never speaks, automatic movements, no expression on her face. She has to be dressed and fed like a young child. She sits with her hands in her lap, staring in front of her. Frances and Jurek have just arrived. They are in their outdoor clothes, with their bags and suitcases around them on the floor. Frances stands apart whilst Jurek embraces his mother. The old woman is very moved to have her son back. Tearful but happy.

*Jurek speaks to her in Polish. As they separate she
turns to Frances and smiles. Jurek gently propels her
towards Frances)*

JUREK: This is my mother—
                *(Introduces them in Polish. His mother smiles—
                speaks in Polish)*

JUREK: She says she is sorry she can't greet you in
                English—
                *(Frances and her mother-in-law face each other. They
                smile. Frances puts her arms out and they embrace.
                The mother stands back, puts her hands on Frances's
                cheeks, speaks to Jurek)*

FRANCES: What does she say?
                (Pause)

JUREK: She says you are pretty, and—*(Laughs)* she
                hopes there will be grandchildren before she
                dies.
                *(He puts his hand on his mother's shoulder. Laughs.
                She too laughs. Then she looks at Krystyna, and
                speaks to Jurek in Polish)*

JUREK: *(To Frances)* She doesn't want you to be upset
                by Krystyna—*(He goes to his sister. Touches her
                cheek. There is no reaction. Turns to Frances)* This
                is my sister. I should say, what is left of her.
                (Frances slowly approaches Krystyna) My mother
                has to feed her, dress her. *(Pause)* I told you.
                (Pause) She was nineteen when she was brought
                home from Ravensbruck. She has never
                spoken, never recognised anyone.
                *(Frances puts her hands on Krystyna's shoulders.
                Looks into her face. Krystyna shows no reaction.
                Slowly, Frances puts her cheek to Krystyna's)*

JUREK: She was arrested in the street early one
                morning. Quite at random—

FRANCES: *(Softly)* Krystyna—

JUREK: *(Bitterly)* My mother prays for her. *(Pause)*

Who would want to stop an old woman
praying? *(Pause)* They are confronted by the
actions of men—and plead for the mercy of
God!
*(Frances lets her hands fall slowly down Krystyna's
shoulders, down her upper arms. She is wearing a
short sleeved blouse. The camera follows Frances's
hands until we see a concentration camp number
stamped on Krystyna's forearm)*

Scene 12

Viewing Theatre in a Warsaw Film Studio. Two weeks later.

*On the screen a film is being shown. Shots of
German planes dive bombing. Quick following shots
of the destruction of the city. Then the 1944 uprising.
A silent line of German troops confronting a crowd of
silent Poles in a ruined street.*

*Film of contemporary Warsaw. The old town is re-
built exactly as it was before the war. The new town
with broad, tree-lined avenues and modern buildings.
A compressed visual portrait of the city as it is now.
The frame recedes. The film comes to an end. We see
that we are in a small projection theatre. Present:
Jurek and Frances. The lights fade up.*

*Slowly Jurek turns to Frances. She is very much
affected by what she has seen. He puts his arm along
the back of her chair, loosely takes the hair at the nape
of her neck in his hand.*

JUREK: Well. You asked to see those films. *(Pause)*
Now you have. *(Pause)* We must thank Maciek
before we leave. He's going on location in the
Tatras to-morrow. *(Smiles)* To make his first
comedy—

FRANCES: Comedy!
(She sits with her head bowed, puts her hands to her face. She is unable to express in words what the films meant to her)

JUREK: *(Gently)* We experienced the war. Then afterwards, we lived it again. In films, books. It was a national obsession. *(Pause)* It was necessary. *(Pause. His manner lightens)* Now I think it is time for some comedies—
(Maciek comes in. He is a slight, wry, gnomelike man. Jurek goes between the seats to greet him, followed by Frances. Jurek and Maciek exchange a few words in Polish. Frances comes up to them)

JUREK: *(To Maciek)* You met my wife, didn't you? At the writers' club?

MACIEK: *(Shakes Frances's hand, smiling)* Yes—

FRANCES: Thank you for showing me the films—

MACIEK: Please. I was glad to.

FRANCES: Jurek says you're going to start shooting a comedy to-morrow—

MACIEK: It is all about a pig. And why not?
(He looks innocently at Frances, who starts laughing. Maciek laughs. He takes Frances and Jurek by the arm, leading them to the door. He is very gay and affectionate)

MACIEK: I once knew a lady animal doctor who—

JUREK: A vet—

MACIEK: Yes a vet, who came back from a mountain village in such a state of mind collapse. Those poor horses and cows, she said, you'd better send them a priest for the peasants think a vet is the messenger of the devil!
(Maciek hugs them to him as they laugh, and they go out)

Scene 13

Jurek's Flat. Morning, Some weeks later.

Jurek is in his study typing. Krystyna is sitting by the table in the living room. Frances has made coffee —the tray is on the table—and she is holding a cup to Krystyna's lips, one arm round her shoulder. Jurek gets up from his work. Catches sight of Frances through the slightly open door. Stands watching her and Krystyna. Krystyna drinks once or twice then closes her lips and refuses the rest. There is a trickle of coffee down her chin. With a handkerchief, Frances dabs away the coffee. Stands back. Looks at Krystyna.

Frances takes an opened airmail letter from a shelf, picks up the tray and goes into Jurek's room. He is now sitting by his desk. Frances puts the coffee near him, holds up the letter.

FRANCES: A letter from my mother this morning.

JUREK: How is she?

FRANCES: I'll leave it here for you to read. She's all right. *(Pause)* But she hasn't heard from Colin for over six weeks.

JUREK: *(Abstracted, sipping his coffee)* I thought he was in West Berlin—

FRANCES: He was. *(Pause)* He has a friend there. A German sculptor.

JUREK: I would hate to be an intelligent young Englishman with left-wing ideals, I must say!

FRANCES: Oh would you! *(Pause)*

JUREK: One would be rather in the position of a man whose dearest relative had died. The funeral is over, and he comes back to find the corpse still in his house.

(Frances pulls a face. Jurek smiles)

JUREK: You might even say it's the English burden, to
             live with the embalmed remains of their efforts
             to become human—

FRANCES: Oh? And what's the Polish burden?
             (Pause)

JUREK: The effort to remain Polish.
             (Pause)

FRANCES: You're different since we came to Warsaw.
             (Pause) Did you know you're different towards
             me? *(Pause)*

JUREK: Yes.
             (Pause)

FRANCES: What is it?

JUREK: *(Turning away)* I've always thought it would be
             better if we let Krystyna go somewhere to be
             looked after. *(Pause)* My mother will not have
             it. *(Pause)* I used to watch her caring for
             Krystyna and think: what are you nursing?
             (Pause) In my mother's heart, the meaning of
             the world is in God. And authority is in Rome.
             (Pause) We try to create a new society with
             the incense reeking in our nostrils. *(Pause)* I
             can't see you hold a cup to my sister's mouth
             without wondering what you make of us. Of
             me. I'm afraid of making you unhappy.

FRANCES: *(Softly)* I don't understand you. *(Pause)* Are
             you telling me you feel callous about Krystyna?
             Jealous? *(Pause)* What?

JUREK: *(Turning back to her, half smiling)* Nothing so
             uncomplicated!

FRANCES: In any case, what have your feelings about
             your mother and sister to do with your feelings
             about me? *(Pause)*

JUREK: I bring you here, to an old relic of a woman.
             And an automaton. You are gentle with
             Krystyna. Deferential to my mother. *(Pause)*

The love you withheld from your family you give to us. Everything goes well with you and me. *(Pause)* Yet I feel involved in some strange kind of deceit.

FRANCES: *(Going to window, looking out)* I know what you mean.

JUREK: Do you?

FRANCES: You try to avoid coming to the point. You're afraid that I mightn't want to stay in Warsaw. *(Pause)* Yet why should you be? Is your attitude to what's being done in Poland ambiguous after all?

(Pause)

JUREK: No. *(Pause)*

FRANCES: I'm happier now than I've ever been. *(Pause)* If I'd never met you . . . stayed in London . . . I'd have become sour. Waspish. *(Pause)* To despise everything around you is corrupting. *(Pause)* You've heard a lot from Colin and me about our grandfather. He lived to see what he understood by socialism abandoned. He detested it, but he didn't become hollowed out. He was angry but he had some idea what was going on. *(Pause)* We grew up in relative luxury. And all we saw was the disintegration in full swing. *(Pause)* There was a stink emanating from everything, and it's got worse. There's no wonder we're a suspicious generation. We trust nobody and we're fooled by nobody. All the claptrap about freedom and democracy and defending values, we know it isn't true. It's just so much political bad breath. England's still the same old family business with enough sense of self-preservation to bring in the very people who ought to have destroyed it. *(Pause)* I'm glad to be out of it.

JUREK: *(Goes to her, looks at her)* There are times when
             you sound disturbingly like your brother—
FRANCES: Do I? Well I'm not like him.
JUREK: And Krystyna was a little like you—
             (Pause)
FRANCES: Is there . . . is there anything you should have
             told me that you haven't? I don't like this
             talking round and round—
JUREK: You think I am . . . what's the precise word?
             Oblique!
FRANCES: That's the precise word!
JUREK: *(Neutrally)* I think you are naïve and im-
             mature. A fairly severe case of political roman-
             ticism. *(Frances opens her mouth to speak but he
             holds up his hand)* To your mother, to her friend
             Peter and most people, you were harsh. Some-
             times violent. *(Pause)* By this, you extracted
             from them a kind of grudging respect. *(Pause)*
             And wasn't your left-wing militancy as much
             a psychological weapon as anything else?
             (Pause) I wish you could have been here a few
             years ago. Imagine the anguish, the self-
             examination, the painful search for honesty.
             Whilst the western sovietologists and satellite
             experts bent over our entrails like prophets.
             What would happen next? How far would it
             go? Weren't they brave fellows over there in
             Budapest and Warsaw, those revisionists?
             (Pause) And this unwelcome scrutiny became
             a weapon in the hands of our own enemies.
             The liberal claque itself sharpened our con-
             flict. *(Pause. Harshly)* We do not exist to
             vindicate our system you know, but to make
             it work. Whilst we were dealing with risk and
             pain and death, you were permutating ab-
             stractions. When I say 'you' I mean those you
             probably dislike as much as I do. But think.

To marry me and come to Warsaw leaves *you*
exactly as you are. How is that? What is that?
Are you wanting what is here, or simply
evading something else?
*(He has struck through to something Frances would
have preferred not to face. She sits down limply, as if
defeated or guilty)*

FRANCES: I don't know. *(Pause: turning her face up to him)*
I love you. *(Pause)* Evading? *(Pause)* I don't
know—
(Jurek goes to the door. Turns to her)

JUREK: Come through—
*(She follows him into the other room, where Krystyna
sits with her hands clasped on the table. Jurek pulls
out a chair, motions Frances to it. He sits opposite)*

JUREK: She is reality. *(Pause)* For me, Krystyna . . .
and others . . . and the dead . . . are the anti-
dote to hallucination. *(Pause)* My mother is the
past. Krystyna is the war. The outraged bitterness in my own mind is Stalin. *(Pause)* I feel as
if I have been flogged by history and left in
shreds. *(Pause)* If you were a Polish girl of your
age, you might feel a number of things towards
me: compassion, curiosity, a rather guilty
indifference. At least I would be able to
diagnose *(smiling)* the condition. *(Pause)* But
you. The light from the street falls across your
face at night. And I look at you sleeping. You
seem enigmatic. You are not really, but all
that divides us—divides us! You are still a . . .
spectator to what has made me. I want you to
know exactly what I am, and what you are.
Here in Warsaw, in Poland, with that
ideological frontier running down the map of
Europe.
(Pause)

FRANCES: *(Wearily)* You want a great deal then, don't

you? I can't have your memories. Your
suffering. Your understanding.
(Pause)

JUREK: There is such a thing as an act of the
imagination.
(Pause)

FRANCES: You make me feel lost. Bewildered. *(Pause)*
I thought you were self-contained. I thought
we would live together in a . . . in a simple
way. *(Pause)* I would have said that for me,
coming here was an act of the imagination.

JUREK: Poland hardly exists for the purposes of
solving your personal dilemmas!
*(He gets up and moves away from the table, stands
with his back to her. Frances is hurt and confused.
She looks at Krystyna, puts her hand over Krystyna's
on the table)*

FRANCES: Why are you attacking me?

JUREK: I don't know whether I am. *(Pause)* Or
whether I attack something in myself. *(Pause)*
You must get it firmly in your mind that
everything here is so much more complicated
than you seem to imagine. *(Pause)* Our freedom is subtle and precarious. We have great
faith in what we are doing, but it is rather
remote from the political fantasy life of a
young Englishwoman all dressed up in revolutionary ideals and nowhere to go!

FRANCES: *(Standing up, tense and bitter)* You've no right to
be so contemptuous.

JUREK: *(Going to her)* It isn't contempt. *(Pause)* It's a
kind of weariness. *(Pause)* The last time I was
in prison, I came to think that since we are all
condemned to death—
(He stops, shrugs)

FRANCES: What?

JUREK: I was once sick. I vomited, thinking about it.

(Pause) It was dark and cold in the cell. I was hungry. I heard myself shouting in the darkness: you are a man. *(Pause)* I was terrified. But terrified because I thought: if you were not here, but warm and well-fed . . . in a comfortable house with your children sleeping, your wife nearby, your books open in the lamplight—you would still be what you are in this cell, minus these physical humiliations. *(Pause)* You could still look round at . . . perhaps some good paintings on the walls, the books on the shelves, and only say: I am a man. *(Pause)* And freeze. Sit there, numb in your house—like a beast in the slaughteryard. *(Pause)*

FRANCES: Not what I'd call marxist optimism!

JUREK: *(Puts his hands on her arms—gentle, softly reproaching)* My dear Frances, the only person really entitled to make a joke about what it means to be Jewish, is a Jew. The same, I think, for what it means to be a communist . . . in certain circumstances.

FRANCES: *(Moves away, goes to the kitchen door, turns)* I don't understand you—and now I'm frightened. *(Pause)* Frightened for us—
(She goes into the kitchen. Closes the door behind her. Jurek stands a moment, goes to Krystyna. Looks down at her. Sits at the table. Takes her hand)

JUREK: *(In Polish)* A poor beast . . . in the slaughter—yard.
(Takes both her hands)

JUREK: *(In English)* A poor beast . . . in the slaughter yard.
(Puts her hands together. Kisses them)

Scene 14

*The East Berlin—Warsaw Train at the Polish
Frontier. Same night.*

TELECINE

*Side of carriage with steam drifting up round board
showing route and destination of train. Beyond the
carriage, the platform of the border station. In the
carriage, Colin and Wanda (a young Polish girl).
Colin is asleep and having bad dreams, stirring and
groaning. Wanda watches him—curious, concerned.
Frontier Guards and Passport Officers board the
carriage. The girl leans over Colin. Touches him.
He tosses from side to side. She touches him again.
He wakes up looking frightened.*

WANDA: *(In Polish)* We are at the border—*(Colin sits up
            and looks at her. She smiles)* You were having bad
            dreams—
            *(Colin moves into the corner. Sits huddled, staring at
            her. He is becoming mentally unstable, his manner
            alternating between severe depression and lucidity)*

COLIN: *(In Polish)* I don't speak Polish.

WANDA: *(In English)* You are American?

COLIN: English.

WANDA: You go to Warsaw?

COLIN: Yes.
            *(The Passport Officer comes in. Asks Wanda for her
            passport. She shows it to him and then he turns to
            Colin, asks for his passport. Colin hands it over.
            The man fingers it slowly, looks at the photo then
            at Colin. Finds the visa and checks the date. Hands
            it over. Stands looking at Colin for a moment, then
            goes out.
            Colin and Wanda smile at each other, a little*

embarrassed. Colin feels in his inside pocket and brings out a letter, opens it, leans across to her and shows her an address written in the letter)

COLIN: Are you from Warsaw?

WANDA: Yes.

COLIN: Do you know that address?

WANDA: *(Reads it)* It is near the centre. *(Hands the letter back)*

COLIN: My sister lives there. *(Pause)* Do you understand me?

WANDA: *(Laughing)* Yes. I understand most.
             (Colin stands up, peers out through the window. He is cold. Flaps his arms. The window is misted over. He looks down at Wanda. Catches her looking at him. He looks away. Looks at her again—and she is looking too. They laugh. He writes on the misted window with his finger: Cuba si! She smiles. Stands behind him. Writes over his shoulder on the window: Yanqui no! They laugh. Both sit down)

WANDA: I will take you to your sister when we arrive to Warsaw. Shall I? *(She rubs at the window)* Poland. *(Pause)* I hope you will like—
             (Colin pulls his collar round his face. Stares at her. She becomes uneasy. Suddenly he leans forward on his knees, his fingers pressed into his face)

WANDA: *(Leaning forward—she is tender)* Tell me. *(Pause)* Tell me. *(Pause)* What is your name?

COLIN: Colin—
             (Wanda stands at the window)

WANDA: Watch—
             (She writes under the previous writing: Colin si! She points at herself and writes underneath: Wanda si! Turns to him laughing. He smiles reluctantly)

WANDA: So I am Wanda—Si?

COLIN: Si!
             (They laugh into each other's faces)

Scene 15

Jurek's Flat. The following day.

In the kitchen, Frances and Jurek's mother are setting out breakfast. Jurek and Krystyna are at the table. Jurek and his mother are speaking in Polish. The bell rings. Frances goes to the flat door. Opens it—is stunned to see Colin there.

FRANCES: I thought you were in Berlin! *(Colin is looking at her strangely. She becomes uneasy)* Well come in. How did you find us?
(Colin enters the room. She closes the door. He stands looking round him, disorientated. Frances realises there is something wrong. Goes to him)

FRANCES: Colin are you all right? Is something wrong?
(He sits at the table, puts his head between his hands. Frances hesitates. Goes to the kitchen door and speaks to Jurek)

FRANCES: It's Colin—
(Jurek comes into the sitting room after her, closing the kitchen door)

COLIN: In Berlin at night if you go near the wall, you hear people calling to each other across it. Traute are you there? Willi are you there? It's Katerin. Katerin here. Werner can you hear me? Where are you? *(Pause)* You hear their voices in the darkness. Sobbing in the darkness.
(Jurek immediately catches the note of insanity. Goes to Colin and speaks gently)

JUREK: What brings you to Warsaw, Colin? We are glad to see you. You look tired. Would you like something to eat? We are having breakfast—
(Frances hardly knows how to deal with the situation. She oscillates between harshness and a sincere attempt to be warm, to understand what is happening to Colin. Goes close to him. Touches his arm)

FRANCES: Shall I get you some coffee?
          (Pause)
COLIN: My mother sent me your address. *(Pause)*
          Should I have come? Shouldn't I have come?
          (Pause) It's easy to go away. *(Pause)* Back to
          her? Back to England? And burrow down . . .
          burrow in . . . burn out my eyes? Cut off my
          ears? *(Pause)* Or a little scratching animal.
          Pen scratching . . . fire burning in the hearth.
          (Pause) As the ink dries, the words disappear
          from the page—
FRANCES: *(Shouting)* Stop that!
COLIN: Do you love each other? I thought so. And me.
          Would you like to hear a story? About how a
          hairy man swung from a tree and made fire.
          He blew on the sparks in the hollow of a stone.
          He blew for a million years, till the fire leapt
          up in a sheet of flame and consumed him.
          (Pause) My mind tilts. I am sane, yet my mind
          tilts. I crossed Europe in a train, entirely
          without incident. A pretty girl brought me to
          your door, and went away laughing. Laughing
          out of goodness.
          *(Frances and Jurek look at each other. Frances goes
          into the kitchen. Jurek sits by Colin)*
JUREK: Do you want to stay with us a little while?
COLIN: I have moments of acute lucidity. I make
          plans. *(Pause)* I see myself walking into some
          cool clinic in London and saying: you've got
          to help me.
          (Pause)
JUREK: We will help you.
          (Pause)
COLIN: Except . . . there seems no point. *(Pause)* Why
          bother? *(Pause)* I know people have to live.
          They must go on living and avert their faces
          when somebody's cheek begins to twitch, in

the street. When the decently dressed man talks to himself in the bus. *(Pause)* Yes. *(Pause)* But I prefer my privacy.
(Pause)

JUREK: I think you can suffer for what you are, or what the world may do to you. But not for what the world is!
(Pause. Frances comes in during this speech with coffee)

FRANCES: The world's done nothing to him, anyway. *(Puts the coffee in front of Colin)* You're dishonest. If you've become a whining neurotic you must find your own way out—
(Pause)

COLIN: Why do you think I came to you then?

FRANCES: *(Softening—she is anxious and worried)* I suppose you feel you've got some kind of right to my sympathy.

COLIN: I could try to live in Warsaw. *(Pause)* Work here. *(Pause)* Find a room.
(Pause)

FRANCES: You could do that in London. Anywhere.
(Pause)

JUREK: You can probably make your life here if you want to. The only question is—why?

FRANCES: Why? Because he's faced the truth that's been staring us in the face for years! *(Pause)* In nineteen sixteen a Yorkshire miner's wife gave birth to a son—and that was our father. He grew up clever and ambitious. He didn't despise the middle classes, he joined them. That's what the English politicians mean when they talk about the disappearance of class barriers. *(Pause)* Colin and I grew up with love and respect for our grandfather, and precious little for our father. *(Pause)* We have a charming woolly liberal for a mother, whom we shamed into sitting in protest against nuclear weapons because she respects what she calls the sanctity of human life. We belong to that great English tradition which owes everything to the sporting idea that social democracies are healthy by definition, and nothing to the fact that most people are politically ignorant and therefore not equipped to choose. *(Goes to Jurek angrily)* As you implied the other day, I am one of the confused products of this situation. But look at him! It wouldn't matter if he was stubborn, or fanatical even. The truth is that he's feeble. *(Goes to Colin)* And you want to come and hide away here, don't you? *(Pause)*

COLIN: Isn't that what you've done?

FRANCES: I married. And I'm trying to live—
(Colin puts his arms on the table. Rests his head on them sideways)

COLIN: The turtles on Bikini Atoll lay their eggs—and die in the sun. They can't find their way back to the sea. *(Pause)* The seabirds' eggs are sterile. *(Pause)* The flying fish go into the trees. *(Pause)* People are shocked, and click their tongues in disapproval. *(Pause)* But I know what we all really want. We want to burn in one last shriek of fire. We long for that split second of incandescence. We can't bear what we are. *(His eyes close)*

FRANCES: I won't have you here—

JUREK: *(Goes to her)* You would throw him out? Your brother? *(Pause)*

FRANCES: I feel nothing for him. *(Pause)*

JUREK: I think you do. *(Pause)*

FRANCES: I used to admire him. *(Pause)* I'm sorry for his pain. But it's unreal to me. *(Bending close to Colin)* Are you asleep?

COLIN: *(Straightening up)* It's unreal to me. *(Pause)* It's embarrassing. Pretentious. There is after all a stable world—for those with the stamina. Its inhabitants have grown almost immune to its terrors. *(Pause)* If they hadn't they couldn't live on, reeling helplessly from one crisis to the next. *(Pause. Stands up. Faces Frances)* Don't you see I've lost the will to oppose? And it was all I had. *(Pause)* We've all acquired a new reflex: that is, how to live without screaming your head off. Leave it to the sombre faced men scurrying about with briefcases. Get on with your life and hope for the best. *(Pause)* Only I can't. *(Pause)* But neither can I get up and incite people to say 'no' any more. *(Pause)* I exist in a kind of twilight. Shiftless, morbid, negative. Wracked with nightmares and hallucinations. I'm startled that people can still laugh, and copulate, and thrive in a little human warmth. I'm always waiting for that last hemisphere of blinding light. *(Pause)* Not assuming myself to be out of the ordinary, I can't understand where my feelings have gone in others. Oedipus put out his eyes and wandered. All I can do is close mine and let the visions whirl. *(Pause. Sarcastically)* What do you two do?

JUREK: It occurs to me that you might have evolved this state of mind in order *(hesitates)* in order not to have to act. *(Pause)* You have chosen the lesser . . . of two forms of distress. *(Shrugs)* As to what I do—I have lived through so much terror, the only thing left for me is to be rational. The duty of those in power is to mankind. They may well fail in their duty. So long as they do not . . . well, we have in Poland at least the beginnings of the kind of society you and Frances believe in. *(Pause)* The task of men such as myself is to . . . humanise what is being created. *(Pause)* You have attempted a similar thing, and feel overwhelmed. But if you cease to act as you believe—then you turn your back on history. You are free—but irrelevant.

COLIN: Very neat!

JUREK: You want to antagonise me and I'm not surprised. One of my weaknesses is self-parody. So long as I am ironically aware of myself, I can be ironically aware of others. A great asset in Poland—
(Pause. Colin goes to Frances)

COLIN: And where do you stand?

FRANCES: *(Moves close to Jurek)* With him. *(Pause)*

JUREK: *(Gently)* You are really very like each other—

COLIN: *(Moves closer to Frances)* Then what separates us? *(Shouting)* We all want the same things—
(A long silence)

JUREK: I believe we do.

COLIN: Then?
(Jurek is strained and bitter—we see in him almost the counterpart of the conflicts which are destroying Colin. He speaks as if making a stark, unwilling confession)

JUREK: I am as exhausted as you are!
(Frances sees the weakness in Jurek that will bind her closer to him—and yet she is appalled. The three of them face each other in utter despair. At this moment the kitchen door opens. Jurek's mother comes through, leading Krystyna. Jurek goes to Krystyna. Looks at her, then at Colin. Looks at Krystyna. Turns to Colin)

JUREK: But I prefer to live—
(He walks out, closing the study door behind him. His mother stands holding Krystyna's arm, looking

from Frances to Colin. She is completely bewildered by the atmosphere in the room. Frances goes to Colin)

FRANCES: You can get out of here!

(She follows Jurek into his study, closing the door. Jurek's mother goes to Colin, who is on the verge of hysteria. She smiles timidly, takes his hand, puts it to her cheek. Gently presses him into a chair by the table. She then makes Krystyna sit down.
Colin and Krystyna are facing each other, staring at each other. The old lady goes into the kitchen, comes back with bread and milk. Puts them in front of Colin—makes signs to him to eat. Puts her hand on his head)

JUREK'S   *(In Polish)* Eat, my son. Eat—
MOTHER: *(Close up Krystyna. Close up Colin)*

Scene 16

A Night Club in West Berlin. Some days later.

Colin and his friend Gunther are sitting with glasses of Himbergeist in front of them. The place is darkened. A young woman is singing on the dance floor: 'Surabaya Johnny'. Her face is spotlit. She finishes, and after desultory applause, goes to Gunther's table and sits down. Colin is lolling back with his eyes closed.

GIRL: Don't you like West Berlin, Colin?
GUNTHER: Shut up. Leave him alone.
            (The next turn comes onto the dance floor. A rather gaunt woman, who begins a strip—very slow and ham. Colin opens his eyes)
GIRL: I am bored.
            (They ignore her. Gunther leans across the table to Colin)

GUNTHER: We are a terrible dream . . . floated on Anglo-German capital. *(Pause)* West Germans are uneasy. Our so-called miracle is devoid of humanity. *(Pause)* And they in the East . . . it is terrible too, because their sacrifices are too much. Too much is required. *(Pause)* It is a joke, isn't it? Stalin said let the Nazis take care of the bourgeoisie, and we will take care of the Nazis! *(Pause)* Now look at us! *(Pause)* The mistakes on all sides—

(He drinks. The girl takes a cigarette from his pack and lights it. They both turn towards the strip act. The woman is down to pants and a bra. As the music reaches a crescendo, she simultaneously removes the bra and her wig—'She 'is a man. Bellows of laughter from the clientele. He withdraws, bowing. Gunther turns to Colin)

GUNTHER: You must go back to London.

COLIN: Yes? *(Pause)*

GUNTHER: I think you are sick. *(Pause)* Perhaps no more than the rest of us but, *(he smiles wryly)* your symptoms are more extreme!

COLIN: *(Vacant and abstracted. Speaks in a whisper)* I'm going to the east side of the wall again to-night—

GUNTHER: No you are not!

COLIN: I wonder what hope there is for some other species. It doesn't look as if ours is going to make it—

GIRL: *(Leaning across to Colin)* Can't you talk about something else, darling?

COLIN: *(To Gunther)* Why do you have to have a woman with a face like a turtle?

GIRL: He's drunk!

COLIN: Yes. And I'd like to know what the turtles have done to man! Or the birds . . . or the fish . . . the innocent face of nature.

GIRL: *(To Gunther)* I don't know why you bother with him.

COLIN: I went to Hamburg first. I got a job in the docks. I found a room. I read in the evenings. I walked out in the streets and stared at the women. *(Pause)* I said to myself: you are doing well. You are picking up. *(Pause)* Yet I felt starved. *(Pause)* It wasn't that I minded being alone—

GIRL: *(To Gunther)* For God's sake take me to dance—

         (Gunther hesitates. Looks at Colin. Colin shrugs. Drains his glass. Gunther and the girl go on to the dance floor. Colin talks to himself)

COLIN: But I did take a girl back one night. I concentrated very hard on everything about her. The fine hair on her arms, the curve of her stomach. We lay in bed awake all night . . . murmuring, loving, silent. At dawn she left me. And came back the next night. And knocked on the door calling my name. Colin? Bist du da? *(Pause)* Liebling? *(Pause)* I sat crouched in my chair, looking at the door and saying nothing until she left. Then I stood up and shouted her name: Katerin. *(Pause)* I went to bed and dreamt of her swollen with my child . . . dragging her heavy body over the hot sand. I called her name: Linda, I shouted. *(Slumps forward on the table, squinting through his glass)* So. *(Pause)* Well then. *(Pause)* Have we tried everything? We have. *(Pause)* And do we bravely plod on? We do.

         (He gets up and makes his way out of the place unsteadily)

Scene 17

The Berlin Wall. Night.

The wall seals a narrow street with derelict buildings on the East side, rubble, barbed wire. On the West side a narrow cobbled street. Colin is on the East side, huddled against a fragment of ruined wall between the barbed wire and the sector wall. He has a bottle and is drinking. Slumps on the rubble, staring at the sky.

Cuts showing:

East German looking round, lighting a cigarette. People calling to each other across the wall in the darkness.
Marie . . . Marie—
Werner . . . bist Du da, Werner?
Bist du's Renate?
Ja, Ja . . . Ich bin's.
Geht es dir gut? Wie geht's den ander'n . . . ?
Was machen die denn?

Close ups of signs:

' *You are now leaving the American sector* '
' *You are now leaving the Soviet sector* '

Close up:

Colin listening to the voices

Gute Nacht, du. Kommst du morgen wieder?
Ja, du . . . ja . . . bestimmt . . . wenn ich's kann.
Colin muttering to himself

COLIN: Frances . . . Jurek . . . Mother . . . are you there?

(The East German trooper is joined by his mate and they light cigarettes. Two Police on the West side are joined by a girl and talk to her. A trooper in a building on the West side looks out of the window, yawns, puts out a cigarette. Now Colin is scrabbling for a hold on the wall—smashes his hand down on the barbed wire, calling out)

COLIN: *(Looking at his bleeding hand)* It's flesh, and bone . . . a human thing. Listen—

CLOSE UPS:

East German guards. West German guard and girl turning. West German guard in the window.

COLIN: Not a concept. Not a free man or an unfree man. Just a . . . a what? *(Pause)* Only a man—
(The East German guards raise their guns—we see along the barrels as they fire over Colin's head.
West German guard pushes the girl round a corner. Advances. The guard in the window raises his gun— fires at East German guard)

COLIN: *(Shouting over the crossfire)* A man, damn you all. Damn you on both sides. Your statesmanship . . . your deceit . . . your contempt—
(A searchlight comes on. There is wild firing across the wall now, in which Colin is trapped. He shouts again above the gunfire)

COLIN: We refuse . . . refuse . . . refuse—
(Colin staggers in a hail of bullets from both sides. Feels his body. Stands with his arms raised. The bullets hammer into him. His shadow is thrown large on an opposite wall, as with arms spreadeagled he slowly curves forward and down onto the wire. Now he is hanging in the wire, blood spurting from his mouth.)

COLIN: Only a man . . . a thing . . . a human thing—

(On the West side of the wall there is a poster with a photograph of an East German guard 'Wanted for Murder', and a wreath on the place where someone was killed whilst escaping. Blood slowly trickles down the wall, over the poster, down to the wreath)

END

Appendix

DAVID MERCER
AND TELEVISION DRAMA

Don Taylor

SINCE the rebirth of television after the war, thousands of hours of drama, comedy and comment have been transmitted. Television is no longer an amusing toy, but a powerful new medium of communication. But the sort of man the child is growing into is a question of controversy, and some concern. Will this be a new medium for artists of every kind to work in, with a new kind of audience, a private audience, denied the cosiness of the group reaction, reacting alone, or in twos and threes; above all, a gigantic and dangerous sociological influence? Or will it be the richest private gold mine in the world, a new industry, capable of making £20 million clear profit in a year, a living image of the values of a society that uses the products of the creative imagination in order to sell soap?

For the future sociologist, the first fifteen years will provide an invaluable avenue of research; but will there be anything at all for the literary historian? Only an optimist would deny that most plays written specially for television are worthless beyond their momentary entertainment value. Of the few that are worth seeing, even fewer are worth reading, and almost none repays analytical thought. There is nothing to analyse.

The plays of David Mercer represent the first major exception to this depressing general rule. Mercer has brought to the television screen a seriousness that formerly it lacked, and a depth and subtlety of thought that cries out for publication. The trilogy of plays included in this volume constitutes a single work of enormous scale and wide implication, and if it has never done so before, television has produced in this writer a man whose work demands to be read and judged by the highest standards of contemporary literature. By entering a medium that is still confusedly trying to define itself and discover its own potential, Mercer is helping to create the framework within which a television drama that is worth the name will eventually exist.

Television as it exists now is the usual sum of historical accidents that is typical of the early history of a new medium of communication. Hardly had it become aware of what it might be able to do, when it fell a victim to commercial interests, who saw in it the possibility of immense financial gain. The resultant ills have been diagnosed too often to be repeated here in any detail, and we have learned to live with the commercial disease that causes them. While half the nation's television is in the hands of commercial speculators, the other half has all but one finger tied. This book is evidence that the finger waggles occasionally, but as in the commercially dominated film and theatre industries, what is achieved is almost always in spite of the system rather than because of it.

The system justifies, and is consequently dominated by the struggle for audiences. In many fields this is a stimulating conflict. No one would deny that competition has resulted in a great improvement in the quality of television journalism and documentary reporting. But the creative arts are notoriously undemocratic in their judgements. We live in a society socially and culturally split, and the kind of drama the majority wishes to see, is not necessarily the best drama. For people working in television drama, the results of the conflict, in aesthetic terms, are almost always bad, encouraging slickness, superficiality, and simplified conclusions about people and issues.

The competitive system also produces practical results that militate against high standards. Firstly, in an attempt to satisfy an apparently insatiable demand, too many new plays are transmitted, as many as a hundred a year, not including serials and series. An optimist might hope for ten new plays a year, in any medium, that might have some kind of positive and individual value. Consequently, some 90% of what is transmitted is hardly to be taken seriously, varying from the competently entertaining, to the unbelievably appalling. This situation has produced a popular image of the television play; entertaining, a more or less accurate picture of the surface of life, satisfying the audience's desire for incident and involvement, and demanding almost nothing.

The demand for material creates, in its turn, a situation in which there is never enough time. Television plays are rushed on to the air too quickly, without sufficient time for thought. Television directors are lucky if they ever get the opportunity to lie fallow, to recoup their creative energies. Too often they must put a play on the air in the most obvious way because there is no time for second thoughts. They fall back on techniques they used last month, or last year. Multiply this by twenty plays in three years, and staleness is not surprising. Television, for reasons beyond the control of its creators, is organized like an industry, not as a creative enterprise.

The primary result of these restrictive conditions is that there has been insufficient thought about what creative television is. What, in fact, is the purpose of television drama? Is it merely to entertain audiences, to pass the time as pleasantly as possible between work and sleep? This is a small conception of drama, whose aim has always been, to misappropriate a phrase of Sir Philip Sidney, 'both to delight and teach'. It is also essentially a patronizing attitude, assuming that people want no more than a display of coloured lights passing before their eyes. But even when a social purpose has been defined, how best should it be attempted, in artistic terms? Is there a television drama aesthetic, does it differ from film, and if so how? There has been no time to ask these questions, nor perhaps, in some quarters, any great inclination. The obvious conclusions have been accepted and transformed into dogma. The fact is that we still do not know what the medium is capable of. Short of the wide screen epic, there is no kind of drama of which television is provenly incapable. We must not assume the answer to be no, when some of the questions have never been properly asked.

Artistically and socially, we don't know where we are going, or why we are going there, and until the system is radically changed, and television is organized so that the medium if used for the sake of what it can do, I cannot see how things can be much improved. Perhaps the allocation of new channels will provide an interim answer, and some release of the competitive pressure. Certainly at the moment television lets itself be led by its audience, instead of leading it, and there are no objective dramatic standards in operation. The world is topsy-turvey when what is popular is valued more highly than what is good.

All in all, it seems fair to say that television is not interested in the creation of a specifically televisual drama at anything other than the most superficial level. This ties up with the fashionably prevailing conception of the medium as journalistic rather than creative. Worthwhile plays have little to do with journalism. They are concerned with the inner life, not its shell, interpretation, not reportage.

It is not surprising then that television drama is not taken very seriously as a medium for any kind of creative statement, and the most pernicious result is that television writers are considered as not quite the same as real writers. They have, apparently, chosen the second rate. Ask anyone living and working principally in the theatre what he thinks of current developments in television drama, and he will probably apologize, and say that he didn't know there were any.

In fact, there are. To rehearse the economic and political background of television doesn't tell the whole story. The world that David Mercer entered one year ago has a rudimentary artistic climate of opinion, a climate that his work is influencing and will ultimately, I hope, help to change.

Most television drama is aimed at little beyond entertainment, and its standards are the standards of high professional competence rather than creative statement. More often than not, the camera will merely watch a storyline, and reveal nothing more than a sequence of events. In fact, until quite recently, a storyline watched by a camera was about all that could be said for the aesthetics of television drama in fifteen odd years.

Then in nineteen-fifty-nine, the BBC instituted a small experimental group, under the leadership of Anthony Pelissier, to try to work out new techniques for television drama, which was known as the Langham Group. The Langham Group represented a definite step forward in television, not so much because of its conclusions, but because of its attitude. It formulated, for the first time, an explicit conception of television drama, by stressing the visual nature of the television medium. At the time its productions were largely laughed at, or ignored, because television as a whole did not want to know. It wanted to turn out the same old stuff in the same old way, to keep the public happy. In fact, to a large extent, Pelissier has the last laugh: the visualist clichés common among the majority of television directors now, the fashionable ideologies of 'writing in pictures,' have their origins, more often than not, in his originally unpopular ideas.

But the ultimate failure of the Langham Group was more interesting than a mere inability to interest the creators of popular television. It was an artistic failure, and a very revealing one, because it was based on an aesthetic misconception.

Pelissier's approach can best be summarized by quotation:[*]

'If Television is not primarily a visual medium, what on earth is it? Here in Britain, and everywhere else as far as I can make out, it is merely illustrated sound radio . . . it is surely in one's visual approach that any individual artistic statement can be made in the Television medium. For me, this was first revealed when one day in an empty studio I found a camera that for some reason was still live. It was pointed at nothing. All it showed was a blank image.

[*]The Journal of the Society of Film and Television Arts, Spring 1962).

Suddenly I realized that any individuality in its use lay in filling that blank image not with whatever happened to come before it when the actors got together in front of some conventional sets, but with what I might devise for the viewer to see. It might be a thumb, a face, a composition of light and shade, a crowd, anything at all, in focus, out of focus, upside-down, what have you. Here to hand was a magical paint-box giving immediate results, not just a recording machine, but a new self-contained medium, potentially creative in its own right. And it wasn't being used, not at all, by anybody. Nor is it now.'

And in summing up, most revealingly . . .:

'Directors could then begin to work entirely within the medium. They could learn how to score their sound and pre-record it, so that they would then be free to concentrate on making the pictures the prime centre of interest and dramatic suggestion.'

This is an immediately attractive philosophy, and it gave a much needed punch on the nose to the conventional televisors. But the group's own work was disappointing. By cutting dialogue to a bare minimum, using stills, and a thick and overloud soundtrack consisting of almost everything except words, it tried to tell its story in a series of carefully planned pictures, using common sounds and objects for their associative and emotive value. But the result was vagueness, an assault on the ear, and worst of all, irrelevance. It looked fine, but it didn't succeed in conveying much more truth than the old-fashioned ways. It became obsessed with its own techniques, and forgot that it was supposed to be telling us something about something. Pelissier seized on half the truth as if it were the whole gospel, and created only confusion. Sound is not merely something that can be pre-recorded, leaving the producer free to concentrate on telling his story in pictures. It is one half of the instrument of communication. Television is not primarily a visual medium. It is not primarily anything. Sound radio is purely aural, and silent film is purely visual. Television, like film, is an equal partnership of the

two. If either half possesses a greater power of communication, it must surely be the aural half, which is the vehicle of
the word. Man gave up picture writing for the expression of
complex thoughts forty centuries ago, because it was not
precise enough. Man didn't give up painting pictures. But
nor did he, if he wanted to tell stories about men in detail,
become a painter.

We are forced back against the wall of primary questions,
and definitions. A play is a created series of events, the product of a writer's mind, in which a group of imaginary people
act and behave in a way more or less imitative of life, for the
express purpose of revealing the attitudes towards people and
beliefs about life in general of the author who created them.
A television play qualifies this generalization in two ways.
It is performed intimately to a small group of people in their
own home, and it has the additional facility of bringing a
selective eye to bear on the characters, attitudes and events
imitated. But the illogical step is to think of the selective eye
as a replacement, rather than an addition. For what it truly
is, is an immensely powerful extra weapon in the writer's
armoury. Not only can he tell you things in words, and
demonstrate things in action, he can also show you things in
pictures. And if 'a thumb, a face, a composition of light and
shade, a crowd', can best express what at any moment he
wants to express, then he cheers for the extra facility it gives
him. It would be very silly of such a writer to be so pleased
with his new glasses that he cuts out his tongue.

There are of course as many different kinds of play as there
are writers, and there are doubtless many who will find great
possibilities in a purely visual approach. They will explore
the texture and shape and significance of things and events
as they can be appreciated purely by the eye. But a story becomes an excrescence in such a case, because we will always
want to know more about the relationships between people
in action than pictures alone can tell us. What is normally
understood by a play demands some sort of story, so one is
tempted to talk of some separate form for the pure visualisers.

The word writer itself is inappropriate for one who is really a seer. As there are poets who write purely in the sonnet form, so there will be artists who will wish to restrict themselves in this way. But it seems to me that this sort of approach is more suited to film than to television. Television's great advantage over film is the continuous performance of actors; this is irrelevant if your main interest is pictorial anyway.

For the play, the story about people, told to point a meaning, the picture remains a means, not an end. For there is a limit to what a picture can express. To create a feeling, to suggest deep emotion, to make a satirical point, to stir complex associations, to reawaken for a moment half remembered things lost in the files of the brain, a picture has tremendous power suggesting things that cannot easily be put into words. But one cannot argue in pictures, and for complex thoughts the picture is too imprecise and open to interpretation to be fully effective. To show a picture of a negro sitting on a station seat marked 'White City', will make a strong and direct impact, and will have a satirical effect that words could hardly match in economy. But to pretend that the problem of race-relations is as simple as that, or simple enough to be expressed in any picture, is only to become dangerously superficial. People are the material of drama, but if drama is to have any serious relevance at all, people must be explored in greater complexity and depth than is possible with pictures alone. All the weapons of psychological understanding and poetic expression must come into the fullest play. In an ironic way, it may well be that creative thought about picture making is partly responsible for the terrible superficiality of television drama. The picture must certainly be made to speak, but it must speak in a context. The words of the play must have told it what to speak about.

David Mercer therefore entered a world in which the power of the word was fearfully underrated. It was merely the necessary means for the characters to explain the development of the plot, and by imitating the speech of life, to reveal themselves in a limited way. It was emphatically not a means of creating an intellectual structure as a framework for creative thought, nor was it a vehicle for poetic images. The use of the image as a poetic device, or of the dialogue of analytic thought was looked on with horror by the Ted Willis/Armchair Theatre school of television writing. Language itself was not conceived as a weapon at all. Merely the thing that characters had to talk in. Mercer knew nothing of the 'rules' of writing for television, and he wrote as he wanted to. The result was a series of plays that demand complete and intense concentration on the part of the audience if the viewing is to bear fruit. Language is in itself a weapon in these plays, as it is in poetry, and it doesn't expect to share the viewers attention with the kettle or the evening paper. Many people, doubtless, could not take this unexpected thickness of texture. Television viewers have been crammed with the obvious for so long that the subtle tastes strange to them.

I first heard of Mercer in the Autumn of 1960, when an actor I was working with showed me a copy of a play called *The Buried Man*, Mercer's second, and asked my opinion of it. I found it interesting and immediately rang his agent, Margaret Ramsay, to ask if I could do it on television. As it was under option for the stage, the answer was no. But she did send me a copy of Mercer's first play, called *A Death in the Family*. It seemed to me to be full of good things, but it covered 154 full quarto pages, and would have run at least three hours. I asked Michael Barry, who was then head of television drama, if I could work with the author in making it suitable for television, and he agreed that it was worth the try. I subsequently met Mercer for the first time at my flat, and we spent a couple of hours taking the play apart. The result was a rough synopsis of events, really the same play to be written in half as many pages. The play that appeared some months later, entitled *Where the Difference Begins*, seemed entirely successful to me, and it was bought by the BBC. Mercer had managed to escape any of the books on television playwriting. He had merely watched a little of my camera rehearsal for David Turner's *The Train Set*. Consequently, what resulted was almost naïvely his own, and to my mind, entirely original in television terms.

While the play was at the discussion and analysis stage of rehearsal, two things struck us all very clearly. The first was that the rather forbidding appearance of the play on the page was an illusion. The thick dialect prose and the long speeches were built on a base of human beings truly observed and truly motivated, and the verbal expression relied on an instinctive ear for rhythm. Though much thought was demanded, the play was ultimately easy to act. The second thing was that the relationship between Margaret and Edgar was an extremely significant and interesting one, and capable of further development. When Mercer and I talked together about another play, a further fact emerged. Mercer was at that time an active member of the Committee of 100, and was very keen to do a play on the subject of civil disobedience, but was convinced that the BBC would not allow it. I thought they probably would, if it were good enough. The two ideas came together naturally enough, and the seeds of *A Climate of Fear* began to germinate.

Where the Difference Begins was a success, and Mercer having given assurances to the Acting Assistant Head of Drama, with whom we discussed the synopsis, that he was writing a play, not a CND pamphlet, *A Climate of Fear* was commissioned. By this time, Edgar and Margaret had become Leonard and Frieda. It was necessary to change the names principally because Margaret's children were too young to be involved in CND, as Frieda's children had to be.

The play was written and scheduled quickly, and was on the screen by June 1962. It represented a considerable growth in Mercer's talents, in that he had become more like himself, and less like other writers. Characterization remained completely truthful, but thought was more complex, and language and rhythm had become richer and more lyrical. There were moments of great verbal beauty in almost every scene, and there was also at least one tremendous challenge, a scene of intense emotional crisis in Frieda, which took place in the middle of the night, in bed. One move only interrupted almost fifteen minutes of what by the end became a kind of fierce interior monologue. To my mind, the great strength of the writing, its relevance and absolute truth to the character made the scene successful. It could not be done on the stage, and a film could never match the growing intensity of the continuous TV performance. Pauline Letts as Frieda, held in almost continuous close up, laying bare her deepest fears layer by layer in a restrained and terrified whisper, seemed to me to catch at the essence of television drama.

But Mercer had left the comparative simplicities of *Where the Difference Begins* behind him, and, it must be admitted, some of his audience too. The Television critics also, a sadly old-fashioned and unthinking bunch, were lost in the new land Mercer was exploring. Most of them, of course, hated the implied political attitude. This was no longer the simple and rather quaint old socialist of *Where the Difference Begins*, safely buried in a past situation, but a vital plea for personal involvement in society, not last year, or to-morrow, but now. Supposedly reputable critics deposed all critical standards, and substituted personal bias. 'I must hit back at David Mercer' cried Peter Black . . . hardly the respectable critic's function. Most concealed their dislike of Mercer's position by attacking his technique, too many words, slow, undramatic, humourless etc. The reader is now in a position to judge for himself.

As I was reading the first draft of *A Climate of Fear* it struck me very forcibly that a third play, about Colin and Frances, would complete the pattern. We would then span three generations, and three classes: the northern working class, hardened in the thirties, the middle class liberal intellectuals, in their youth as the war began, and the rootless and less deceived young, in some of whom the passions of their grandfathers are reborn. I phoned Mercer immediately, and he was deeply excited by the prospect. The word trilogy was then first mentioned, and the project had a final shape, and an end in view. Mercer spoke at some length to the principal actors in *A Climate of Fear,* telling them his ideas as to how the characters should develop, and eventually a new synopsis was commissioned, for a play to be called *The Birth of a Private Man.* This was to be the most ambitious play yet, taking the conflicts of the first two plays, and putting them into a fully European context. Now it was not just people who were divided, nor even families, or nations, but the whole world. The expanding pattern of the trilogy was to be brought to its logical ending, and the significance of the agonies of the Waring family put into the greater context of the agonies of twentieth century man, trying to find a way of living that will not end in inevitable destruction.

The new play was to include, as one of its main characters, Jurek Stypulkowski, a Polish Communist intellectual, who was to marry Frances, and take her to Warsaw in the second half of the play. Without much more than hope, we asked if we could visit Warsaw together, to try to get a better understanding of what we had taken on. To our great joy, the BBC considered this a worthwhile project, and in August 1962 we duly spent five days in Warsaw, talking to Polish writers and intellectuals, and two, on the way home, in Berlin, looking at the wall, from both sides. There is no doubt at all that the character of Jurek became immensely more complicated and interesting as a result of this visit. Some of our more simple preconceptions proved to be incredibly naïve, and we became very aware of the specific atmosphere of Modern Warsaw, a phoenix of a city, razed to the ground by the Nazis, rebuilt from its own ashes, an emotion and a sense of pride and purpose that can only be felt on the spot. Our personal gratitude to the BBC for the trip is enough, but its artistic value, both to Mercer's writing and my production, is beyond estimation.

Perhaps this is the place to point out that the BBC can only be praised in its treatment of this writer. So far the plays have been performed with only those cuts agreed by the author and director, and every one of them has been allowed to overrun its scheduled time, the first two by five or six minutes each, and the third by half an hour, in order to preserve its unity. Though this was not accomplished without much blood, sweat and tears, it is still a fact to be stated with some complacency.

With a writer like Mercer, a director's main task is to understand and interpret. Television technicalities are really no more than two or three simple principles wearing complicated electronic disguises. The important task is to direct and shoot the play so as to make the author's meaning clear. What follows is therefore my interpretation of Mercer's work and substantially how I tried to direct it. If it reads like literary criticism, this seems to me a good thing. Television conspicuously lacks and despises literary standards, a fact which accounts for the quality of so much of its output.

On the evidence of this trilogy, it is fair to call David Mercer a political writer, provided, and it is an extremely important proviso, that the word is very carefully defined. The economist writes about facts, the politician about probabilities and the propagandist about ideologies, but the writer of plays always writes principally about people. Mercer's concern in his writing, is not to help defeat the Conservative Government, or to change English nuclear policy, but to try to communicate to us his vision of how people live in the twentieth century, and why they live as they do. Every creative artist has his own methods of revealing the truth as he sees it. Spenser chose fairy stories in order to talk about morality, and Milton seized upon the classical epic and the old testament to dramatize his own religious conflicts. Similarly, Mercer uses the world of political situations and the thought behind them as his creative convention. Of course people do not talk about politics as continuously as Mercer's characters do, we know that. Nor does the Devil speak blank verse.

When Mercer's characters engage in political controversy, they take us out of the arena back to the meaning of the word itself. Politics is the science of government, and is concerned with the way people organize themselves into societies in order to improve their manner of life. To the average Englishman it is a kind of game, not to be taken too seriously, and he is, on the whole, rather above it. The chairman always sums up by saying there's much to be said on both sides, and let's carry on over a friendly glass of beer in the pub. Mercer's plays do their best to shatter this complacency. Our lives, the way we live them, even if we live them at all, are at the mercy of political controversies, and a disagreement about the way in which man should organise his society may yet prove to be the executioner of civilized humanity. To David Mercer, political conflict is a question of basic universal choices, not who's building the most houses this year, or who can dangle the most eye-catching bribes at election time.

At certain times in man's history, certain subjects have been dominant. For two centuries after Luther, it was how to worship, and when blood was spilt, it was more often than not in the name of one of the faces of Christ. By analogy, this is becoming a political century. Wars, from 1917 onwards, have increasingly been fought not for motives of patriotism, or economic gain, but for reasons of ideology. Ideology has divided the world into two armed camps, and one half, it seems, is prepared to destroy the other to ensure that its ideology is victorious. This tragic division is the subject of Mercer's trilogy, and this is the way in which they are political plays. In them we see an analysis of our dominant political conflicts worked out in terms of people, and it is Mercer's peculiar talent to be able to talk intelligently and subtly about political questions while remaining true to the psychology of the people involved. His work demonstrates the convincing marriage of subtle political thought with exact personal psychology, and the result is that his people, while remaining individual, take on archetypal attributes. The past and present sufferings of the Waring and Crowther families are the agonies of twentieth century mankind trying to live. It is the business of drama to observe the particular and make it general, and in telling the story of the Crowthers and the Warings, Mercer is also telling the tragic story of fifty bloodstained years.

Where the Difference Begins takes as its subject the history of the radical impulse as it has been expressed in socialism, and demonstrates it in the life of a Yorkshire working class family. In attitude it is basically simple, and in style basically realistic. It is very much a beginning, a point from which to continue.

The play is, in effect, an inquest. In the first fifteen minutes Alice Crowther dies, but the body that lies upstairs throughout the rest of the play is more than merely the remains of the mother of the family. It is the past which is dead, a way of life that Wilf and his wife represented typically in their time; and it is also a radical impulse, which seemed in the thirties to be building a road to the new world, and which in the fifties died of material suffocation. A typical situation is presented in the play, working class father, uneducated, a natural socialist, for reasons that can easily be guessed:

'At eleven year old I were scrattin' coal for me living. What I made were t'difference between eating and starving in our family. Sixteen year old I were cleaning out boilers. Come home, get washed, drop into bed and start all over t'next morning. And socialism? Tha's reight. I knew nowt, but in them days you didn't have to be brilliant to know which side tha were on.'

The father stands pivotally between the two sons whom the the sweat of his labour and the sacrifice of the woman dead upstairs have helped to educate. Edgar, the elder son, has taken his father's exhortations to education very much to heart, and in acquiring knowledge, he has also acquired the middle class values that all too often go with it. Richard, with his knowledge, has taken a large dose of disillusion. He cannot believe as his father believes, much as he would like to, because his intellect tells him that simple belief is out of place in a complex social situation, and has been proved inadequate. Yet he knows that the morality of his father's position cannot be challenged. Two other characters stand

on the sidelines of this conflict, watching, and adding their
own stories to the revelation of the past. Margaret, the intelligent middle-class liberal humanist, lulled into acceptance
of a life of family, home, personal concern, the decent English
virtues, is approaching the crisis of middle age, and cannot
keep her questioning mind quiet any longer. For her, it is
her own past that comes under the microscope, and she can
never be quite the same again. Uncle George is senile, almost
raving, but he is all that is left of an even remoter past, the
first generation of English socialism, the generation of Kier
Hardie, and the bitter struggles of overt class war. His in-
coherence is broken by one flash of illumination, almost the
most moving moment in the play:

> 'It hasn't been nowt but bloody wars, when you come to
> look at it. Has it? Still, with a bit of luck we shall be under
> t'sod afore t'next one. Capitalists has got to go on making
> wars, tha knows. That's Marx, that is. Marx said that.'

One can say nothing, except that for a man of George's
generation it is the awful truth.

At the end of the play, nothing is changed. Wilf, Edgar and
Richard still stand in the same relationship to each other,
believing and disbelieving the same things, Margaret has
done nothing, and George is one day nearer his grave. But
the past has been illuminated, and the social reasons which
made the characters what they are, have been explored in
thorough and passionate detail.

'Ah were as red as John Penny's eye after a night on t'beer'
says Wilf, and,

'Socialism had some guts in it in them days'
But at the end he is forced to recognize that:

'Summat's done. Summat's finished. Summat's gone.'
The theme of the play is the reluctant acceptance of that fact,
and a series of questions. What was it worth, that way of life,
that structure of belief, what was it worth in social, ideological and personal terms? And, most of all, if it is indeed a
thing of the past, what is there to replace it? When Wilf too
dies, must we choose between Edgar's enlightened but ultim-

ately self-interested Toryism, and Richard's overwhelming sense of failure?

The play is summed up in Richard's speech to his unborn child, as embittered a fairy story as has been told for many years. It was easy for the little socialist person to see the lines of conflict when it was a question of fighting the capitalist devil who ran everything. What socialism was seemed obvious:

> 'Dad wanted the people to own everything, and everybody to have an inside lav. He said that was socialism, in case they didn't know it.'

Ideological subtleties seemed unimportant when bellies were empty and hands were idle. The bellies must be filled, the hands put to work. But when the little socialist went away to be educated, he saw that the simplicity of his father's beliefs was not enough. For needs can be satisfied if their basis is a merely material one. What about socialism when everybody's got an inside lav and is voting for Macmillan:

> '... and practically all there is left to do is to shout, where do we go from here? Shout: where do we go when all the cities aren't fit to live in, when we all have everything to live with and nothing to live for? Where do we go when all the black men have got their independence, when all the coolies are riding around in mini-cars? When we're all fed and innoculated, where do we go? When the life expectancy's raised to 150, where do we go?'

Richard's answer is the black answer of his depression. Earlier in the play the same mood is evident, but Wilf has an answer for it:

> '*Richard:* You know what your sons are right enough! One solid conservative, and one shagged out political idealist. ... It's a question of where to begin again dad ...
>
> *Wilf:* Tha mun find thy road, same as we had to, Richard. Nobut, tha's an educated man. Tha mun do it better than we could have done, with all t'will in the world. And happen being educated, tha'll not let them pull t'wool over thy eyes.'

The question of where to begin again is the question of the rest of the trilogy, and the first play leaves it unanswered. But it is Wilf, not the question, that remains in our mind. We know he belongs to the past, and we know that his simple belief is irrelevant in the modern context; but he is a figure of immense strength and dignity, and in social terms, the father of what material progress the working class has made. Wilf's last scene is, as never before, the testament of the uneducated workman, a savage and dignified epitaph on a breed of rank and file socialist now vanished or vanishing, and the way of life that was lived by them. As the play closes, there is no doubt where our sympathies lie:

'Sitha—t'goodsyard. Work it out for thisen. An average on nigh fifty hour a week for forty year. How much time does that make? I know every siding and signal and permanent way over t'county. I've gotten as far as I can go, and happen I know no more for all that. Canst not think what I wanted for thee two? I'm dumb, but dost think I've never wanted to say nowt? Me head's gotten nowt in it, but dost think I've never wanted to fill it? And I waited for thee two to grow up and make it reight. Eh, when I were a lad we thought it a marvel to go fifty mile an hour. Now they're barn to t'moon. It's all come about in fifty year, and it'd take a good 'un to keep up with that. Tha's left us old 'uns behind reight enough. But I can fire an engine, and drive it. I can cop a pike with a spinner. My eyesight's going now, but I could nick a rabbit at twenty yard with yon old catapult, from t'footplate . . . It's not dignity tha misses Edgar lad. It's knowing I've no place in thy world.'

Much has been written about the dignity of the working man. I doubt if it has ever been better expressed in modern drama than it is in that scene.

In style the play is firmly realistic, but within that convention one can sense a potential conflict between the imitative and the purely creative. Creative writing, in this sense, is almost unknown on television. Most television writers, even the best, are concerned with depicting as accurate and truthful a picture of people's lives as possible. In that sense their work is imitative. There is no connecting philosophy to interpret the sometimes accurate pictures they draw. Their characters can do anything, as long as it is consistent with their personalities as created. Mercer, from the start, has known what he wants to say. He has a definite conception of the human personality, and its relationship to society, and every one of his plays, even the more stylised ones that follow this trilogy, attempts to communicate the same interpretation of humanity in its present condition.

But *Where the Difference Begins* is a first play, and in it Mercer is not completely clear about what he is good at. An added interest of the trilogy is the way in which Mercer finds out what he can do best, and creates, in the third play, a highly personal and compressed style, eminently suitable for the sort of communication he is concerned with. There are passages in the first play where the characters are developed purely for their own sake, interestingly, but not always in a way relevant to the play's main theme. There is also an element of personal involvement, which is missing from the other plays. Richard's insecurity is not purely related to the play's demands. It reflects the insecurity of the unrecognized author, not sure if his talent is genuine. It is significant that there is none of this personal involvement in the other two plays. The writer is objective, creating characters and situations for a purpose, not writing to sublimate his own needs and unfulfilled desires. There is indeed a kind of art which grows from that kind of creation, but it is not David Mercer's. What is written is written with passion, but passion distilled to an essence.

Where the Difference Begins was a simple play, strong in dramatic outline, richly characterized, argued in relatively direct terms, and written with a passion that gave it a direct emotional appeal. It could have constituted a formula for three or four similar plays. But Mercer did not wish to repeat himself. His mind was already exploring different avenues of thought in subject, attitude and style. In subject, he was trying to answer Richard's question, 'where do we go from here', no longer summing up the past, but trying to grapple with problems that changed almost as he wrote about them. His attitude was necessarily much more complex. These plays are not aimed at the man who is prepared to take up simple positions about the issues raised by CND, or the state of modern socialism. The simple positions are almost by definition false. In style, the play represents a transition, feeling towards a method of writing which fuses political conflict and personal psychology in an absolute and indivisible way. This can only be done at very high pressure, just as poetic drama in verse requires a very high level of compression to be successful, and there are perhaps moments in the first quarter of an hour of *A Climate of Fear* where the pressure is not high enough, and some of the joins show. But in the best scenes there is no doubt that the fusion is achieved, and that the characters are revealed through their political commitment in a manner which is both subtle and original. In addition, the play is more spare than its predecessor. There is nothing included that does not have direct relevance to the theme, no development of character for its own sake. The mind must always be at its sharpest focus, for what is being said is always relevant.

The subject of the play is commitment, the nature of commitment, and its consequences. That the commitment is to socialism and against the sort of society that tolerates nuclear weapons, is taken for granted. A moral choice at the most fundamental level, about the whole nature of man's existence, determines whether a man is a socialist or a conservative. But socialists come in many shapes, from Public School to Peking, and a consideration of the question of how to change society, (the fact of wanting to change it is assumed) creates the principal complexities of this play.

A Climate of Fear takes its shape from the story of Frieda's change of position. It presents her at the beginning, living outside society, fundamentally unconcerned, and shows how the actions of her children, by playing on her own sense of purposelessness, involve her more and more in her society, to the final point of overt political action. In addition to this demonstration of the theme in action, we are also invited to consider the nature of commitment as it expresses itself in five characters.

In the simplest of the five, Tom Driffield, we have a direct link with *Where the Difference Begins*. There is tremendous sympathy in all Mercer's writing for these old men who knew what the class struggle was like when it did not need to be subtle, who were on the receiving end so often, and yet who accomplished so much. They are written with love, all the more so perhaps because they do belong to the past in everything but the morality of their beliefs. Even their bluntness and disrespect for authority is principally one of the defence mechanisms of the oppressed, the Englishman's way of putting up with fools in power. Tom's definition of English socialism in the fifties:

'The British left is like a kipper: two faced and no guts.' though splendidly apt is a kick in the pants rather than any contribution to the problems that need to be solved. The creation of the first socialist country in 1917 is an object of great emotion, but the emotion is retrospective. The motives that caused the same socialist country to put down a rising in Hungary in 1956 are more complex and difficult to understand. In that world Tom is out of his depth. But as with Wilf, Mercer has tremendous sympathy for Tom as a man, and as a valedictory gesture, he gives him the best single piece of writing in the play, the superbly rhythmical and restrained epitaph on Surry Waring:

Yon was a man with a right heart. Yon was a man that put little Leonard on the table when he was nobut a bairn, in front on some of the pit lads. He runs his hand through Leonard's hair and says: I shall make him speak with tongues. T'bairn looked up at him. Surry says: the tongue of dignity, the tongue of community, the tongue that the illiterate man who fathered him to his mother never had. Surry's heart isn't stone. Surry's heart's rotting in a flooded seam under Broughton Colliery this many a long year. It's gotten t'worms in. And so has your Leonard's.'

This, with its biblical rhythm and rhetoric, and its strange Lawrentian period sense, is not merely reminiscent of *Where the Difference Begins*, but a development of it. The working class fathers of socialism are seen as almost legendary figures, of heroic stature. Yet at the same time, Tom himself knows their limitation. They produced so many Leonards and Edgars. Surry's impassioned hopes for his son, his rhetoric, brought forth not the new world, but Leonard's smallness of mind and father-hatred. Tom is sadly aware of his own irrelevance.

Frances appears very simple on the surface, but in depth reveals more and more, becoming, by the time the third play is complete, one of the most interesting characters in the whole trilogy. In *A Climate of Fear*, she is presented to us as an extremely intelligent girl of seventeen, at the height of the rebellious stage. She is full of the excitement of her newly born intellect, and with it she can demolish what she pleases. Her rebellion against parental authority is typical and harmless enough, but it is complicated by strong feelings of what we must almost call disgust, and by her worship of her elder brother. Her attitudes are largely his, but she has taken them without their complications, and the result is a black and white view of life. At seventeen, everything is simple, and the intellect is at its most arrogant. Perhaps it is Frances's lack of a father she can respect and the resultant insecurity that makes her choose definite positions and attack constantly. The feelings of admiration that her father should have had, have been shared between Colin and her grandfather. Certainty is the armour of the insecure.

Her purpose in the early part of the play is mainly to act as an irritant to Frieda's conscience. She grows into a real character during the scene at Peter Driffield's flat. This scene, which contains as much dramatic impact as anything in *Where the Difference Begins,* and is infinitely more subtle in thought and character motivation, is dominated by Frances's brutal reading of Peter's letter to Frieda. As Frieda begins to open the innermost doors of her personality, Frances watches her with an amused distaste, building the fragile house of matches that she has already decided to destroy. In the midst of her mother's courageous attempts to understand the things that have made her what she is, and are still driving her now, Frances, feeling very grown-up, burst in with her crude revolutionary song, which she follows with an even cruder view of her mother's situation:

> 'You're getting to be great at self contemplation. But you don't change. Even my father's more consistent than you are. He thinks like a puppet, and lives like one. You live like one, and indulge yourself by thinking like a human being where it's no challenge, inside your own head. You're not honest, you're simply inventive.'

She goes on to read the letter on the flyleaf of Aragon's poems, which to her is a confirmation of all her worst suspicions about her mother and Peter. How could they be so soft! The great struggle for freedom was being fought under their noses, and all they could think of was their petty emotions!

Then comes the horrific moment. Her mother never received it. It wasn't communication, merely Peter talking to himself, trying to be convinced. For her mother, this last chapter of her abortive relationship with Peter is being written to-day. Once more Frances is out of her depth. At seventeen she can deal with ideas but human emotions and motivations are beyond her. She can only attack even more viciously to cover her confusion. When this attack is at its height, in a moment of parental insight, Frieda perceives Frances clearly:

> 'You can't bear to have me love you without being on your side.'

For Frances, as Colin points out in the third play, this would be a strain too great to be borne.

Our feelings for Frances are the variable feelings we have for a real person. Her cruelty to her mother would in a mature person be difficult to forgive but in her case we are prepared to accept that it grows from great concern allied to great ignorance. This kind of cruelty is not uncommon in an adolescent and if it is only her age that is the villain of this scene we can see the scene from Frances's point of view, as one of the battle grounds of growing up. But there are other suggestions. Frances's passion, a faint sense of wretchedness within the enjoyment of assertion, suggests that there may be other reasons that make her act in the way that she does, and that her actions are not merely the result of inexperience but deeper and more compelling needs. If so, her position is a complex and serious one and it is this trend of her personality that provides the foundation for her development in the third play.

As this play comes to its climax, all the main characters are forced to recognize new things about themselves, with the exception of Peter. The tragic thing about Peter is that the events of the play only confirm what he has known about himself for a long time.

'For weak and doubting people, its painful to act . . . I've had over twenty years of it.'

Peter's attitude is that of the radical intellectual. But the intellectual virtue of being able to see every side of an argument is in Peter so pronounced as to be almost a vice. As an observer he is perhaps brilliant and can record in his books and articles a balanced yet intensely radical view of life. But faced with the reality of living he becomes his natural timid self, unsure how to act, or if action at all is called for. In the world of political action he is nothing more than a rather remote don who attacks the socialist right in political journals, and in his relationship with Frieda he is unable to do anything more than write long impassioned letters that he is too timid to send. Deeply afraid of the betrayal he sees evidenced in Leonard, he tries to keep a sense of continuity by bringing his miner Dad to London to live with him. Colin

attacks him for the very betrayal he fears, for reducing pole-
mic to scholarship, for making a profession out of his commitment, instead of a life:

'PETER: Well? Why so rattled?

COLIN: There's a soft too reasonable centre in you.
            Caught a glimpse of it just now. You're just as
            dug in as my father is. Your tutorials, and
            your books, your articles about the New Left
            defining itself. You're dusty. You need a beat-
            ing. The way you blather on about fathers and
            sons! Man, you're way out!

PETER: Your mother thinks I've influenced you and
            Frances.

COLIN: My mother mistakes your ineffectualness for
            depth.'

This outburst is a product of Colin's incipient neurosis, and
is by no means unanswerable. But Peter's only answer is:

'You're partly right about me.'

Partly! The eternal qualification that destroys action. When
Peter admits that he has not achieved all the things he
dreamed of, a life of involved political action, the changing
of society, Colin is at his most severe:

'PETER: Leonard knows I'm a parody of what I ought
            to be.

COLIN: (entering) You're a parody of what you never
            were.'

Peter accepts the blow, as he always does, with nothing more
than the mildest rebuke. He is a weak and doubting person,
it is difficult to act, and Colin is partly right. He presents the
interesting spectacle of a character paralysed by intellectual
self-knowledge.

For Peter we can only have a sad affection. His reasonable-
ness is the result of genuine humanity and concern, and it
breaks our heart. We feel we know him intimately, and yet
the fact is that he only appears in two scenes, of which the
first is perhaps the stiffest and least successful in the play. In
one scene he comes completely and convincingly to life, and

gives an excellent demonstration of Mercer's method of revealing the truth about a person through his political position. Peter is his politics, for it is the very psychological make up that we are interested to see revealed that has determined his political choices. The two things are inseparable; the political attitude reveals the psychology, and the psychology implies the political attitude. The author's final comment is left until the third play, but we have seen enough in the second to know what inevitably that must be.

At first sight, Colin appears to be merely the character who plugs the CND line. Passionately concerned, rigourously intellectual, absoluteley committed to a fierce moral position, which expresses itself in Marxist terms, he seems the archetypal young radical. But the political attitude is not as simple as that, and it reflects the expected psychological complexity. Every statement of position that Colin makes is closely followed by a qualification:

'Here am I, a passionate socialist. Which is a very difficult thing to be at this time et cetera et cetera . . .'

It is a joke at his own expense, but it is also the truth. The story of Colin in the last two plays is the story of how difficult it is to be a passionate socialist at this time. It is difficult for two reasons. Firstly, because how to be a socialist is by no means a settled question, and secondly, because the vast weight of society as it is now constituted militates against social change. Colin is a revolutionary without a revolution, a leader with no army, hated by the conservatives, expelled by the Labour party, sceptical of orthodox communism, a man who dreams of the genuine socialist society that he sees rejected on every hand. One of the scattered band of dissenters in whom a contemplation of the English political scene since the war induces almost despair, what will he do? Will he fit himself in, take a job, get a wife, settle down? Will he preserve his beliefs, but express them merely among friends, or will he modify them gradually, to suit society as it is? Or will he continue to fight against a society he hates with every atom of his strength, for almost no reward? Such questions can only be answered in psychological terms, of each individual person. Colin is too intelligent to compromise his beliefs for the sake of personal contentment without incurring his own contempt. He must hold to his adopted positions, or break. But the first long scene in the prison makes it quite clear that his psychological constitution is not built for endurance. He feels things intensely in personal terms, and at the back of his mind is always his disgust at his father's betrayal of all he was educated to achieve. *A Climate of Fear* shows the approach of a personal crisis in Colin, which is fully revealed in *The Birth of a Private Man*. Colin, Christ-like, takes on his head responsibility for the sufferings of humanity, and their restitution, but finds that that cross is more than he can bear.

Colin's first big scene, his father's visit, presents to us his positions, but it presents them with such passion and disgust, that the seeds of what is to follow are plainly planted. He emerges from prison tormented by doubts, and what seems to be a desire to jeer and destroy. He hammers Peter's intellectual inaction, and even jeers, though lovingly, at the old Yorkshire shock-worker in the kitchen. His socialist position has become a complex one certainly, but the unease lies deeper than that. It is not even the intellectual problem of reconciling the conception of the individuality of man, which has been the root of all Western thinking since the Greeks, with the communist conception of man as a single minute cell within the body of the social organization. It is deeper still, more dangerous, less curable. Colin has come to doubt not the moral justification of socialism, but the worth of men. What is beginning to grow in him, is the cancer of nihilistic despair, and prison is to him its image:

'I didn't mind jail. I'll go as often as I have to. But I never realized before how a prison is my society in action. I knew it, but I hadn't felt it. You feel like a fly in a man's fist. And behind the fist there's the arm, the shoulder, his total strength. A prison doesn't make you doubt your moral position . . . it makes you doubt men.'

When Frieda questions his doubts, he replies:

'I've as much despair and hopelessness in me as anybody has.'

In fact he has more, and for him it is a tragic fact. Within him, the desire to give up is getting stronger and stronger:

'I'm going to get me a nice chick with a leather raincoat, a cosy bed-sitter done out in Victorian, no landlady, and move in.'

And at a deeper, more destructive level:

'It makes you want to turn your face to the wall. To withdraw your complicity from all life . . . and be damned.'

Colin ends *A Climate of Fear* beating his head against the cubicle wall of the Black Maria, in a despairing determination to be strong. But a man can only beat his head against an unyeilding wall for so long. In the third play, the desire to withdraw becomes even stronger, and the continuous beatings begin to take effect.

If *Where the Difference Begins* is Wilf's play, *A Climate of Fear* is Frieda's. Colin shows a crisis point being prepared for, in a man in his early twenties; Frieda shows, in a middle-aged woman, the actual moment when the crisis erupts into action, the one moment of decision after which life is irrevocably changed. This moment of decision occurs in the last scene with Leonard, and the following film sequence, and the last scene of the play begins to show some of the consequences of the action. The whole play is centred round Frieda, and shows how her emotions are screwed up by a series of events to the point where action becomes unavoidable.

Margaret in *Where the Difference Begins* has been forced into the position of asking questions. Her children no longer need her, her mind has been laid asleep too long, the change of life is approaching, she feels useless, pointless. Her husband is sinking into a middle-age she feels unready for, and she is sexually frustrated. Before her eyes is the example of Richard and Gillian, patently all the things she and Edgar are not, and death, as it always does, has brought all these things into sharp focus.

Frieda in her first scene is in the same position. Colin's imprisonment wakened her from a sleep of twenty years, and she can never pretend complete unconcern again. She is at her most sophisticated with Peter, and staunchly affirms her vaguely liberal-humanist position:

'I can assure you, having no political beliefs is an absolutely painless sacrifice. I keep my respect for people who are human beings first, and idealists second.'

But only a few minutes later she is admitting:

'Do you think I'm not baffled about what one ought to do? Do you think I wouldn't be grateful to be passionately involved along with my own children?'

Her uneasiness is obviously something which runs deep.

The first half of the play comes to a climax in the bedroom scene. The preparations for Edgerton's party and the party itself have been needle-pricks to Frieda's awakening conscience.

But in bed after the party, unable to sleep, she is at last brought face to face with herself and compelled to recognize all the things she has hidden or ignored for twenty years. The first and worst thing is the emptiness of her own marriage.

'If you were to die or be killed, I'd cry. I'd be wretched with grief. And what would I be mourning? Or if I died, what would you mourn? Human loss, but what is it? When we can touch neither our own children, nor each other?'

The feeling of uselessness and irrelevance that afflicted Margaret is made explicit in Frieda, in a memorable way:

'We live, but we've no real connections with life. What are we afraid of? Fire? Burglars? Burst pipes? Accidents? Human beings should have more dignified fears.'

She proceeds with an attempt to remember what has made them what they are, ending with a summary of Leonard that is brutally true, but at the same time infused with the charity that befits his wife. This is the subject of *Where the Difference Begins* again making itself heard, but here, through the eyes of one who was personally involved, we see not so much betrayal, as misdirection. What to Colin seems a cynical sell-out, is seen by Frieda as a gigantic but understandable mistake:

'Oh, you're a paragon of normality. Britain's new man on the decline. The brainy working-class kid who puts his head down and swots. And looks up one day to find himself created in his own absence. Who made him? What is he? A bit of a Christian, a bit of a Tory. Doubtful about trades unions and United Nations, living harmlessly. Whose creation is it? Didn't know it was happening. While the world goes to pieces over his bewildered head.'

By the time the scene is half way through Frieda has accepted one thing at least, that she is in need of redemption. The days when she could sit back in her pleasant house in the country, surrounded by good things, and be the wife of a highly respected scientist are gone for good:

'You love me—and inside love, I'm starved. I have a nice house—and inside the house I'm frightened. We have friends, neighbours—and among them I'm appalled by them. I love you—and inside that love there's hysteria, because I want to live before I die.'

Frieda may not take action but whether she likes it or not she has become a different person from the one who began the play. She has seen through not only her whole situation but also herself. She has spiritually left her husband but has gone nowhere. At this point Colin enters the play and it is in this mood that she goes to the homecoming party at Peter's flat in Camden Town.

When she arrives she is more than half on her children's side. She has come to realize that she has been to all intents and purposes dead for twenty years, and she now sees her children as epitomizing all the qualities she lacks. But straightaway Colin shatters her simplified preconceptions. It's not all flag-waving and convictions. It's concern and despair. Once again she is back in the melting pot. There is no simplicity, and she recoils from entering life if it is merely to be exchanging one complex situation for a worse:

'There's part of me that would almost welcome death, an end. I don't necessarily mean a war. Not physical dying. There are other ways. Bovine tranquillity. Failing to be outraged by the little you've made of life.'

It upsets her to think that her children, whose lives she thought were so definitely directed, are prey to a disillusion as great as her own. She is thrown further back towards despairing inaction and a desire to defend Leonard, and obliquely, herself:

'You talk about prison. I think you are trying to say it crushes the love in you. But me. The prisons are in me. The bars are in my bones. The locks in my own doors. I am embarrassing myself and you. You both want to connect it with your father, but you mustn't. Oh, I came in here and found you three men . . . together. And your father going north in that train with a heart like a stone. He knew I would see you.'

She knows how much Leonard needs her, and she is reluctant to leave him undefended. In an attempt to find some sort of balance, she even dismisses her own questionings as no more than indulgence:

'There's no real substance in what I say. One imagines tensions.'

When Frances launches her attack, the effect on Frieda is twofold: to show her, in passing, something about her daughter, and to encourage her retreat into despair. By the time the scene is ended, she has taken such a hammering that she is prepared to give up. The world she wanted to enter is a real world and no easy path to fulfilment is there for the following. She would rather stay sleeping, let man go to perdition in his own time. She will disengage herself, and live out her life as comfortably, and with as little fuss as possible:

'I really do believe you're all wasting your time. If people were determined to live, then they would insist on it, demand it. But they accept the possibility of annihilation already. And they're learning to live with the certainty. What's the use of saying they're lied to? Or mislead? Or ill-informed about the alternatives? They know the facts. There's only one conclusion. Death must be less of a strain on us than our humanity. I see your beliefs as an emotional trap. I don't reject them. I've no energy left for them. No hope. I feel as if my life has flickered out.'

Frieda decides her flirtation with the world is over. She will return to her middle age, with the sour consolation that Leonard probably feels as much bewildered pity for her as she feels for him.

But though home looked very tempting from the open spaces of the world, when she is back in it, it is unbearable. She is a changed person, she cannot pretend otherwise. Her old life bores her to distraction. Then, for a moment, Leonard blazes into anger and reveals the feelings he has repressed so long, the love-hate relationship with his father, the emptiness of the middle class life he has chosen, and secretly hates, all the frustrations and furies of twenty years. Though she is the object of the attack, for a moment Frieda sees hope. But before her eyes Leonard consciously denies and represses the truth he has inadvertently admitted:

'It was anger talking. Nonsense. You grin and bear it for years, and when you finally open your mouth, you come out with a lot of drivel . . . It is muck. It's not true.'

Within seconds he is engaged in a discussion of ridiculous banality with the pathetic Rawson, back in the world of lawnmowers and good neighbourliness. As Frieda listens with increasing horror, she realizes that it will take more strength than she has got to save Leonard from the full consequences of the life he has chosen, and that the certain result is her own destruction. In a moment of hysterical protest the decision is made and the irrevocable step taken. She must act or consciously destroy herself as Leonard is doing.

Her confusion is made quite clear in the last scene, shut in the coffin-like Black Maria, hysterical with fear and realization of what she has done:

'I don't know what it was. But rather this than anything else. I'm sure of that. No one should . . . leave it to someone else.'

She knows nothing except that her old life is dead and she must try to live a new one. Her last word is the simple: 'I'm here.' She has reached this point in her life and suddenly she must begin again. She has nothing but herself, and life to be lived. All one can say of it is that it will be lived honestly.

One could write many pages yet on *A Climate of Fear,* and still leave unsaid much that the play suggests. I have done no justice at all to Leonard, a most subtle character, and emphatically not a cardboard opponent stood up to be shot at. But the play is the story of the turning point in Frieda's life, and that I have tried to interpret. Though in a different, more stylized way, she is as completely realized a character as Wilf, explored in great subtlety and depth and springing immediately to life through every word of her complex speeches. Those critics, most of them, to their shame, who saw in this play no more than an arid and verbose political display, seem to me to have been guilty of the most crass and stultifying insensitivity.

The Birth of a Private Man is in every sense a climax. It deals with the largest issues of the modern world, in a European, even a world context, with a penetration of thought and a brilliance of language that has never been equalled on television. It is a work of the most remarkable concentration. There is no scene, hardly a speech that is not directly relevant to the play's main theme, and yet the characters are minutely and exactly observed and drawn, truly understood from within. It is richer, and more dramatic than *A Climate of Fear,* more concentrated in every sense, and it shows a growing power in the use of poetic images that suggests the most exciting things to come. It seems to me that in this play Mercer has completely mastered his own style so that it is now an instrument in his hands to be used as he wishes. He has indeed created his own language. What we read is not observed English. It is the English language as recreated by David Mercer.

The theme of the play remains commitment but it is seen from a new angle. We are not concerned with the necessity for contracting in to one's society, but the price of contracting out. Just as the plot of *A Climate of Fear* is Frieda's conversion to an acceptance of responsibility for her society, the plot of *The Birth of a Private Man* is, as the title suggests, Colin's renunciation of responsibility.

The play begins with what is surely Mercer's final farewell to the old guard. The first two plays are both dominated by the militant fathers of Socialism in the north of England, for whom the lines of battle were clearly drawn, and who, tragically, produced the confused generations of the fifties and sixties. As this play begins, the last of them is laid in the earth, with the reverence we would expect. But even at the graveside, the division those old men fought to destroy cannot be overcome. The old miners and the visitors from London are two separate groups. There is little between them, except grief for the one that's dead. It doesn't escape Colin:

'Those miners at the graveside—we weren't just strangers to them. We were alien. My grandfather was a friend of Peter's dad. Both men had worked with those miners. Boozed, sweated, got families. What am I then? Where's the human link from me to them? Who could be more isolated nowadays than a man who still believes in the things they once passionately wanted?'

Colin is obviously where we left him at the end of *A Climate of Fear*. Frieda rubs it in:

'Well. Tom's dead. Your grandad lost his life in the pit. Soon they'll all be dead. And there'll be no Grand Old Men of Socialism left to bother anybody's conscience.'

Within a few seconds Colin announces his decision to withdraw from all his political commitments. His girlfriend wants a child, and a life of quiet, he will become a private man. But the vision he sees is significant:

'All she wants is babies and peace. Not peace movement peace. Peace in a room with a child on the floor. It would be strange wouldn't it? To stop agitating. Turn your back on everything. Watch your wife grow pregnant, take a job, furnish a flat, keep your head well down. In a world you believe the public men will destroy.'

It is not an alternative choice, but a retreat. A retreat out of the world, into a room, with the back turned and the head well down, waiting for destruction. With this vision in his mind, Colin hears the porter's news of a suicide up the line: the ultimate withdrawal from life. ·

The station scene defines Colin's disillusion, and shows the degree to which it is becoming neurosis. As was made clear in *A Climate of Fear,* it is not disillusion with socialism that is at the root of Colin's agony, but disillusion with men. He has struggled, and failed:

'I've marched. I've been on sit downs. I've been arrested a dozen times, and in prison twice. I've worked in the Labour party and the New Left till I couldn't stomach the one and the other disintegrated. I've hovered on the brink of joining the Communist Party like a hesitant virgin. I couldn't ever quite bring myself to do it. I've read and argued and talked, factories, dockyards, turned my home into a bloody office, refused to give my girl a child, which is what she wants more than me even. I've dropped my Ph. D. I live on handouts from people who are sympathetic to the movement. I'm poor, and tired, and rapidly turning nihilistic. You talk about history! All I want to do is to crawl away and laugh.'

All Colin's values and standards are upside down, and there is nothing for him to hold on to. His wild pilgrimage round England comes to an end in a transport cafe, where his feelings are only confirmed. What contact is there between Colin's socialist ideals and the workmen for whose sake those ideals were formulated? None. They don't want to know. His disillusion is complete, and he phones his mother to announce his discovery:

'The most incorrigible force in the human personality is destruction.'

It is a terrifying conclusion for a man of twenty-four to come to, and his reason for returning to Linda to give her a child:

'I believe in spitting in the face of the executioner.'

hardly suggests that his withdrawal from commitment is a

rational act. What drives Lear insane, and paralyses Hamlet into immobility, is the horrifying thought that perhaps man is a purely selfish, utterly worthless creature, a collapse of all objective standards of morality, and a triumph of destructive impulses. Like Hamlet, Colin is burningly aware of the immorality of the life that surrounds and involves him; like Lear, he is unable to contain it, and it drives him mad. Later in the play, the image of Lear suggests itself even more strongly.

From this point on, Colin's disintegration is an inexorable process. Linda leaves him, unable to cope with his agony in addition to her own bitterness and insecurity, and because she realises that her love has no power to cure his social obsessions. Peter sees the danger of Colin's mental state with his usual clarity:

'It took me half a lifetime to go through the stages he's gone through. To be a shagged-out revolutionary in your early forties is regrettable, but human, I suppose. At twenty-four, or whatever Colin is, it's preposterous. Not because there's hope for socialism, but because the political imagination should be more sturdy. And because to opt out is to threaten the moral coherence of your life.'

Frances ignores such subtleties. To her, Colin is merely being as self-indulgent as her mother. She cannot see that the reasons for his sense of defeat are by now beyond his control. She can only compare her sane fiancé with her partly sane brother, without realizing that different standards apply:

'Jurek has to fight too, you know. For truth, and honesty, for what communism should mean. He's been doing it all his life. He's tired. But he goes on. What stops you, except your preoccupation with your own sense of defeat. You can't afford it. It's a luxury.'

The only advice she can give is to snap out of it.

With his mother, whose questioning and liberal intellect he has inherited and magnified to a dangerous degree, Colin is always at home. In his scene with her, he is almost relaxed, as much concerned about her as about himself. For a moment he is, as Jurek puts it, 'ironically aware of himself':

> 'Well. I've got the single fare to Paris. And five quid.
> Don't offer me more money, because I'd rather go like
> this. I want to be exposed. To whatever else there is be-
> sides obsessions about politics and nuclear genocide. Do
> you know, I haven't been to the pictures for months?
> Haven't read a novel, walked in the park, indulged in a
> friendship.'

This kind of awareness is for Colin the path back to sanity.
But it is a last moment of calm before the mental storm
begins. From now on, although there are moments of clarity,
and the oddly tender episode with the Polish girl on the train,
the clouds of Colin's obsession become thicker, darker, and
more absolute.

When we see him again, he is totally lost in the black
poetry of insanity, licensed, like Lear in his madness, to give
us his warped vision of the struggles of mankind towards
death:

> 'Do you love each other? I thought so. And me. Would you
> like to hear a story? About how a hairy man swung from a
> tree and made fire, he blew on the sparks in the hollow of
> a stone. He blew for a million years till the fire leapt up in
> a sheet of flame, and consumed the man. My mind tilts.
> I am sane, yet my mind tilts. I crossed Europe in a train,
> entirely without incident. A pretty girl brought me to
> your door, and went away . . . laughing. Laughing out of
> goodness.'

This is writing of the very highest quality, on a plane of
poetry, above anything yet achieved in the trilogy. This no
longer a description of a state or analysis of a character. It is a
poetic vision of humankind fused into an image. The most
potent of the poetic images which take over the play from this
point on, is the image of mankind's distortion of the natural
order, his perversion of the natural state of being:

> 'The turtles on Bikini atoll lay their eggs, and die in the
> sun. They can't find their way back to the sea. The sea-
> birds' eggs are sterile. The flying fish go into the trees.

People are shocked and click their tongues in disapproval.
But I know what we really want. We want to burn. We
long for that split second of incandescence. We can't bear
what we are.'

What drives Colin mad is that man has depraved the good,
and created only horrors. The directions of life are all invert-
ed for him, and the moments of lucidity get fewer. The
obsession with the perversion of nature, particularized in the
image of the turtle, continues to the end of the play, and
reaches its climax in the West Berlin night-club:

'I'd like to know what the turtles have done to man! Or
the birds . . . or the fish . . . the innocent face of nature.'

As Colin says those words, we see that the stripper performing
in the background is in fact a man, made up, wearing
woman's clothes and a wig.

Finally, in the extreme vision of the completely private
man, the madman, all the images become one, in a terrifying
juxtaposition: the dying directionless turtles, Katerin, whom
he slept with in Hamburg, and Linda, whose child he wanted
to father:

'I stood up and shouted her name: Katerin. I went to bed
and dreamt of her swollen with my child, dragging her
heavy body over hot sand. I called her name. Linda!'

This kind of horrific vision is beyond endurance. Trance like,
he sums himself up:

'Well then. Have we tried everything? We have. And do
we bravely plod on? We do.

As far as we can. Colin has reached his limit. Jurek has
spoken of these limits earlier in the play:

'In the concentration camp where I was held for . . . for
not long really. A year . . . There was a line some distance
from the fence. If anyone crossed that line, they were shot.
Many people chose to cross it. To those people it was the
only answer to what was intolerable.'

For Colin, the line is drawn across Berlin: the wall, that is
symbolic of all that divides the world, and the struggle that
has destroyed his mind. Colin's ritual suicide is the only way

out of an unbearable situation. With his last screaming words he damns both sides, the agents of his destruction, and dies emphasizing the naked humanity which, as Jurek has pointed out earlier, is all that a man is. Colin has tried to live for the improvement of mankind, and it has broken him. But what dies is a human thing. Mercer reminds us that the purpose of all political thought or action is a humanistic one, for the betterment of men. For man himself is nothing more than: 'a poor beast in the slaughteryard', and he needs to be loved and bettered to the utmost of every individual ability. The end of the play is ironic and savage. The man who contracted out dies a victim of the struggle he tried to ignore, caught in the symbolic crossfire of two great and conflicting social organizations. Mercer's meaning is plain. Even the hermit cannot pretend to be safe in the nuclear age. And life is a path to be followed towards the ultimate betterment of man. One cannot leave the path. One cannot give up living, without, in some way, dying. Krystyna, who was taken to torture quite at random, still breathes, but she is dead, because she lives without purpose. She is a perfect symbol of withdrawal from life, taken to its logical conclusion.

In opposition to Colin stands Jurek, and between them the balance of the play that Mercer intends is achieved. Jurek is in some ways a more tragic figure than Colin. He has been, and still is subjected to far greater pressures, but he doesn't die, nor does he sacrifice his reason. He understands Colin well enough:

'You have chosen the lesser of two forms of distress. As to what I do . . . I have lived through so much terror, the only thing left for me is to be rational.'

Madness is a state of agony and misery. But sanity is perhaps even more agonising in the world as it is now. It is easier to give up than to persevere.

This is Jurek's position as the play begins. His struggles have been in the past, and now he is resolved. As the play develops, we learn more about those struggles, and the true nature of the choice that Jurek has made, but we do not see

him change. Colin puts him to a severe testing, but he holds
his ground. The key to Jurek is that he has come to accept the
tragic attitude to life that Colin finds unbearable. Colin's
sense of human ineptitude is magnified by his neurosis into
universal nemesis. Jurek's vision of man's estate is more
sober, wrung more slowly from him, a realization of the
tragedy of human destiny, the blind attempt to go forward
that ends for everyman in the same gravestone:

'The last time I was in prison I came to think that since
we are all condemned to death . . .
                                        He stops, shrugs.

FRANCES: What?
JUREK: I was once sick. I vomited thinking about it.
                 It was dark and cold in the cell. I was hungry.
                 I heard myself shouting in the darkness: you
                 are a man. I was terrified. Because I thought:
                 if you were not here, but warm and well-fed
                 in a comfortable house with your children
                 sleeping, your wife nearby, your books open in
                 the lamplight, you would still be what you are
                 in this cell, minus these physical humiliations.
                 You could still look round at . . . perhaps some
                 good paintings glowing on the walls, the books
                 on the shelves and only say: I am a man. And
                 freeze. Sit there numb in your house. Like a
                 beast in the slaughteryard.'

What Jurek is describing is the moment in the past when he
had most in common with Colin, the moment when despair
overwhelmed him, when he realized that mankind is im-
prisoned in the cell of living, and the only exit is into death.

When Colin comes to Warsaw seeking help, his passion
reminds Jurek of his own days of struggle, and the reminder
is in itself a temptation to relax into the easy world of non-
committal. Colin will not let him escape with anything less
than the truth. He brings to the surface the agonising
realization:

'Then what separates us? We all want the same things.'
All sane men want peace and the betterment of life, and yet

the frontiers are guarded with sten-guns, and every day the rockets come out onto their pads. For the second time Jurek is forced to look his life in the face, and to admit:

'I am as exhausted as you are.'

At that point Krystyna is brought into the room, as if to remind Jurek of the true nature of the choice: continuing struggle, with its attendant exhaustion, or surrender, and withdrawal. Jurek looks at Krystyna and says:

'But I prefer to live.'

He has chosen for the second time, and he has made the same choice he made before. He still believes in the essential humanism of communism. His own task is to preserve that humanism, as the new society is created. Jurek is the answer to Richard's question: 'Where do we go from here?' and as such, is an image of what future socialism has to offer mankind. The morality of Wilf's beliefs remains unchanged, but Jurek is aware of the complexity of what has to be done, and of the many mistakes that have already been made. The socialist is battle-scarred and weary, but still convinced of the ultimate morality of what he is doing. With that conclusion Mercer leaves us at present, with a mood of resigned continuance that must be common among socialists in every part of the world.

For Frieda and Peter, this play is mainly an epilogue. Peter's choices, as we saw in *A Climate of Fear,* were made a long time ago. He has always been a man who understands himself, and his limitations. Too much understanding is in fact Peter's tragedy, except that tragedy is too strong a word for it. Peter even understands that it is his understanding which betrays him. Characteristically, he writes his own epitaph on the hopes and failures we have seen revealed in both the plays:

'One of the causes of my failure to get what I want from people has always been my paralysing ability to understand why they wouldn't give it to me. I should be more predatory.'

With sadness, and with charity, we can only agree.

Frieda too has left her greatest agonies behind her. Her life has been dominated by two moments of choice. The first was when she married Leonard, and the second was when she left him. That second moment is now a part of the past, and she is fully aware of what it means to her. Her dreams of a flat in London where people wandered in and out discussing Sartre have come to a reality of dandruff, nicotine, a sewing-machine, and an Almoner's office in a hospital, what Frances cruelly describes as middle-aged tat. But the fact is that Frieda, although much of what Frances says is perhaps true, accepts what her life is now, and is almost happy. In *A Climate of Fear*, she wanted to become a person. That she has now done, and she relishes the sense of identity that Leonard stifled in her:

'I think I want for the first time in my life to exist in my own right. To be someone on my own.'

This, as she remarks a few moments later, is honesty. Frieda has recognized her true nature, and is now attempting to live with it. When she needs a rest from her honesty and its subsequent involvement she no longer retreats into the comfort of middle-class wifedom. She returns to the first springs of life itself, in the children's ward:

'I'm not impressed when they smile, or put off when they are angry. I feel a kind of gratitude for their exhuberance ... their craziness. Children speak and behave improbably, and one responds.'

Children represent the blank fact of living. They are life untutored and uncontrolled. They are in that sense an image of the reason why Frieda has left her husband, and entered a world which will give her no kind of mercy or special consideration. She is committed to what they represent. In the end, Frieda stands with Jurek. They have both learned the same things about life, and have both been forced to face themselves in their absolute nakedness. And they have both made the same difficult decision. The choice was life or death, and they have both chosen life, with all the difficulties that choice entails. 'Why do you love her?' asks Frances, in her sour mood. 'She has courage.' answers Colin. This is the best last word about Frieda. The two plays she appears in tell the story of a woman, who, against the enormous weight of convention and background, had sufficient courage not to sell herself out. The end of her story is a sad one admittedly, but the woman who brushes dandruff from her shoulders in a seedy Earl's Court flat is truly alive, and forcing life into her own pattern of meaning, whereas the woman who dispensed sherry in a house in the country was a victim, more than half dead.

In *A Climate of Fear*, Frances was an apostle of commitment in its crudest sense. There was simply right and wrong, and the moral duty of the committed person was to uphold the right and castigate the wrong. This sense of moral duty encouraged her to ride roughshod over personal relationships, tact and sensitivity, but we realized in that play that she was only seventeen, and that the kind of moral ferocity she exhibited is a common attribute of that age. But in *The Birth of a Private Man* three years have passed, and Frances has not noticeably changed. Even her imminent marriage has not softened her. She is as blunt with her mother as she ever was:

'No other society in the world could have produced my
   Mother. Liberally educated, provincially sub-cultured
   and morally confused. She has the Lady Almoner approach to life!'

She is merely more sure of herself now. Now she has Jurek to refer to, she can even be blunt with Colin, and she does not hesitate to show her contempt for his confusion.

By this time it is obvious that her directness has nothing to do with age, but is a fact about her personality. She demands simplicities. As Colin's attitudes become more complex, she rejects him and comes under the influence of Jurek, who stands for everything she approves of. He is a real live communist, and has been involved in life, to the extent of prison, and fighting, and the risk of death. She worships him as much as a romantic symbol as a man, and the list of men condemned to death by the Nazis which bears his name, and which she carries in her handbag, is symbolic of her attitude to him. With such a man, in a communist society, where right and wrong is defined by the party, she will feel utterly secure. It is a dangerously naive attitude, but one she fights tooth and nail to preserve.

When she gets to Warsaw, and finds herself married to her real live communist, in a real live communist world, she is aware that everything is not right. Her dream world has become reality, but it is not what she expected. Gently Jurek tries to make her face life, and the facts of life with him in Poland:

> 'You are still a spectator to what has made me. I want you to know exactly what I am, and what you are, here in Warsaw, in Poland, with the ideological frontier running down the map of Europe.'

Frances is off balance. This is not what she expected:

> 'I thought you were more self-contained. I thought we would live together in a simple way.'

Jurek has got through to something that Frances has never dared to recognise before:

> 'Are you wanting what is here . . . or simply evading something else?'

And later:

> 'Poland hardly exists for the purpose of solving your personal dilemmas.'

He tries, gently, but firmly, to enlighten her, firstly about the political facts of life:

> 'You must get it firmly in your mind that everything here is so much more complicated than you seem to imagine. Our freedom is subtle and precarious . . . We have great faith in what we are doing, but it is rather remote from the political fantasy life of a young Englishwoman all dressed up in revolutionary ideals and nowhere to go!'

Secondly, he tells her about himself, his sense of the human tragedy, his desire to leave the world to itself, and his conviction that he cannot, because he is the world and the world is him, and to leave it is to invite death. This is a very long

way from Frances' romantic conceptions of communism, and
her reaction is immediate:

'I don't understand you, and now I'm frightened. Frightened for us.'

Dimly she realizes that their relationship up to now has been
built on a very flimsy and unreal foundation. Like Othello
and Desdemona, they have both been in love with an illusory
person. Unlike Othello, Jurek is sufficiently self-aware to
realize the false ground beneath them, and his purpose in
shattering Frances' illusions, is to try to give a real basis to
their marriage.

This is the unsteady situation that Colin burst in upon, and
Frances' immediate reaction is to want to reject him. Her
renewed insecurity once more makes her cruel and attacking.
Just as, in Jurek's first scene, she attacks her mother for questioning the simple image she has of him, so in the scene with
Colin, she attacks him for bringing into her house a complexity that might accentuate what she newly recognizes in her
husband. Her desire to defend her husband, overcomes her
natural sympathy for her brother, and driven to desperation,
she throws him out to fend for himself. She realizes that one
week of Colin could well bring Jurek near to a similar state
of defeat.

The secret of Frances is what she avidly denies:

'JUREK: There are times when you sound disturbingly
             like your brother.
FRANCES: Do I? Well I'm not like him.'

She is like him, because she is a product of the same social
situation. Mercer is at pains to emphasize this connection,
and gives her a long speech in each of the two main Warsaw
scenes making it clear. The generation that has seen the
betrayal of the socialist impulse of the thirties, the triumph of
reaction all over Europe, and the mistakes and failures of
communism in its struggle for birth, is confused, embittered
and cynical. In such a climate of opinion it is very difficult for
an intelligent person to preserve genuine socialist ideals.
Colin and Frances choose opposite ways of coping with the

situation. Colin tries to stare it in the face, and accept all its implications. Frances withdraws from the struggle, just as certainly as Colin eventually does, not away from commitment, but into it. Her refuge from life is the simplicity of dogma. Colin understands this, and says so to his mother:

'Frances is only crude because she fears what is complex. She needs to be simple. To believe this, like that, hate something else. She daren't hesitate. It would be a strain for her to love you, for example.'

Jurek too understands the potential neurosis of the girl he has chosen for his wife. To him she is like a fountain of life at which to drink and arise refreshed. She is young, unscarred, and full of simple moral beliefs. But he realizes sadly that he has deceived himself and her by thinking that their marriage could be built on that sort of relationship. He recognizes that he must make her face the truth about the world and herself. He knows the dangers of any kind of withdrawal from reality. And he knows what the price might be for Frances if he fails:

'Krystyna was a little like you.'

At this point we leave Frances, facing truths about herself which it has taken two plays for her to recognize. Her salvation will depend upon Jurek's patience and her own resilience, and perhaps, ultimately, on the history of the next ten years.

The Trilogy comes to an end with Colin's death, and Frances and Jurek trying to cope with the problem of building some sort of socialist future. I won't attempt any summing up of what has been said. I will only say how the pattern of the three plays strikes me, and how strange this is, considering that the growth of the trilogy was largely accidental. It follows an expanding pattern, from a family in Yorkshire, to the world, and mankind, but at the same time returns to the basic human thing that is man, and that the world is for. It couldn't have been better planned by the most rigid classicist, and it is perhaps an interesting comment on how works of art are created.

This appendix has now become very long, and I feel it is time for me to end. I justify my great expense of words in two ways. The first is that Mercer's work is unpopular in content and unfashionable in style, and might easily be dismissed by the unsympathetic and unthinking, hidden behind a few easy labels. I hope I have indicated entries into the work that make it impossible to ignore it.

The second reason is that these works were written for Television, and television drama suffers from a great lack of seriousness. I know of no other TV play that would have stood up to the kind of analysis I have given this play, and still suggest more to be revealed. I would like to suggest that Mercer's work offers a new standard by which television drama must be judged. He has killed forever the idea that television is only suitable for the short story form of drama, and that deep thought and complex language have no place on the small screen. The television magazines are full of soft-headed articles about writing in pictures, as though this offers the only genuinely fruitful avenue of exploration. I challenge anyone, in television or out of it, to tell me how they propose to reveal people and the world as fully as these plays do, by a dominantly pictorial method. If they tell me that they don't aim at the scope and depth of this work, but at something smaller, I will agree with them. What they have seen here is more significant. It is the first writer of major stature television has produced. It is the work of a dramatic poet.

The trilogy completed, Mercer is already following new pathways of drama, and techniques beyond those demonstrated here. I look forward to directing the new plays.* They will, I know, present an even greater challenge to the director, to the actors, and to the audience, than the plays included here have done.

Don Taylor January 1963

---

*A Suitable Case For Treatment, transmitted on Sunday October 21st 1962 on BBC TV, directed by Don Taylor, Television and Screen Writers Guild Award for the Best original teleplay of 1962. *For Tea on Sunday*, transmitted on Sunday March 17th 1963 on BBC TV, directed by Don Taylor.